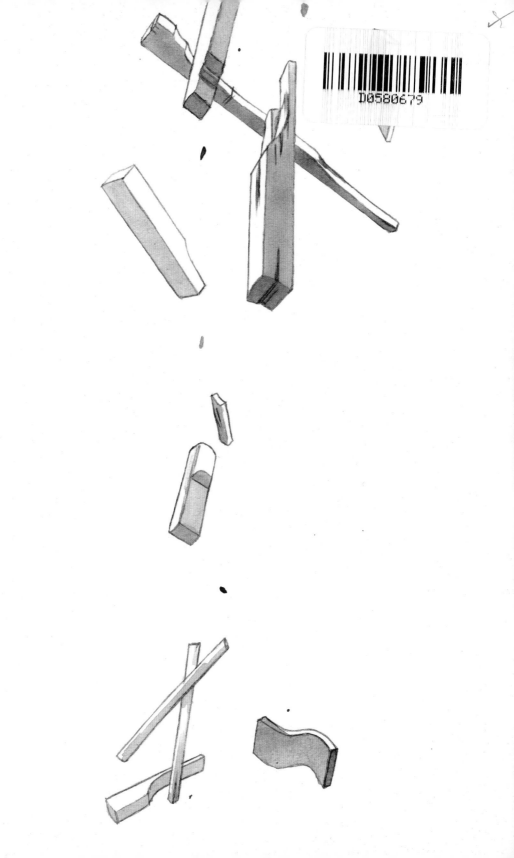

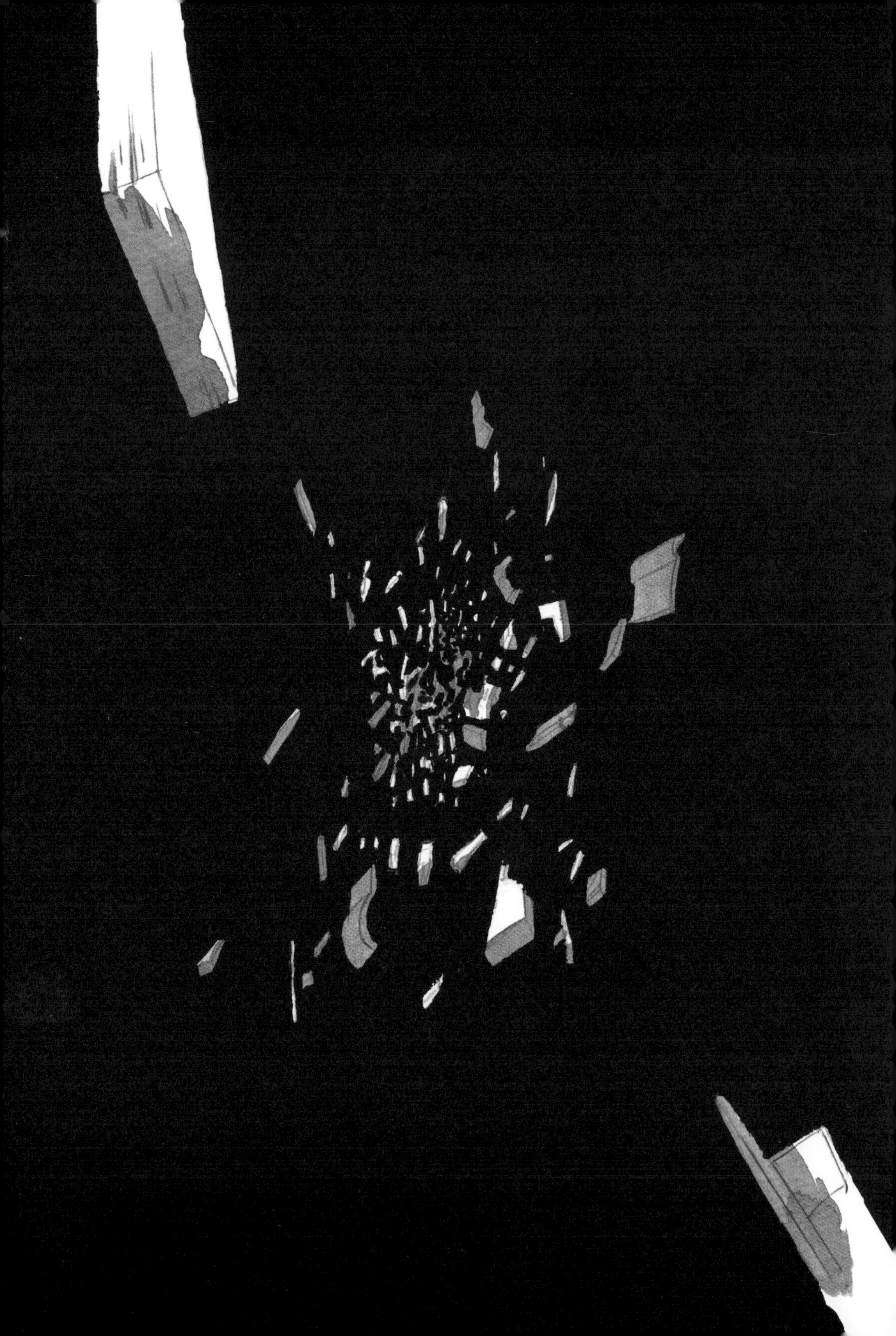

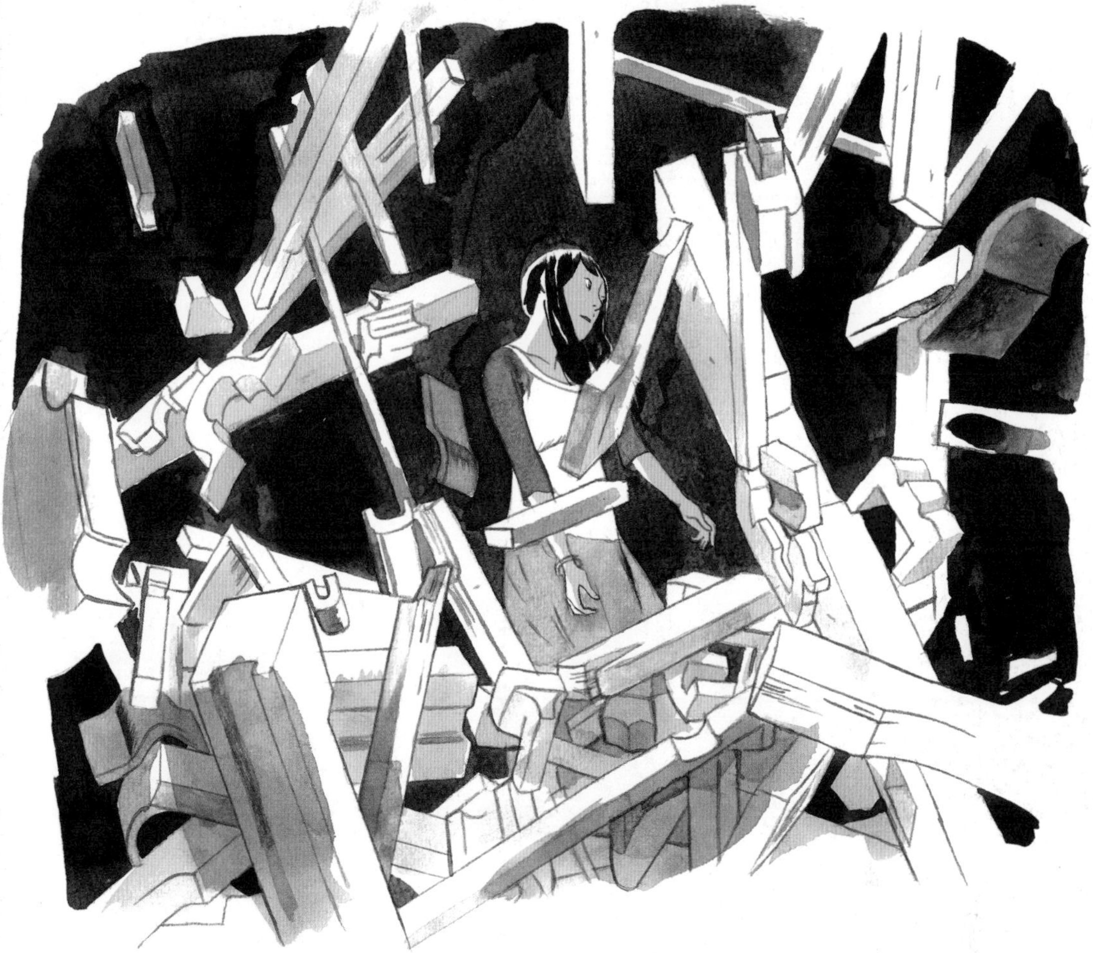

JUST SO HAPPENS

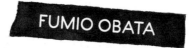

FUMIO OBATA

Abrams ComicArts • New York

Editor: Carol M. Burrell
Designer: Pamela Notarantonio
Managing Editor: Jen Graham
Production Manager: Kathy Lovisolo

Library of Congress
Control Number:
2014948131

Hardcover ISBN:
978-1-4197-1595-2
Paperback ISBN:
978-1-4197-1596-9

Copyright © 2015
Fumio Obata

First published
in the United
Kingdom
in 2014 by
Jonathan Cape/
Random House
Group Ltd.

Printed and bound in China
10 9 8 7 6 5 4 3 2 1

Abrams ComicArts books are available
at special discounts when purchased in
quantity for premiums and promotions
as well as fundraising or educational
use. Special editions can also be created
to specification. For details, contact
specialsales@abramsbooks.com or the
address below.

ABRAMS
THE ART OF BOOKS SINCE 1949
115 West 18th Street
New York, NY 10011
www.abramsbooks.com

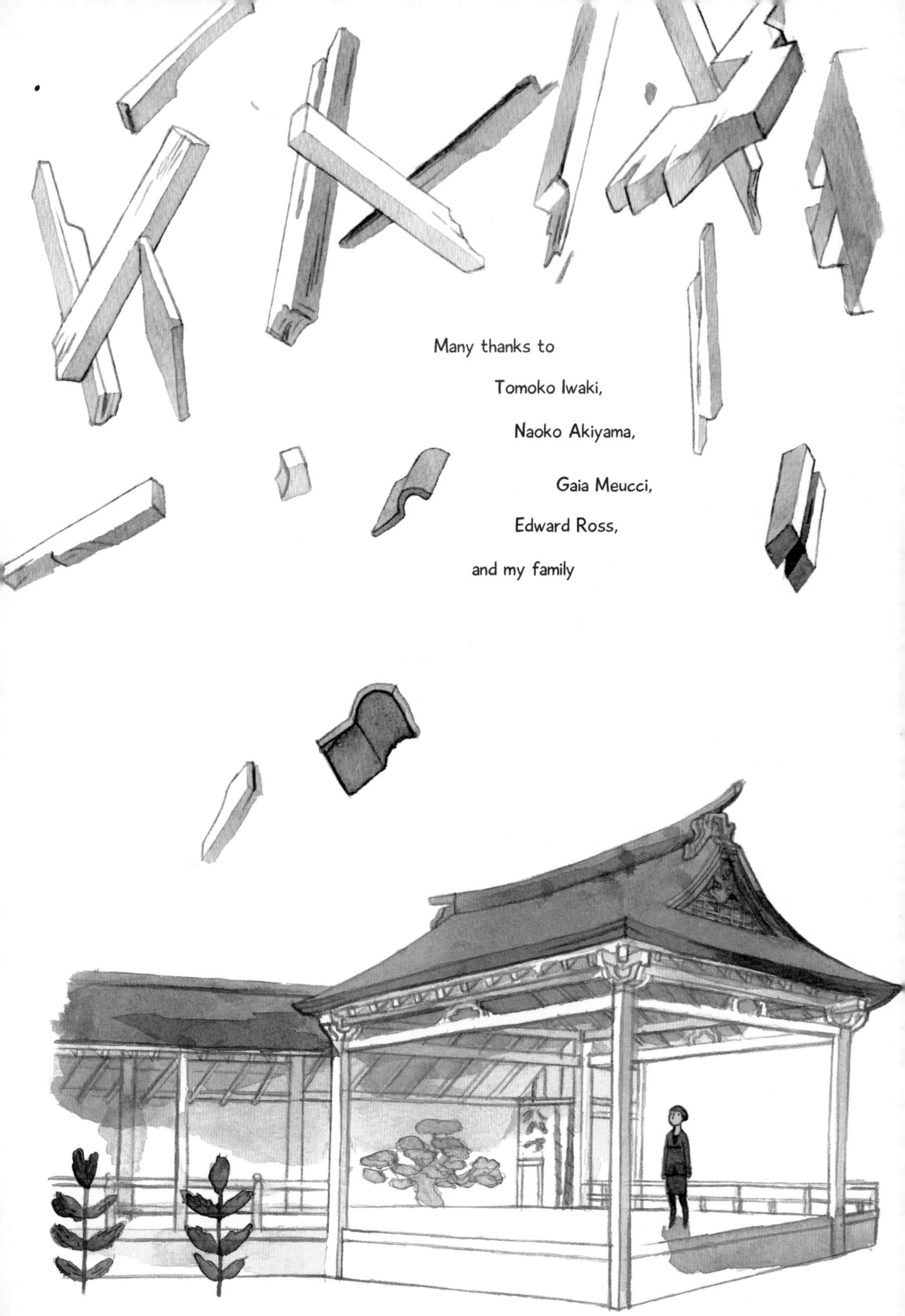

Many thanks to
Tomoko Iwaki,
Naoko Akiyama,
Gaia Meucci,
Edward Ross,
and my family

I

OK!
derma
NO.

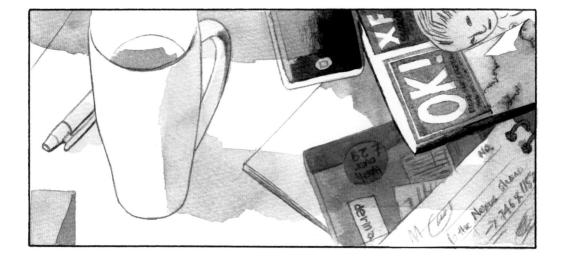

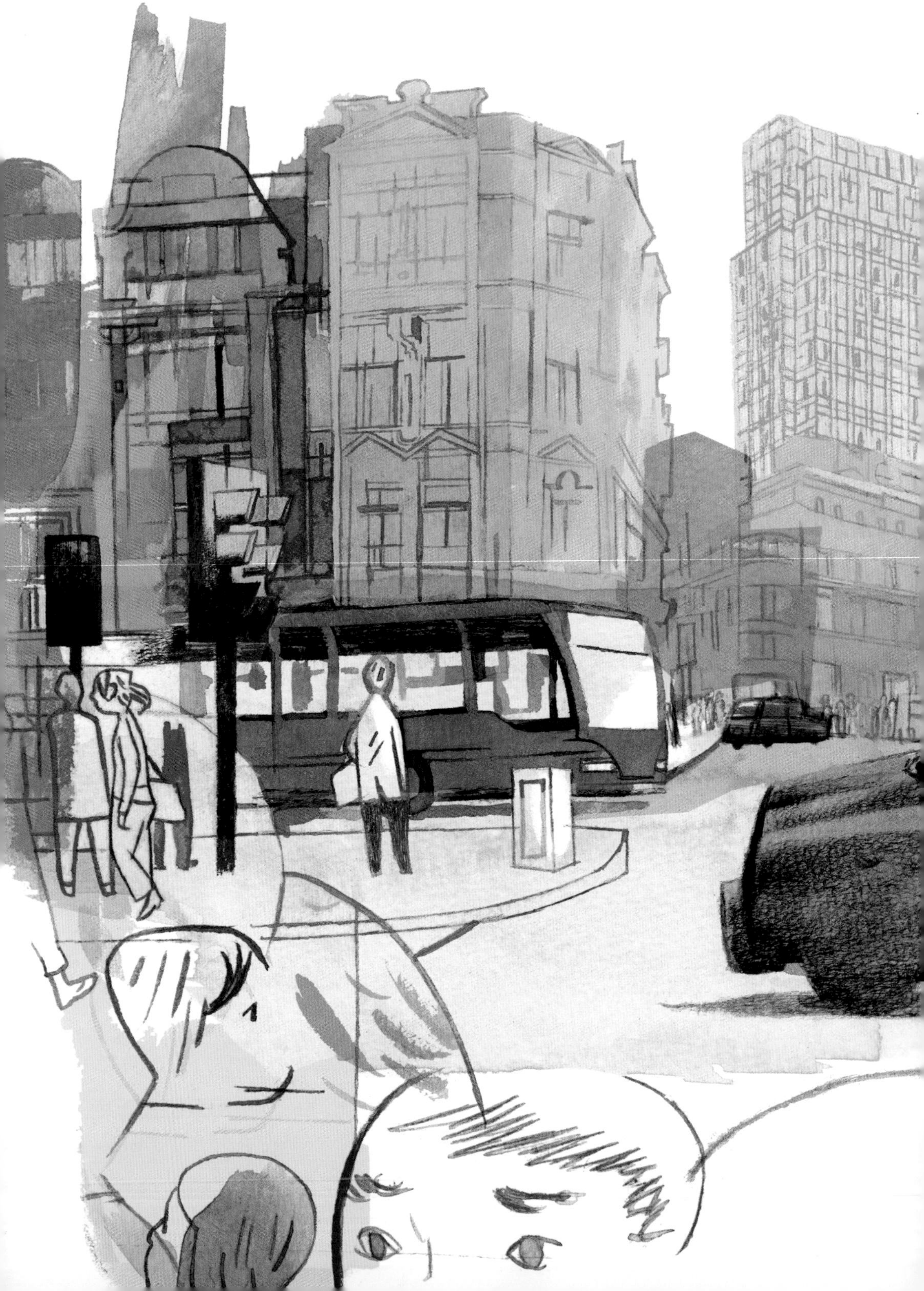

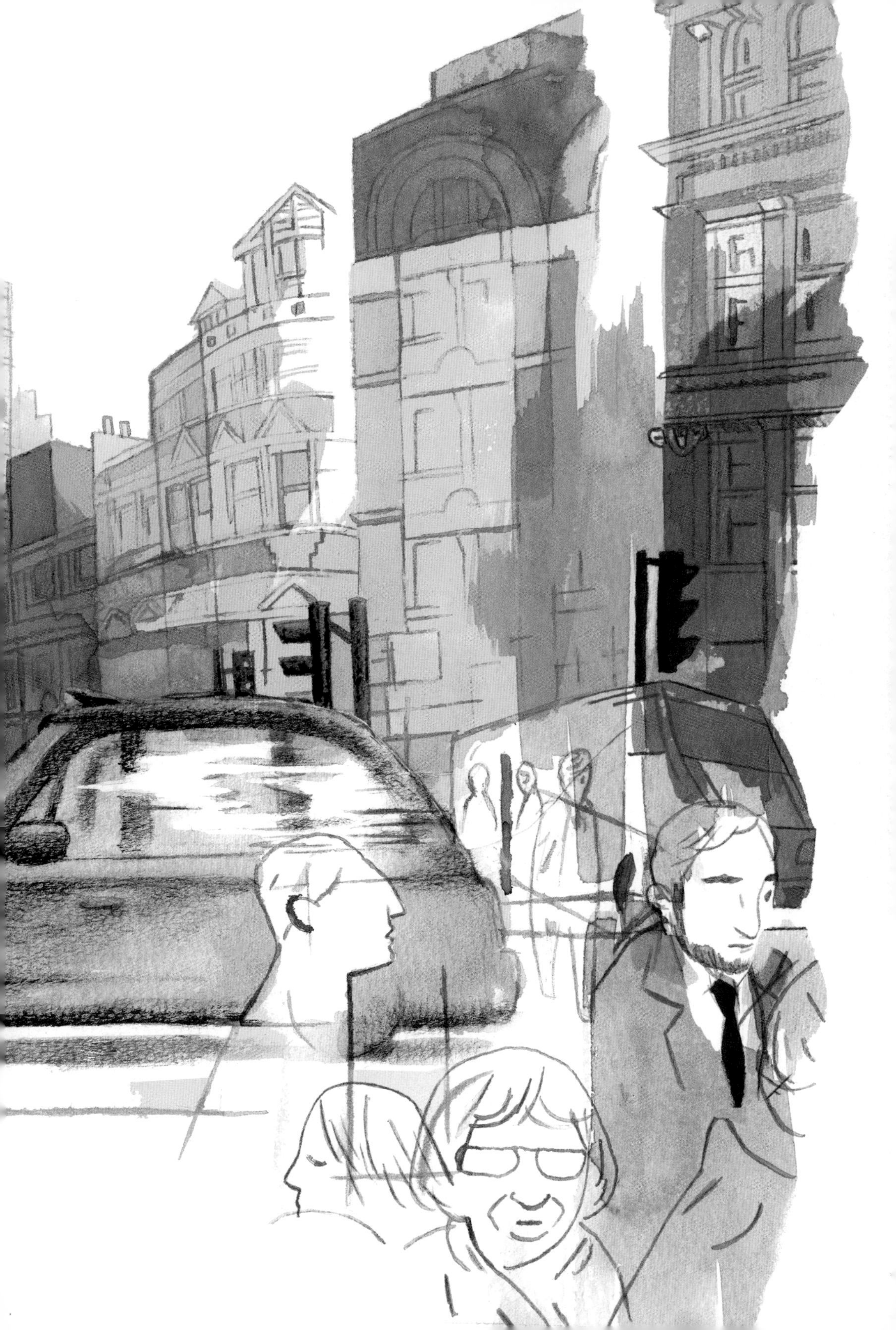

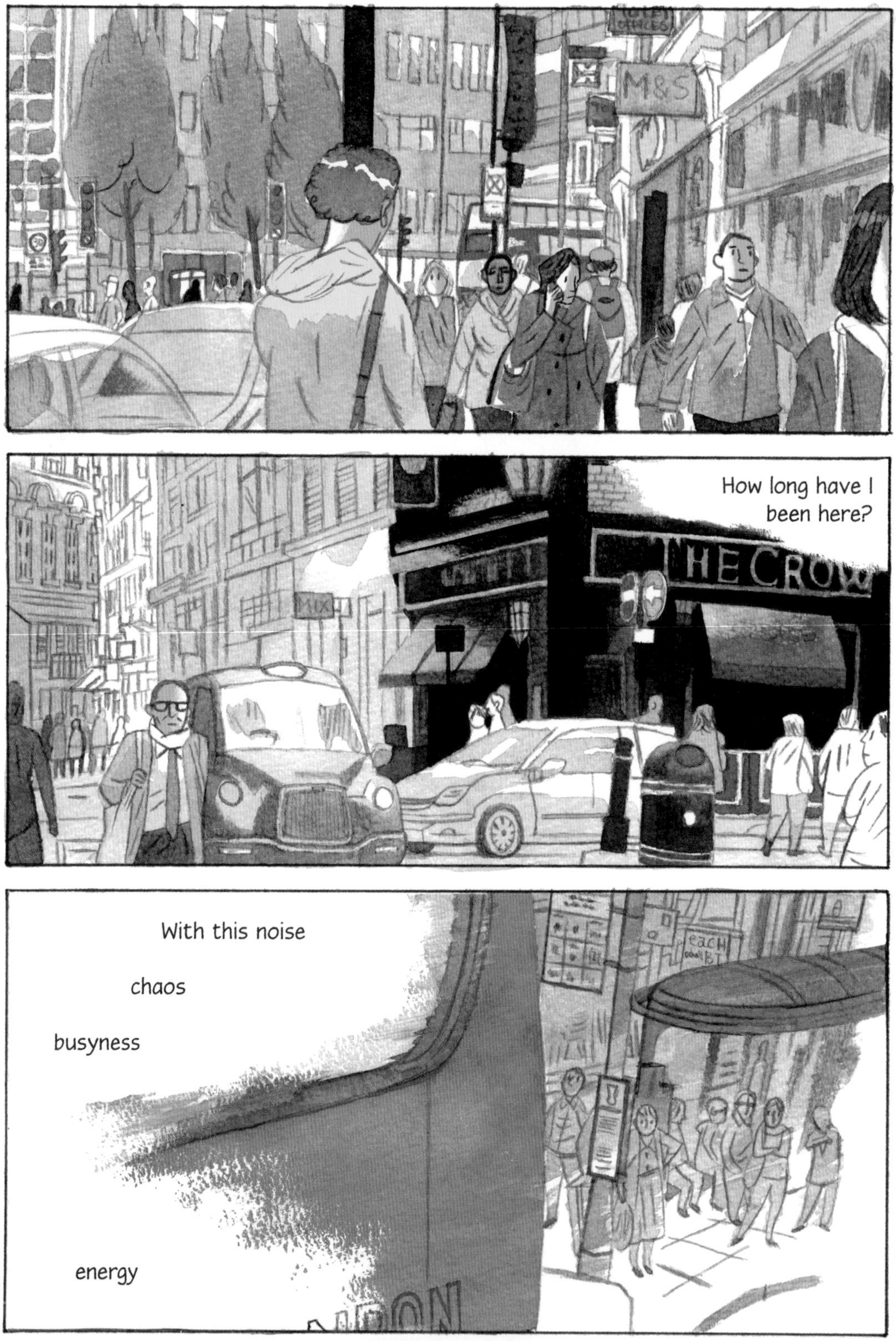
M&S
How long have I been here?
HE CROW
MIX
With this noise
chaos
busyness
energy

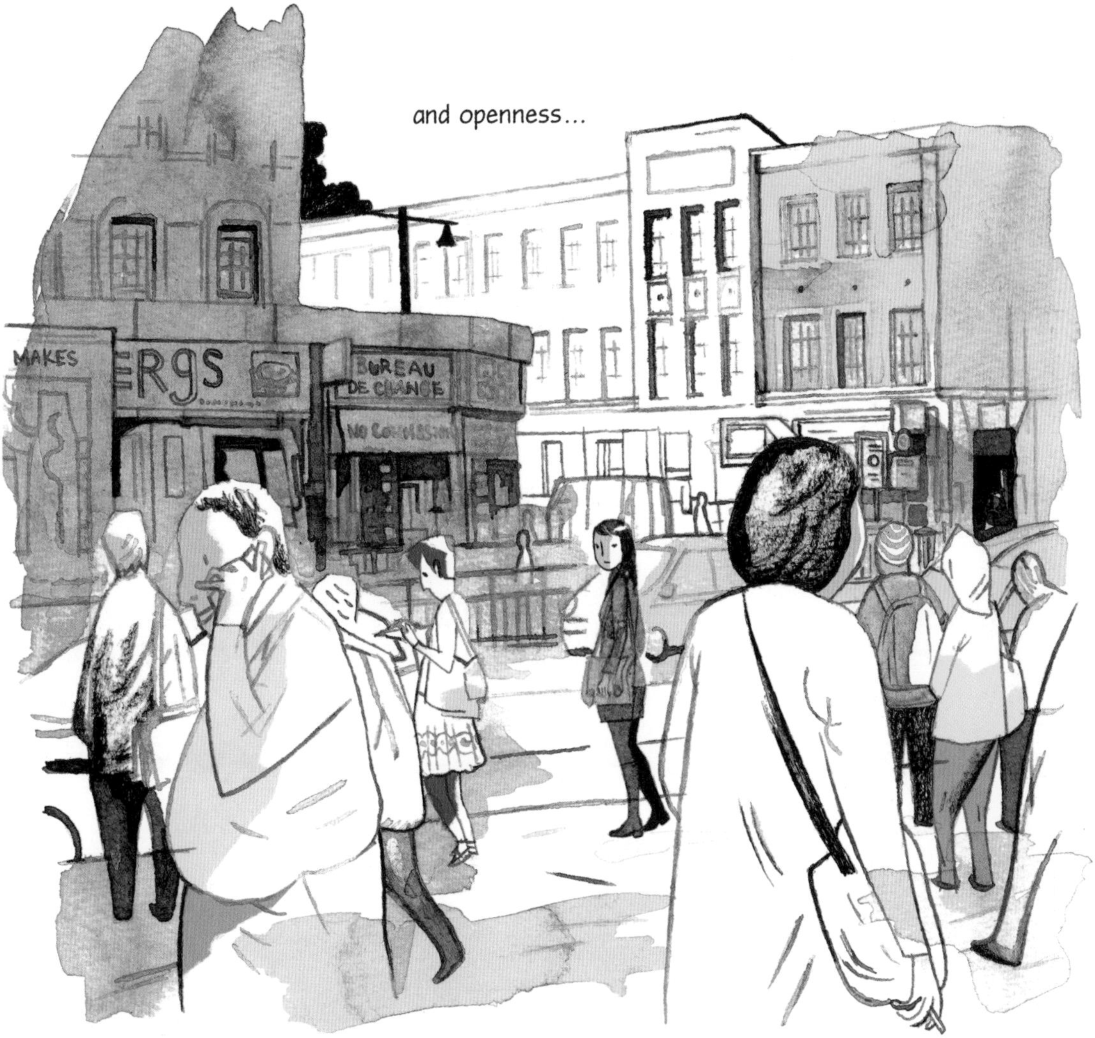
and openness...
MAKES
BUREAU DE CHANGE
NO COMMISSION

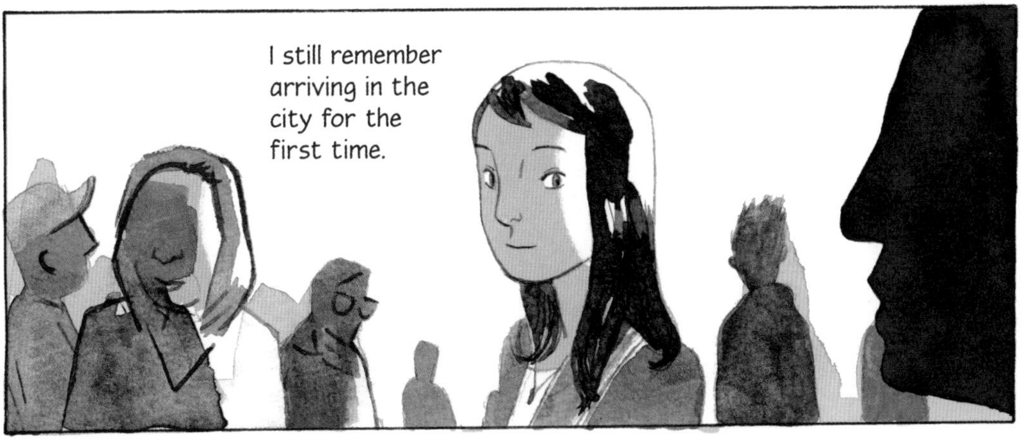
I still remember arriving in the city for the first time.

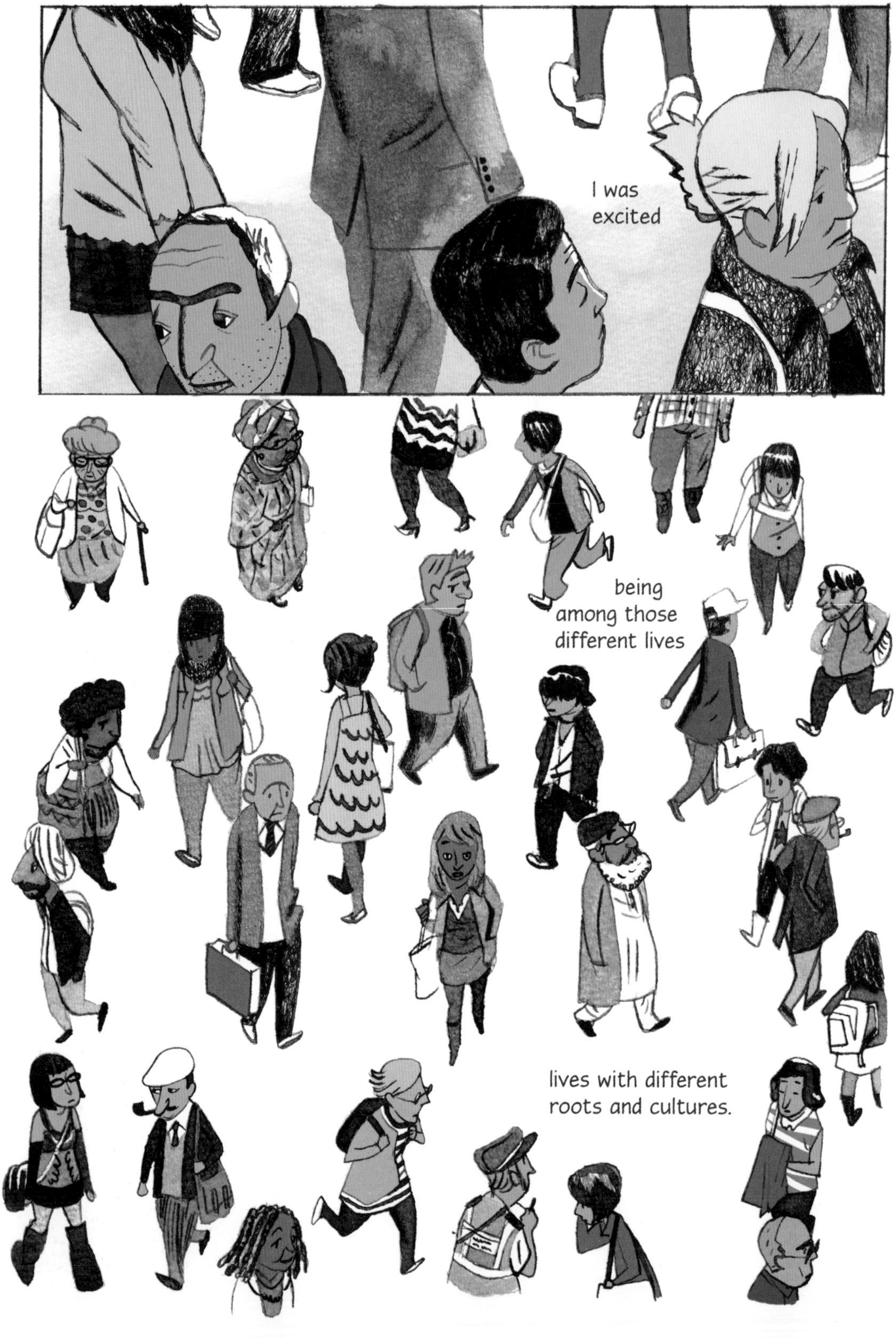
I was excited
being among those different lives
lives with different roots and cultures.

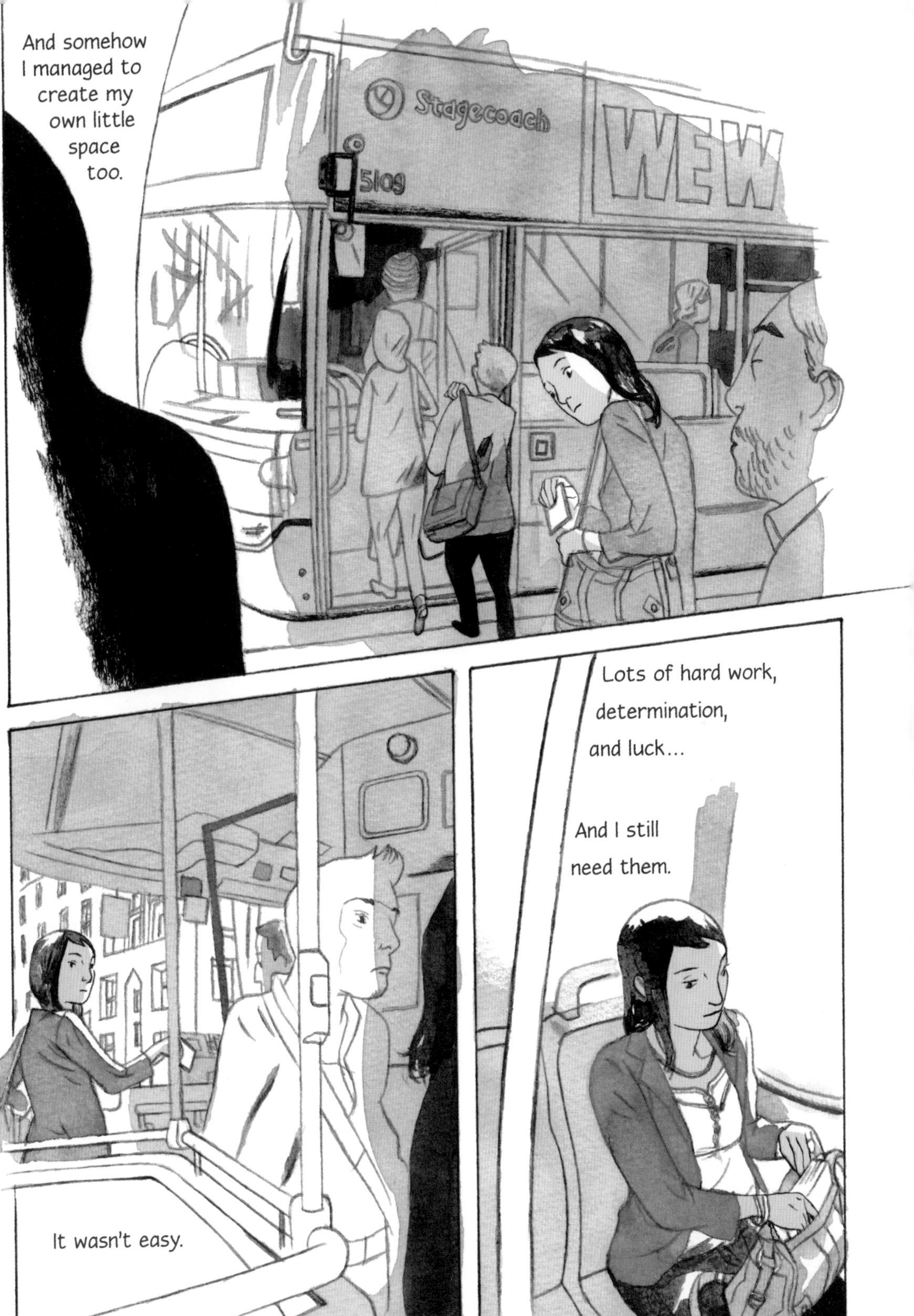
And somehow I managed to create my own little space too.
Stagecoach
5109
WEW
It wasn't easy.
Lots of hard work, determination, and luck...
And I still need them.

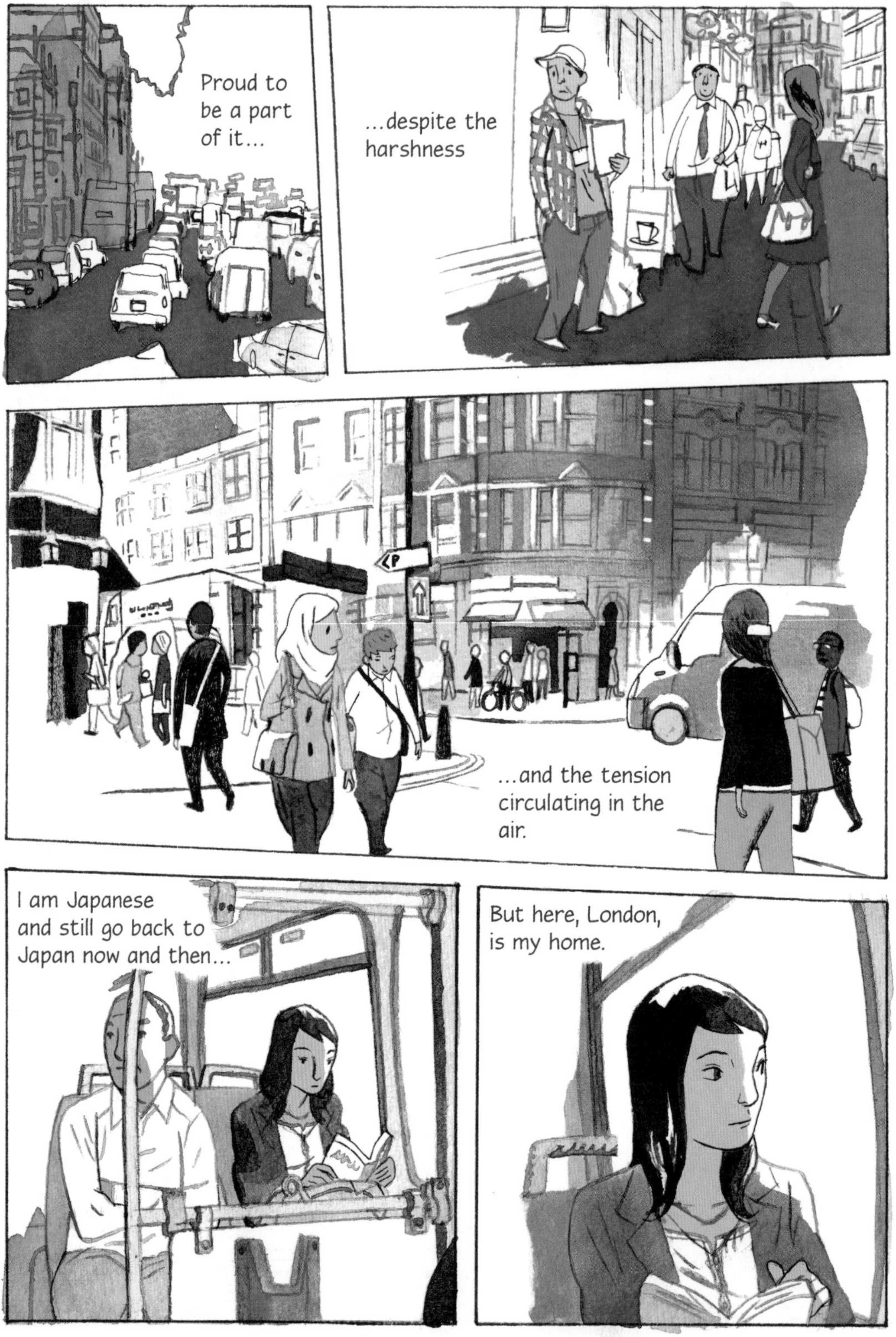
Proud to be a part of it...
...despite the harshness
...and the tension circulating in the air.
I am Japanese and still go back to Japan now and then...
But here, London, is my home.

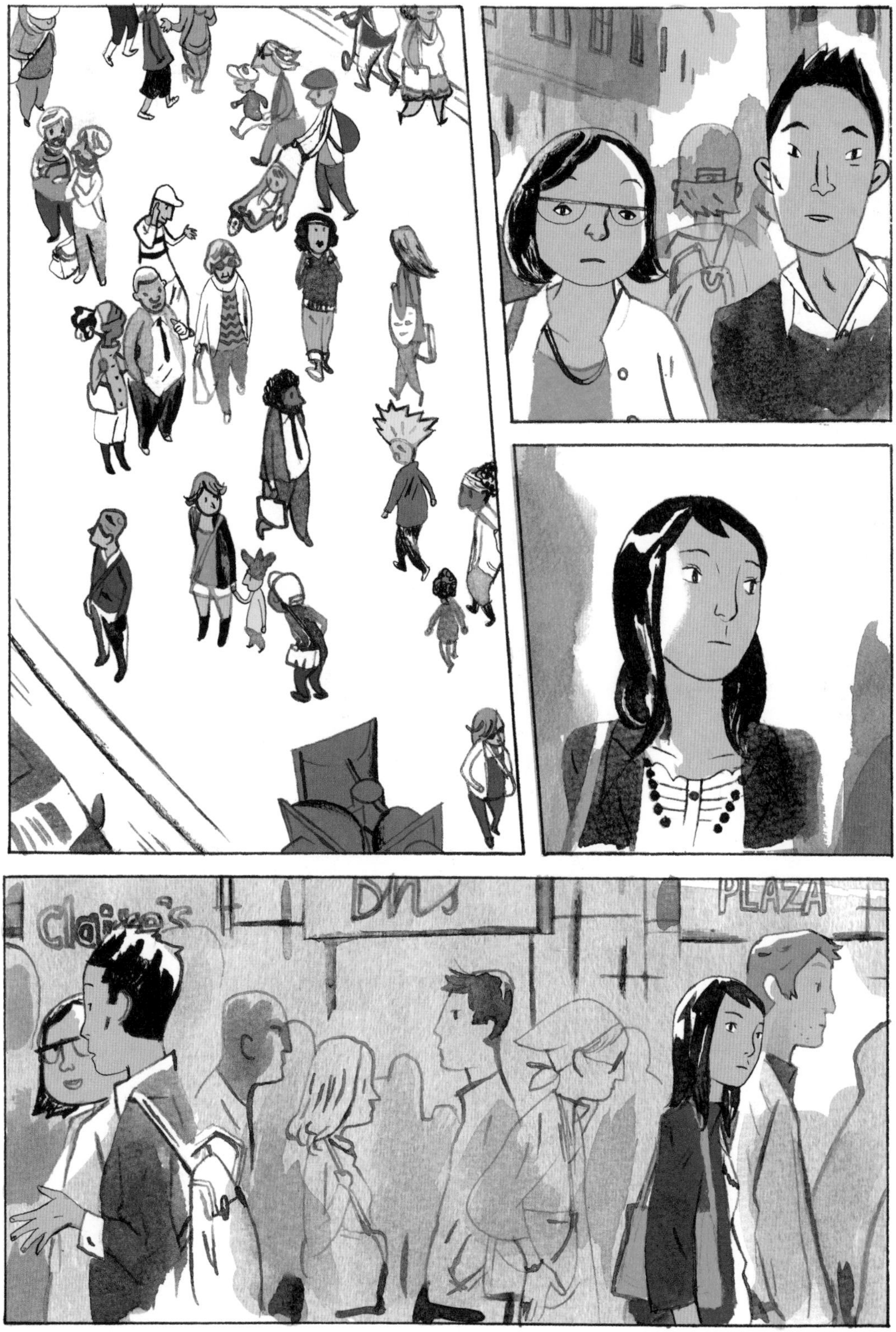
Claire's
Bhs
PLAZA

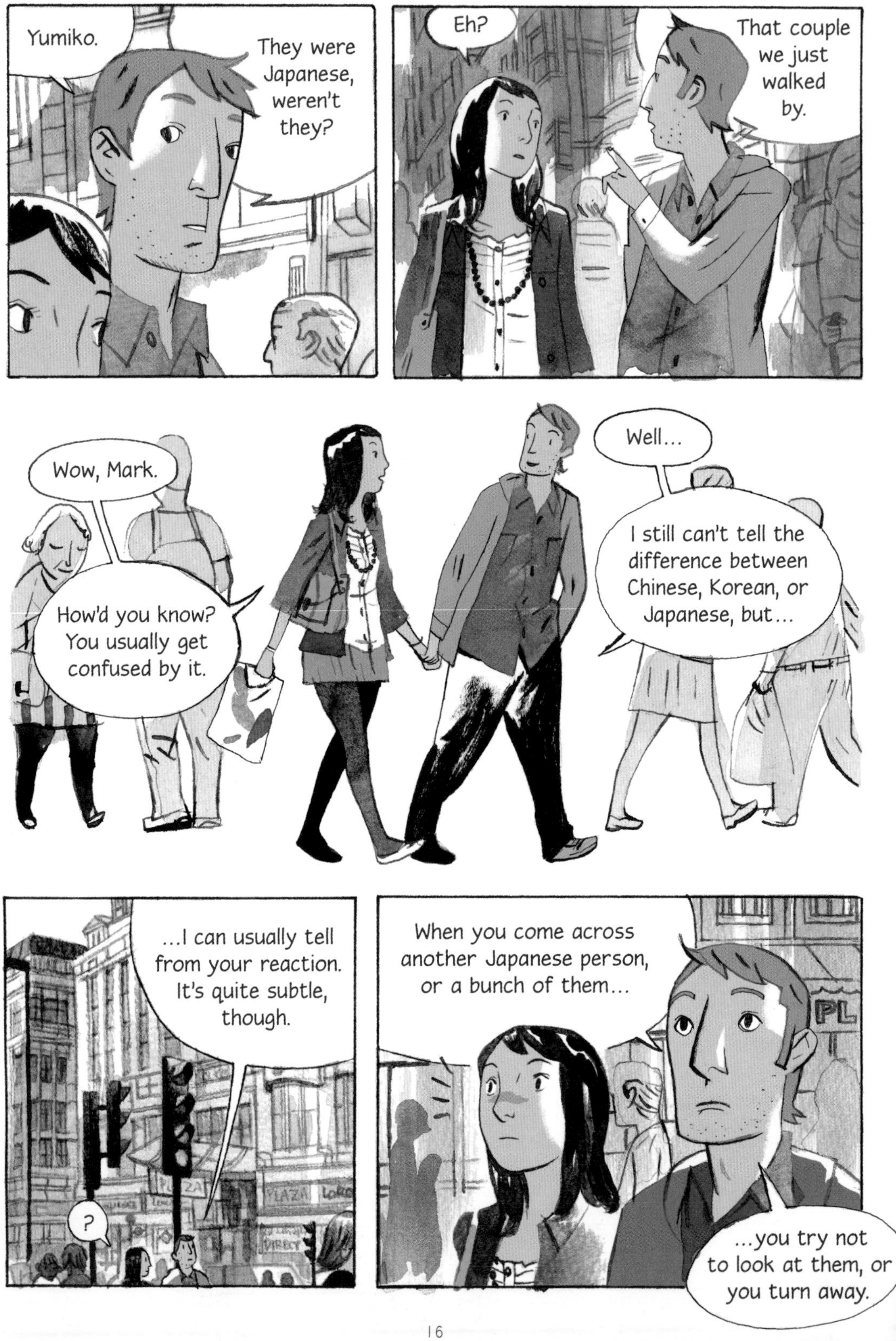

Yumiko.
They were Japanese, weren't they?
Eh?
That couple we just walked by.
Wow, Mark.
How'd you know? You usually get confused by it.
Well...
I still can't tell the difference between Chinese, Korean, or Japanese, but...
...I can usually tell from your reaction. It's quite subtle, though.
?
When you come across another Japanese person, or a bunch of them...
...you try not to look at them, or you turn away.

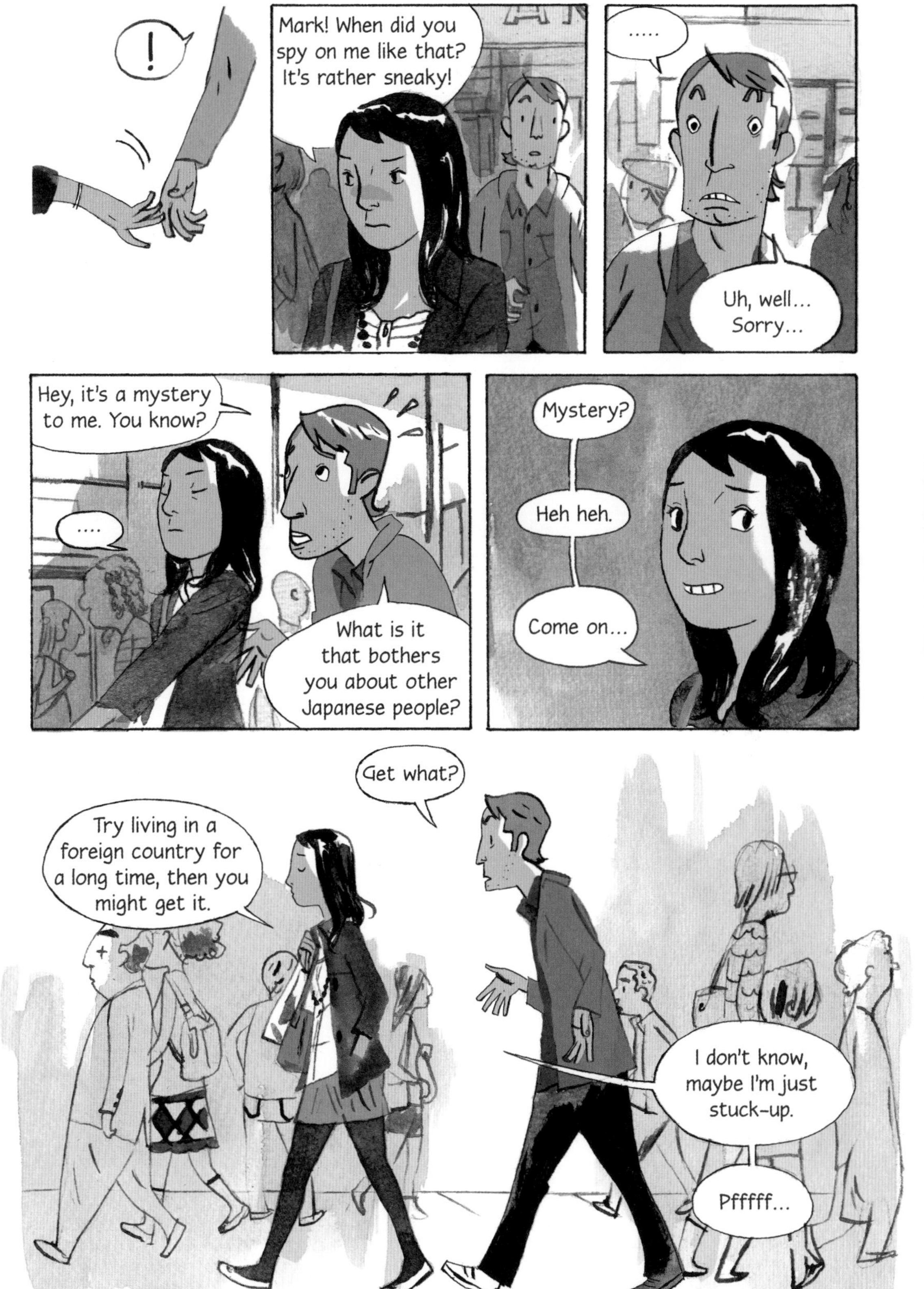
!
Mark! When did you spy on me like that? It's rather sneaky!
.....
Uh, well... Sorry...
Hey, it's a mystery to me. You know?
....
What is it that bothers you about other Japanese people?
Mystery?
Heh heh.
Come on...
Get what?
Try living in a foreign country for a long time, then you might get it.
I don't know, maybe I'm just stuck-up.
Pfffff...

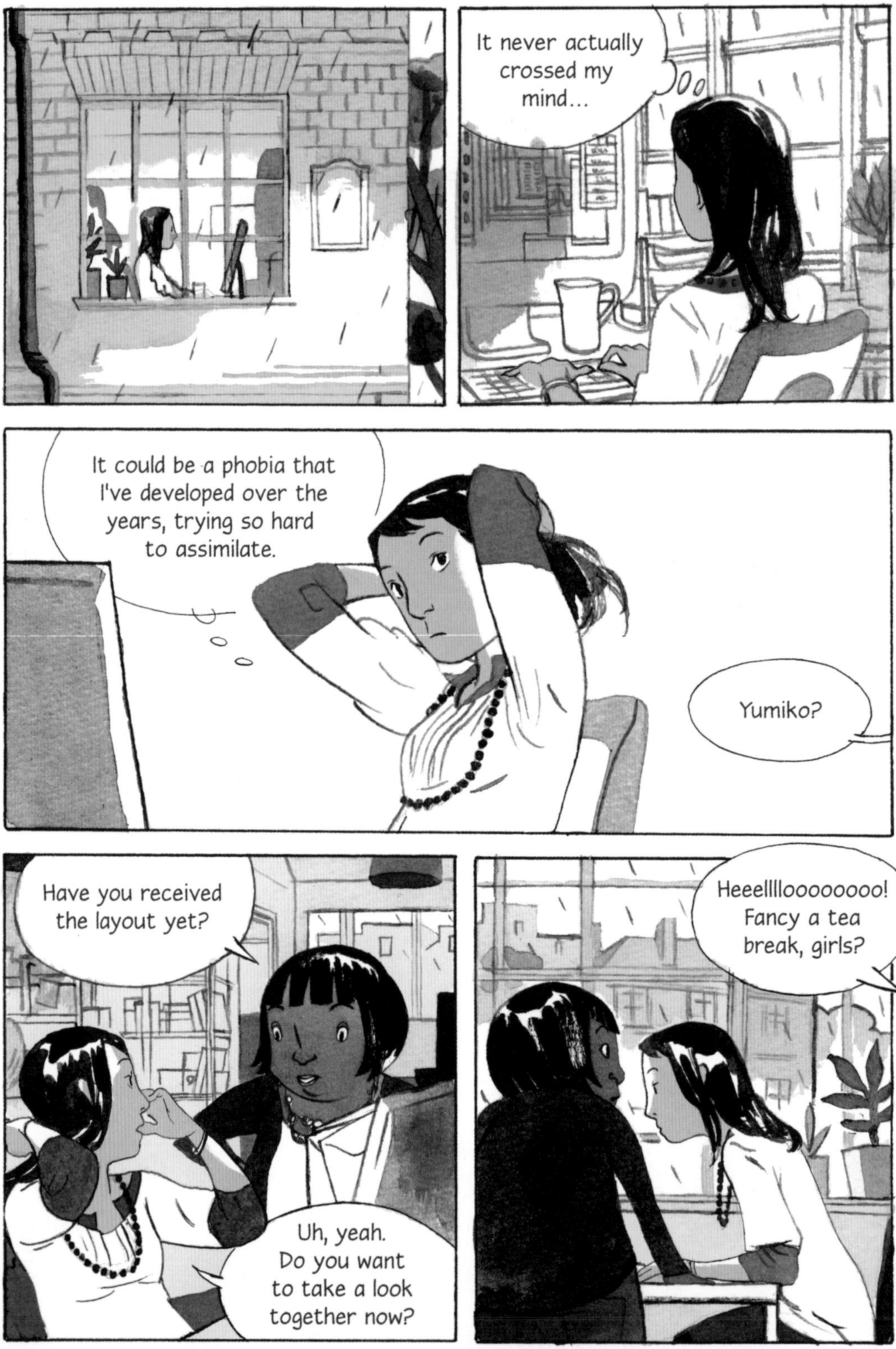
It never actually crossed my mind...
It could be a phobia that I've developed over the years, trying so hard to assimilate.
Yumiko?
Have you received the layout yet?
Uh, yeah. Do you want to take a look together now?
Heeellllooooooo! Fancy a tea break, girls?

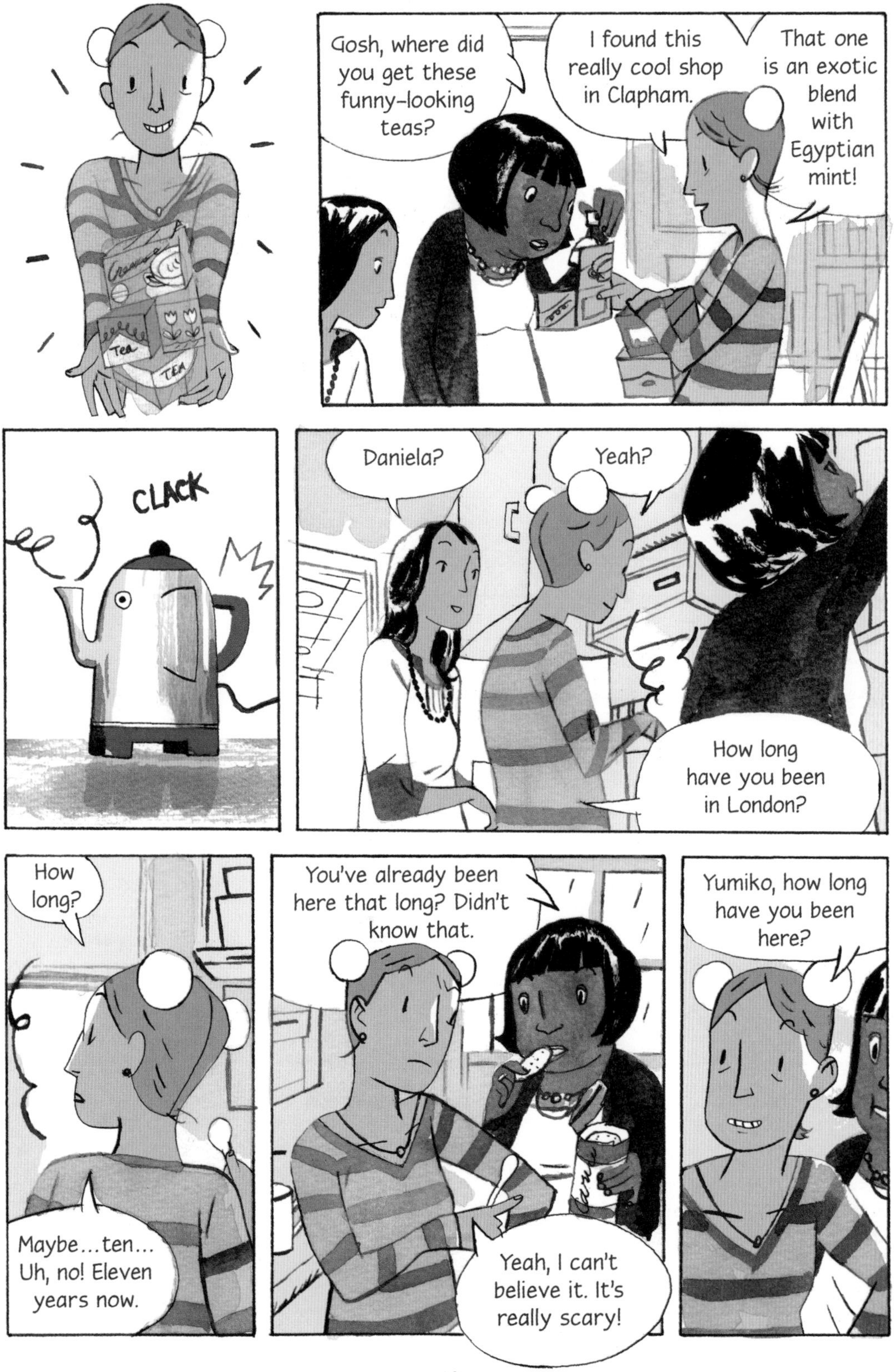
Gosh, where did you get these funny-looking teas?
I found this really cool shop in Clapham.
That one is an exotic blend with Egyptian mint!
CLACK
Daniela?
Yeah?
How long have you been in London?
How long?
Maybe…ten… Uh, no! Eleven years now.
You've already been here that long? Didn't know that.
Yeah, I can't believe it. It's really scary!
Yumiko, how long have you been here?

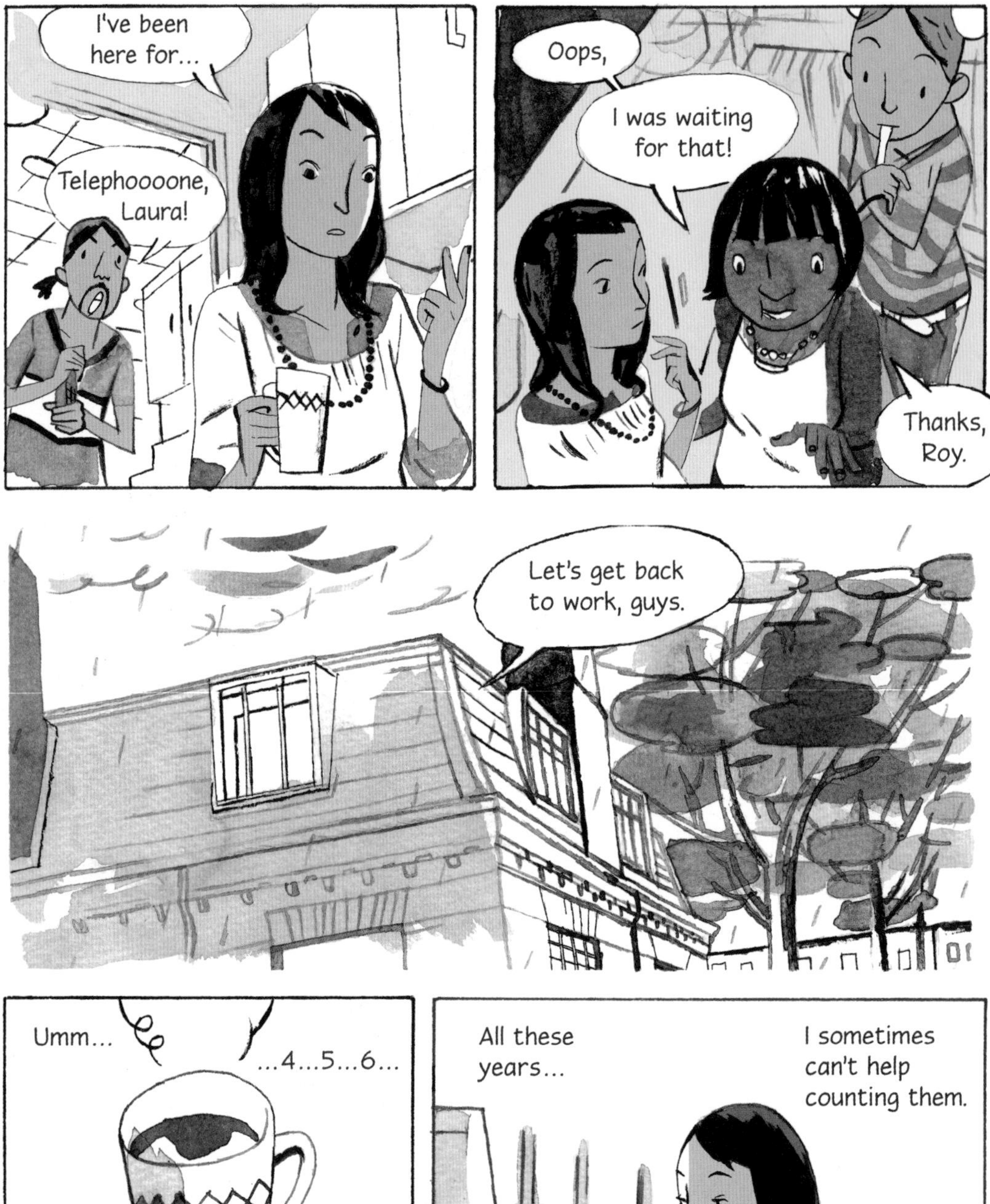

I've been here for...
Telephoooone, Laura!
Oops,
I was waiting for that!
Thanks, Roy.
Let's get back to work, guys.
Umm...
...4...5...6...
All these years...
I sometimes can't help counting them.

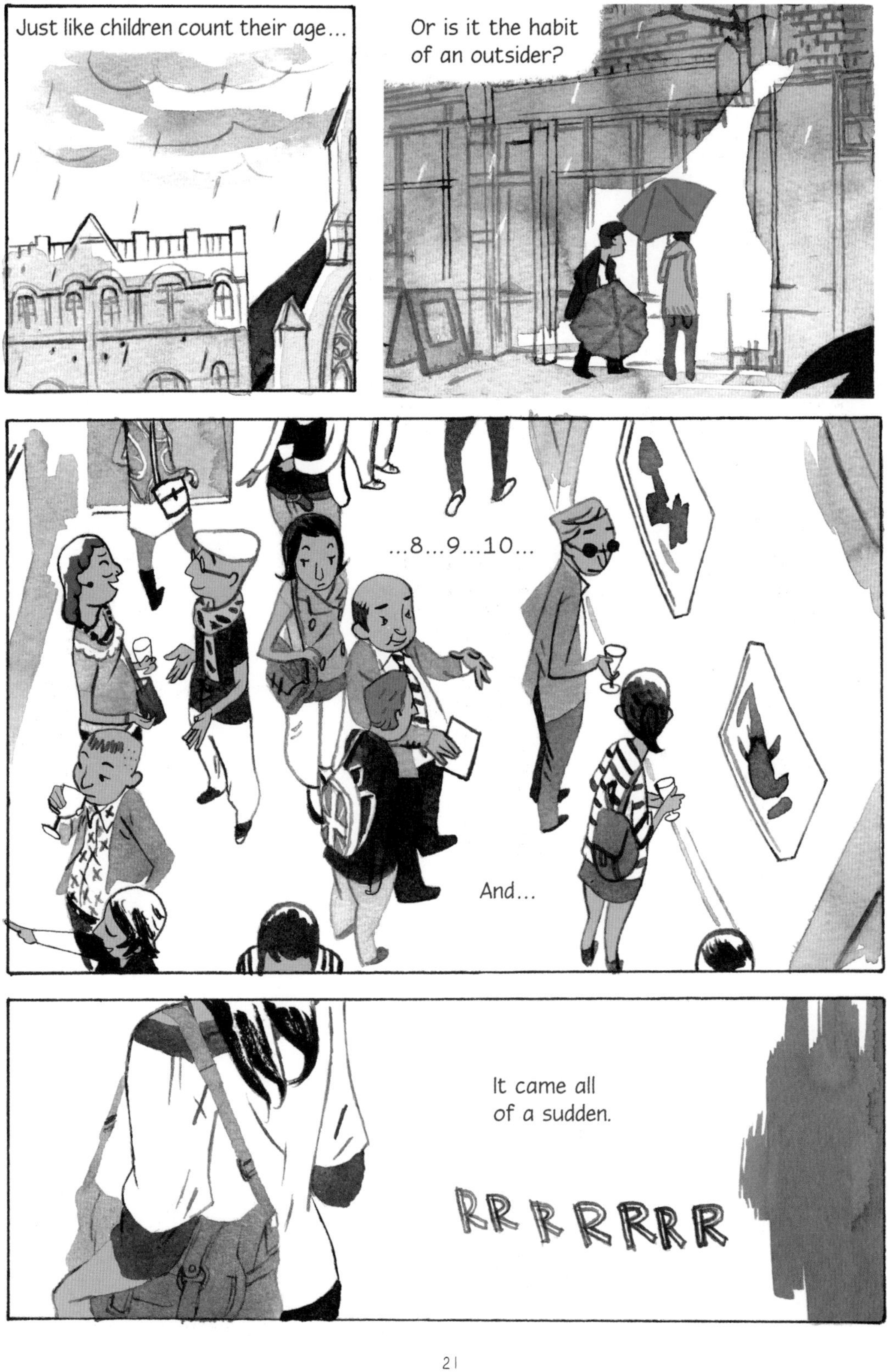
Just like children count their age…
Or is it the habit of an outsider?
…8…9…10…
And…
It came all of a sudden.
RRRRRRR

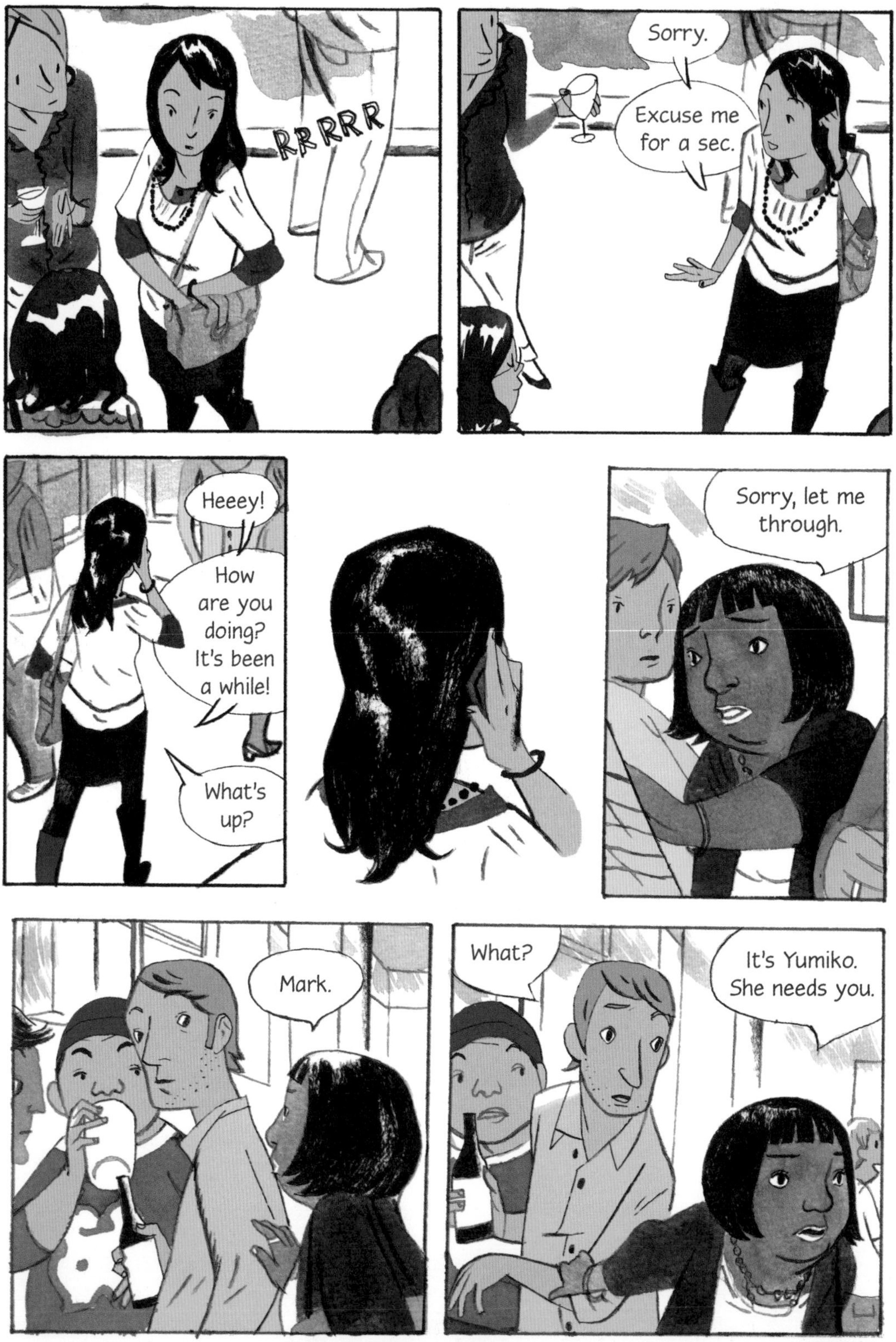
RRRRR
Sorry.
Excuse me for a sec.
Heeey!
How are you doing? It's been a while!
What's up?
Sorry, let me through.
Mark.
What?
It's Yumiko. She needs you.

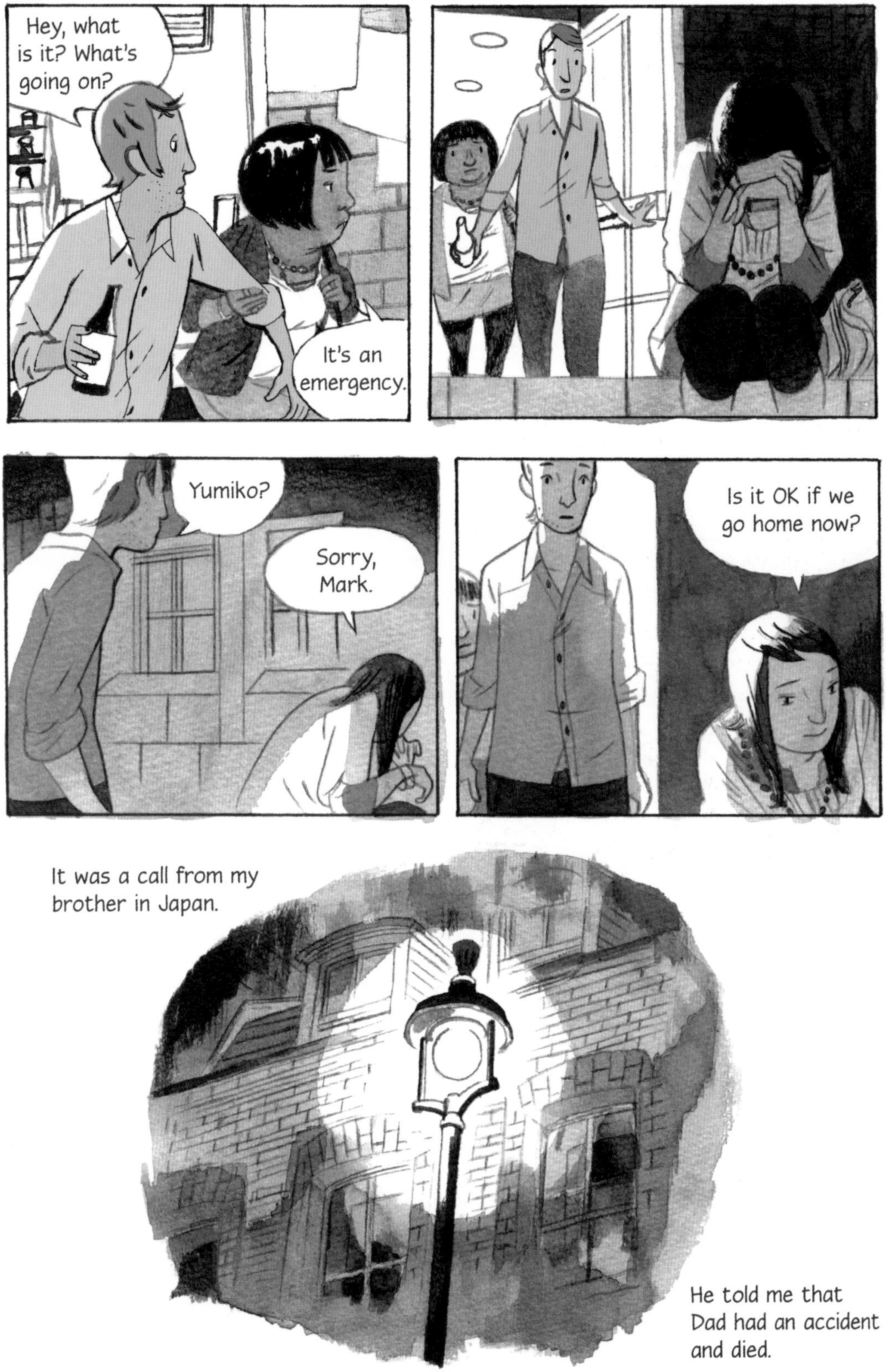
Hey, what is it? What's going on?
It's an emergency.
Yumiko?
Sorry, Mark.
Is it OK if we go home now?
It was a call from my brother in Japan.
He told me that Dad had an accident and died.

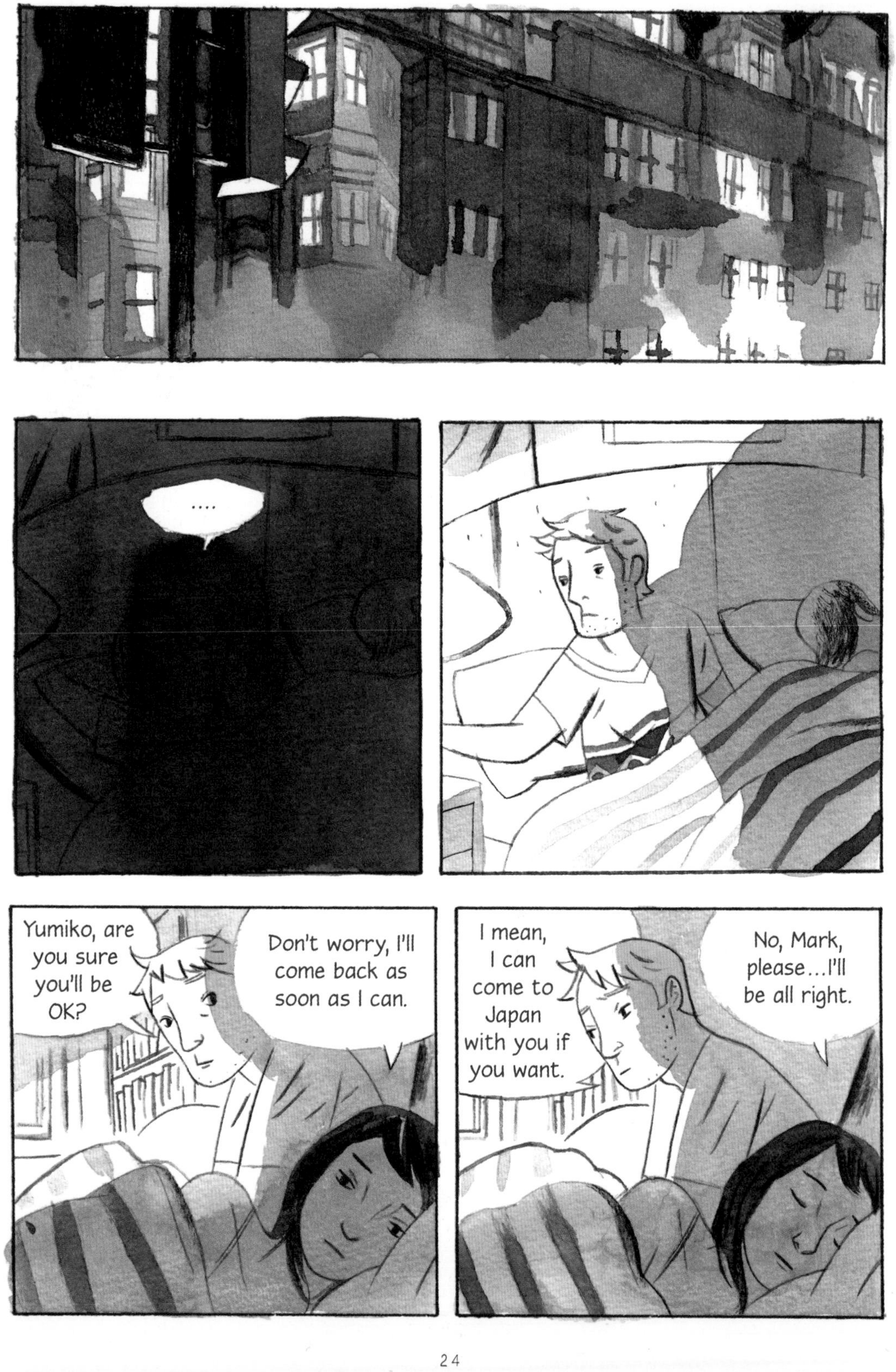
....
Yumiko, are you sure you'll be OK?
Don't worry, I'll come back as soon as I can.
I mean, I can come to Japan with you if you want.
No, Mark, please...I'll be all right.

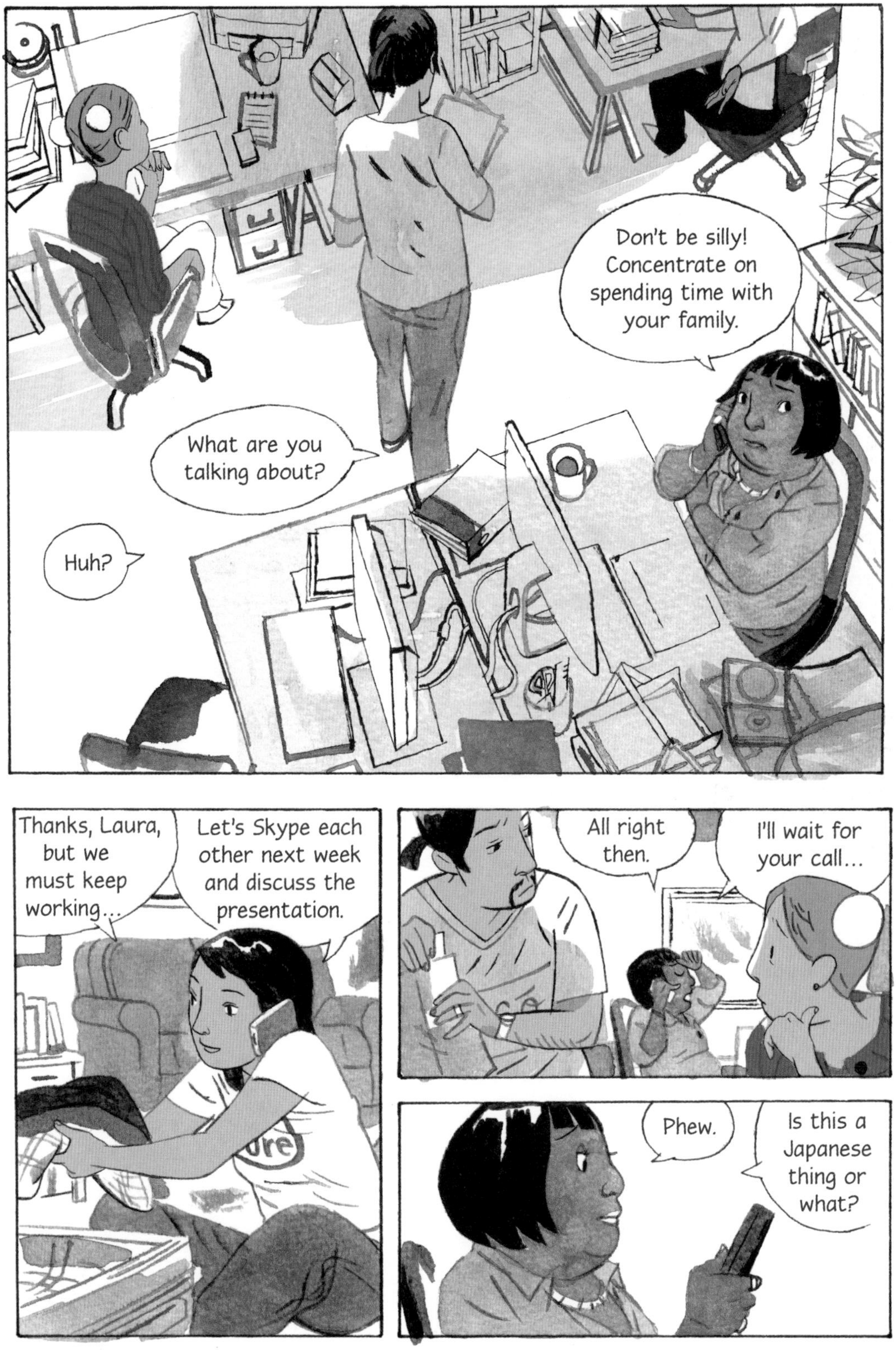
Don't be silly! Concentrate on spending time with your family.
What are you talking about?
Huh?
Thanks, Laura, but we must keep working...
Let's Skype each other next week and discuss the presentation.
All right then.
I'll wait for your call...
Phew.
Is this a Japanese thing or what?

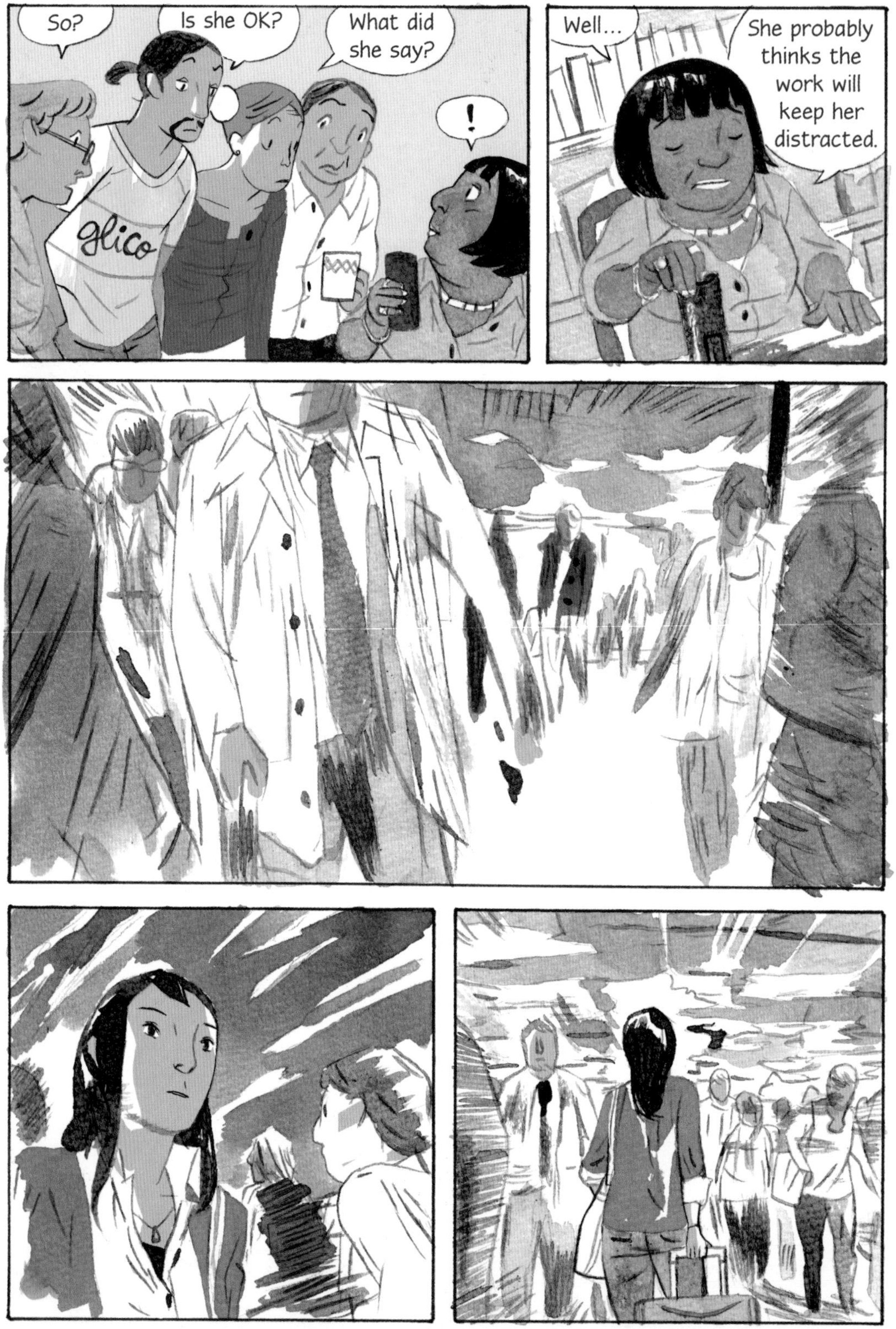
So?
Is she OK?
What did she say?
!
Well...
She probably thinks the work will keep her distracted.
glico

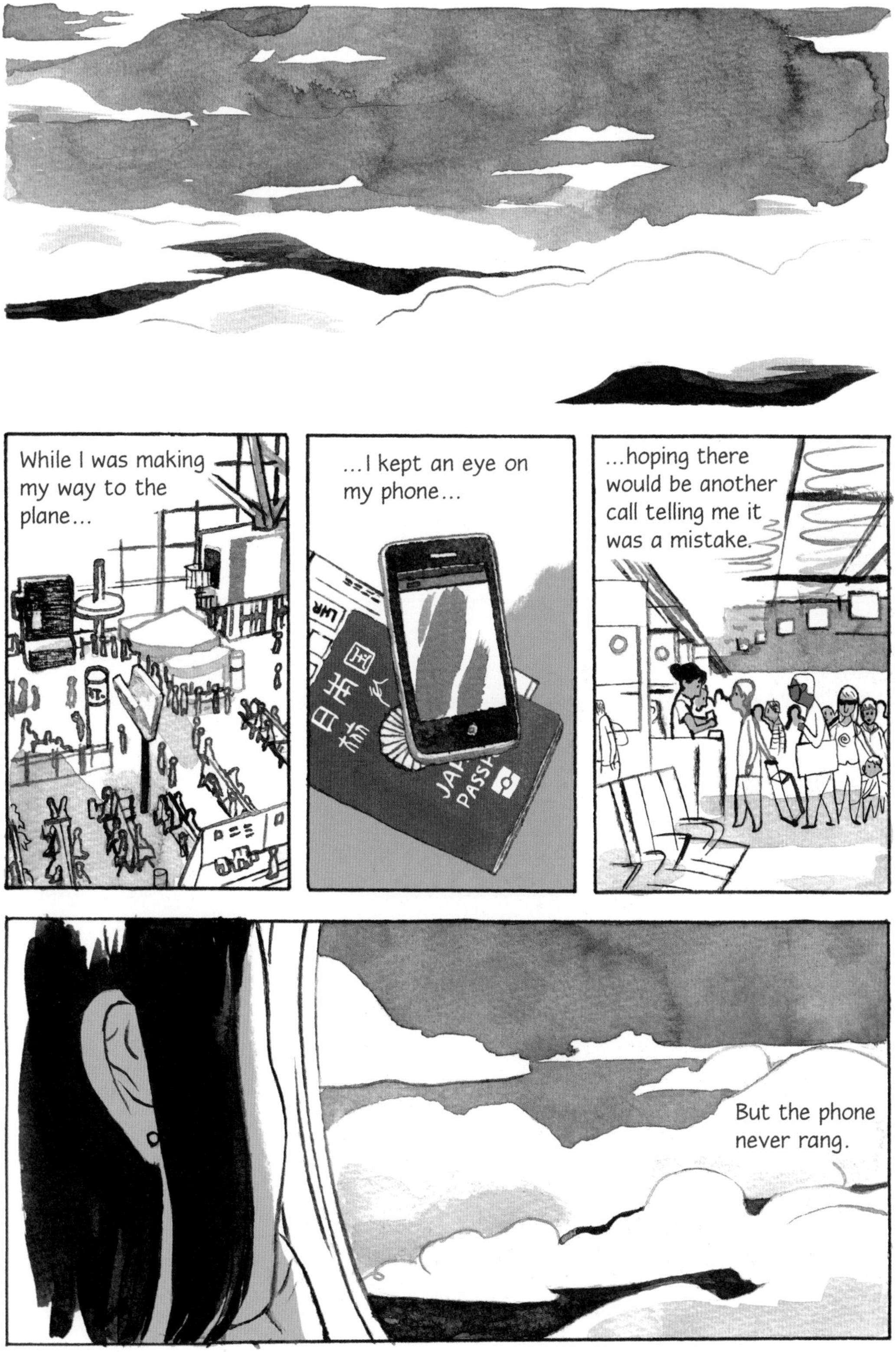
While I was making my way to the plane...
...I kept an eye on my phone...
...hoping there would be another call telling me it was a mistake.
But the phone never rang.

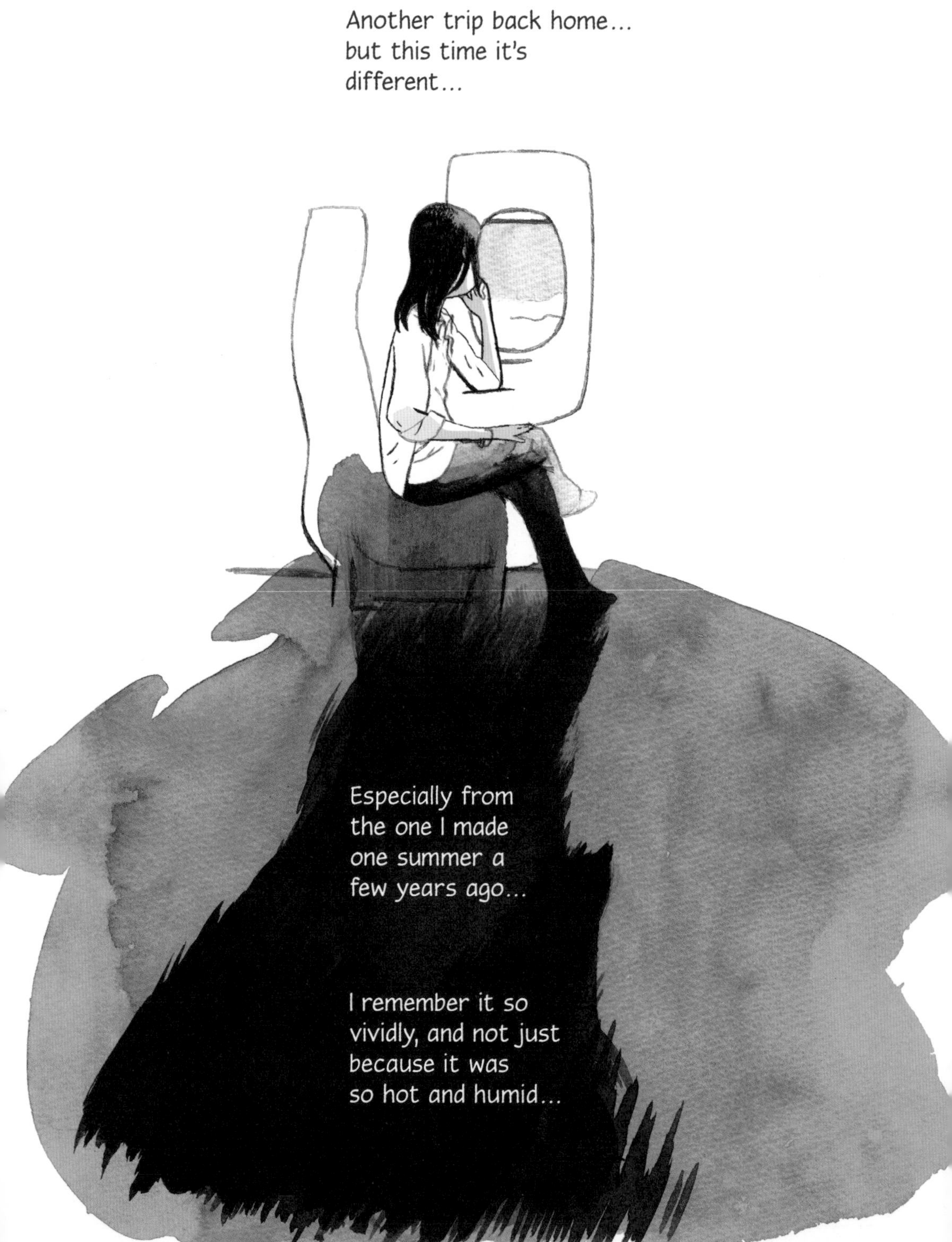
Another trip back home... but this time it's different...
Especially from the one I made one summer a few years ago...
I remember it so vividly, and not just because it was so hot and humid...

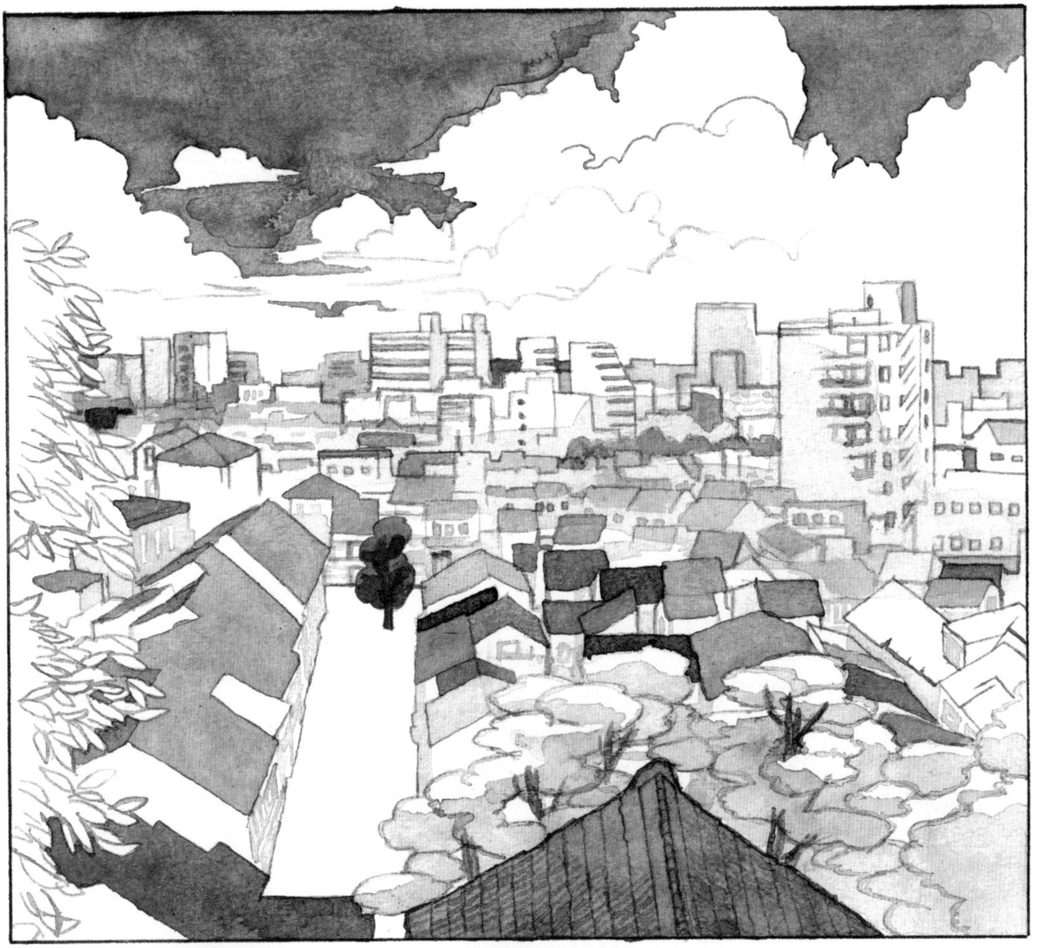

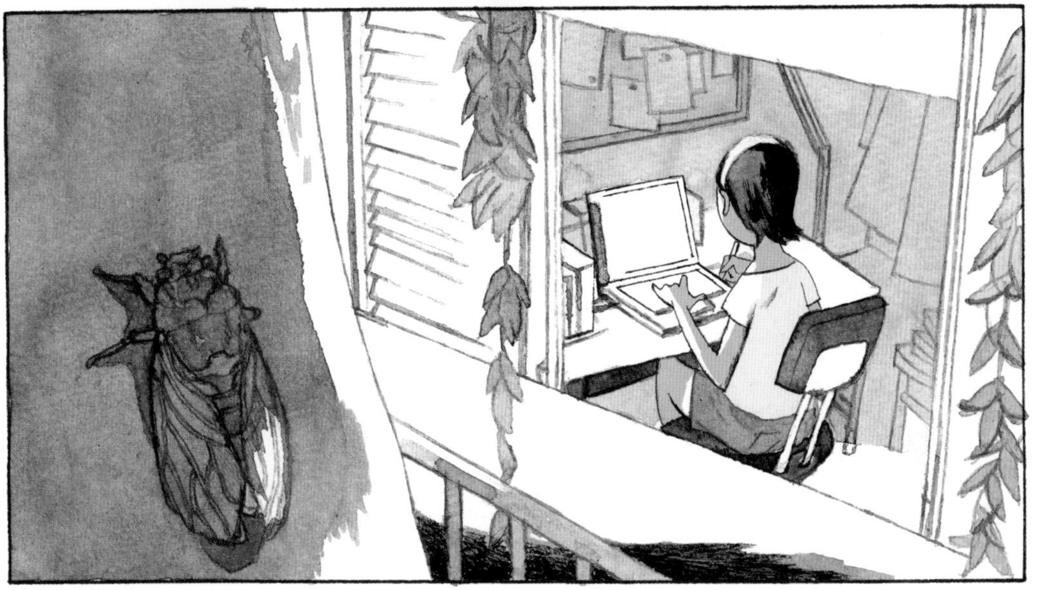

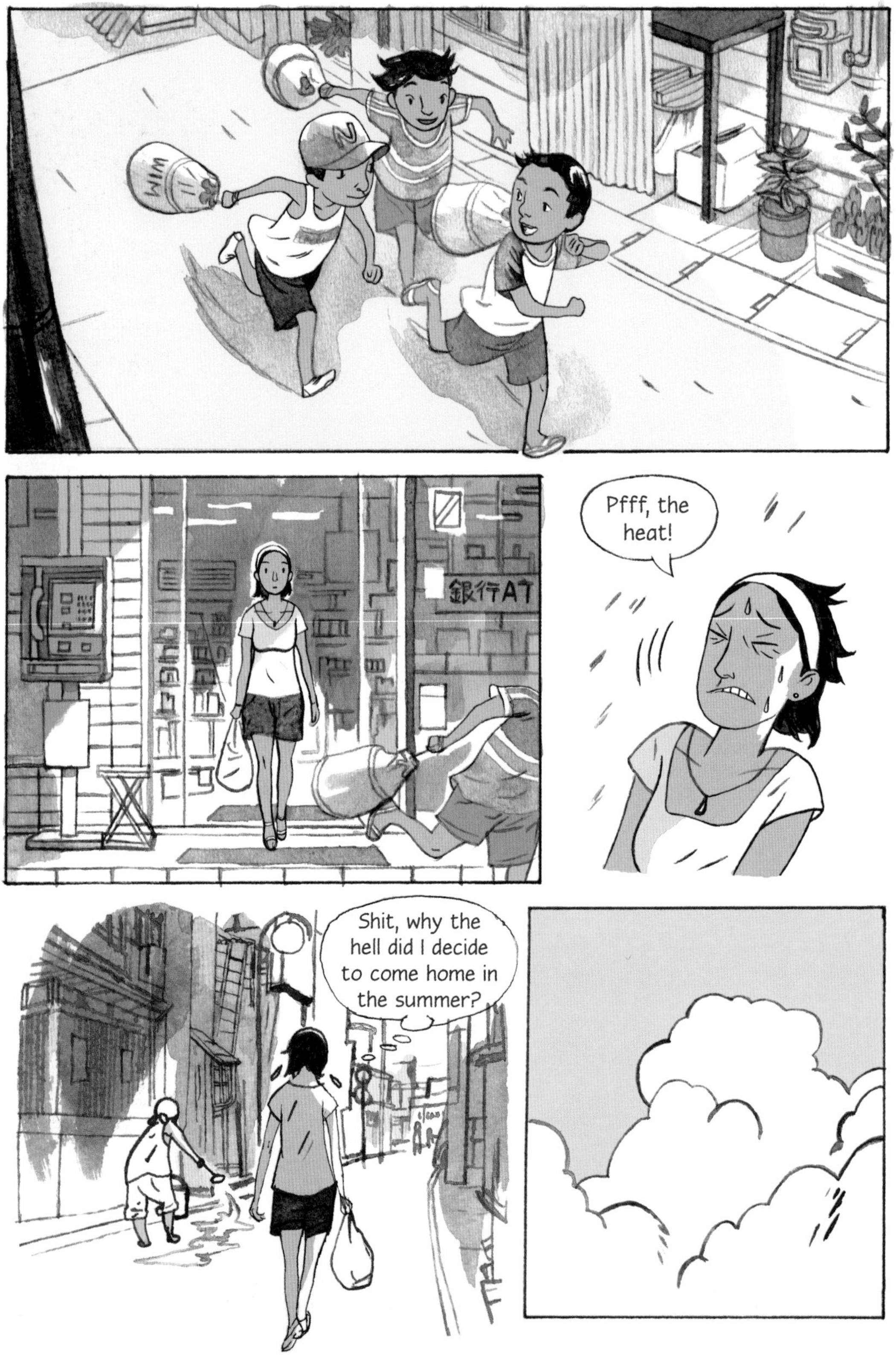
銀行AT
Pfff, the heat!
Shit, why the hell did I decide to come home in the summer?

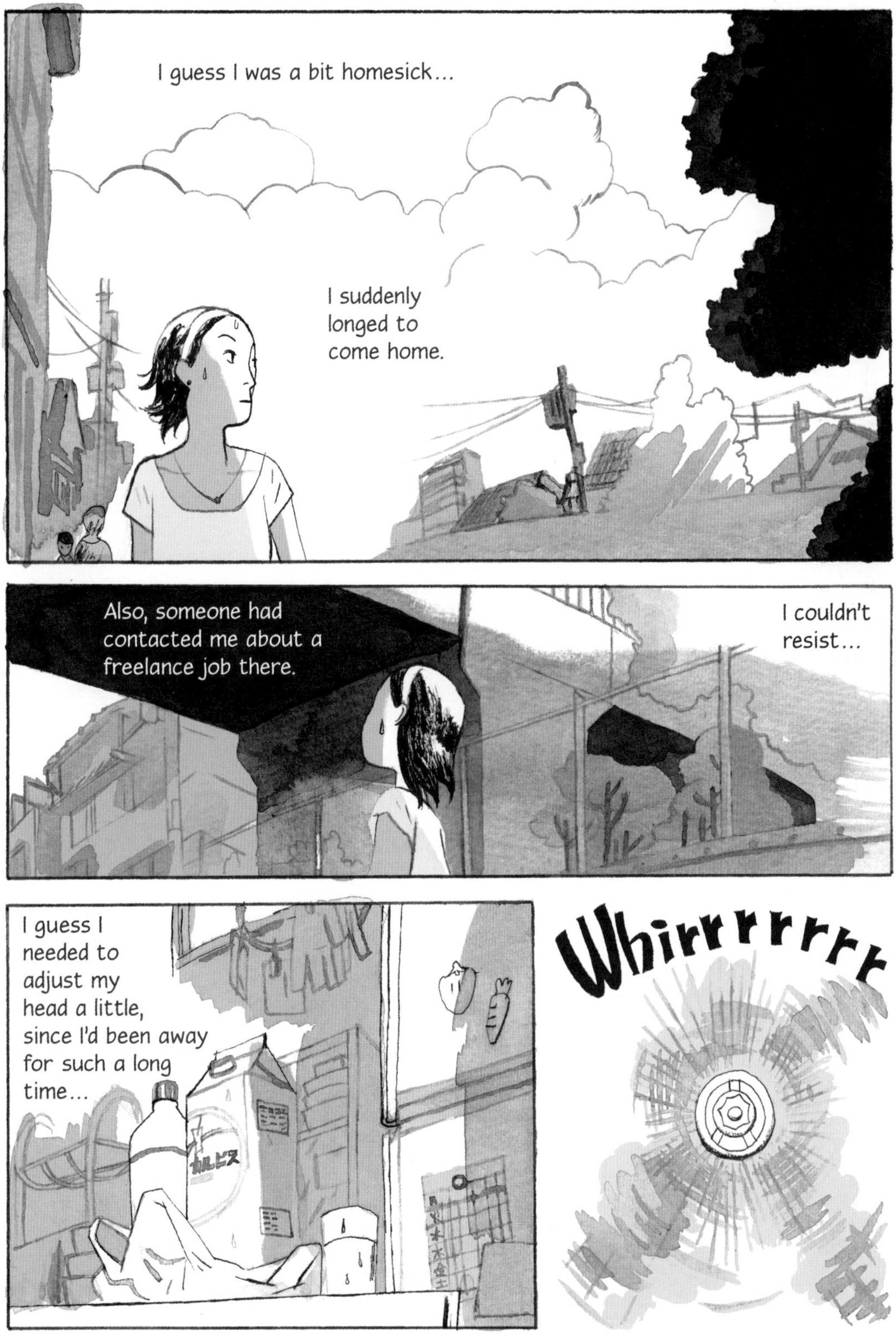
I guess I was a bit homesick…
I suddenly longed to come home.
Also, someone had contacted me about a freelance job there.
I couldn't resist…
I guess I needed to adjust my head a little, since I'd been away for such a long time…
カルピス
Whirrrrrrt

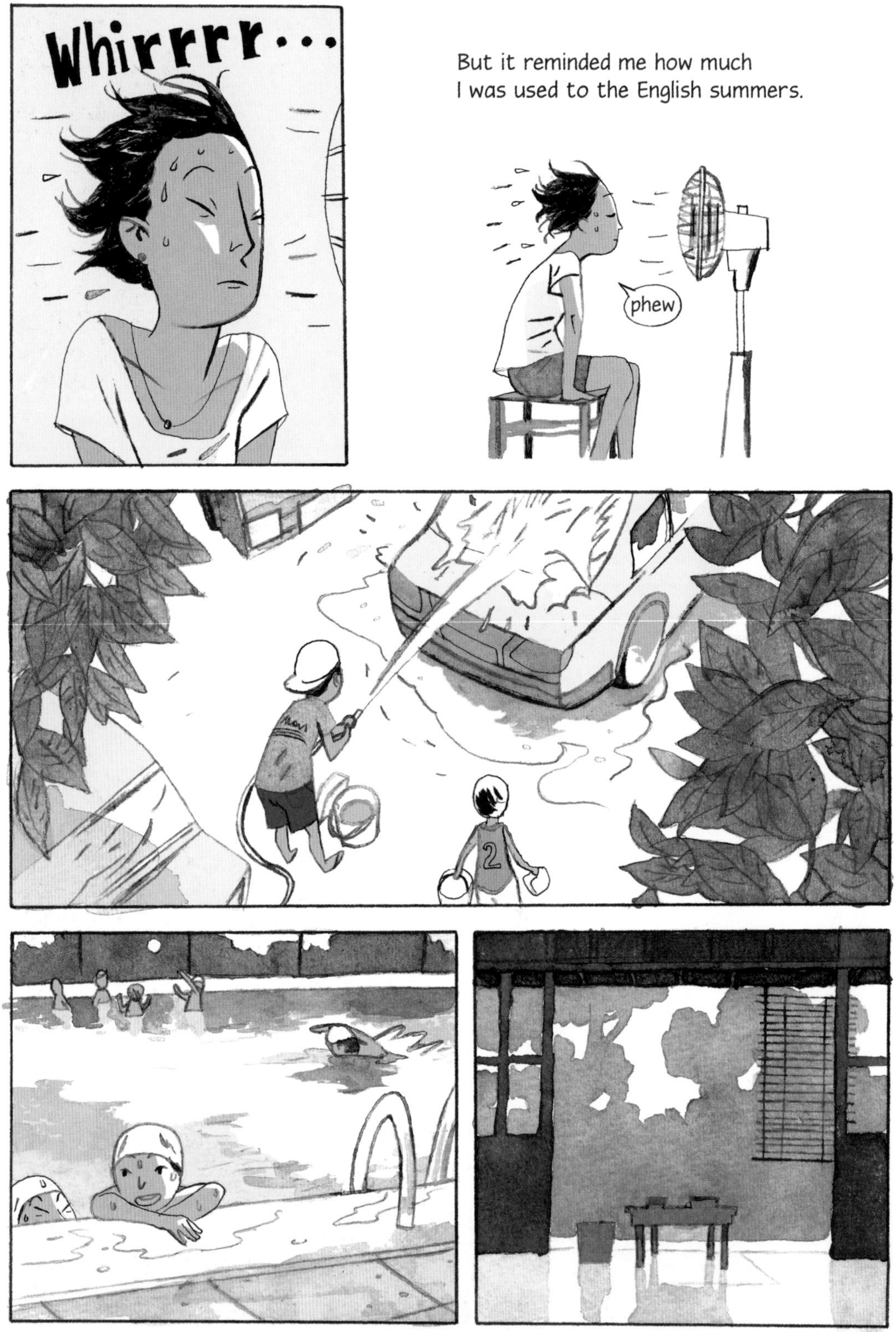
Whirrrr...
But it reminded me how much
I was used to the English summers.
phew
2

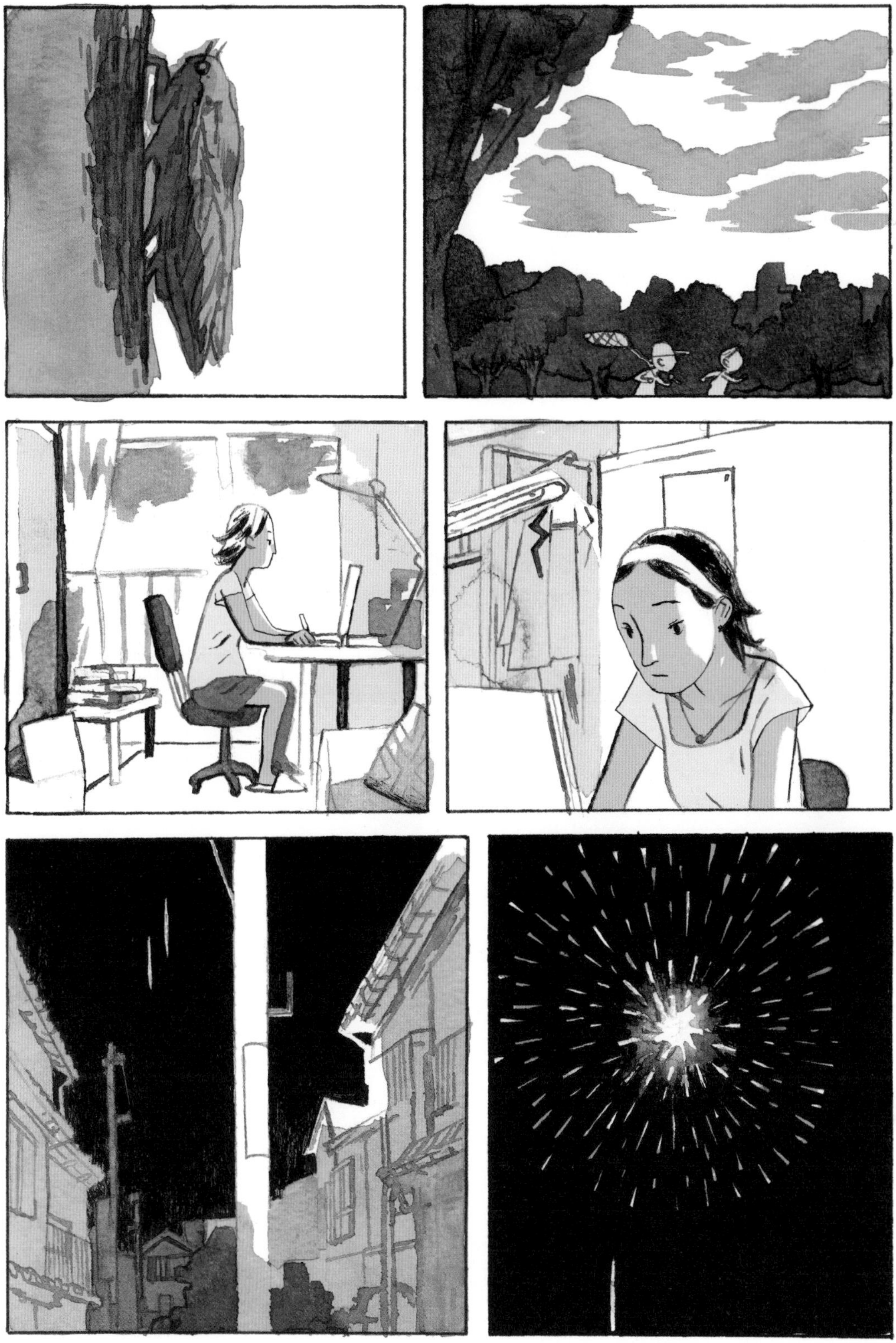

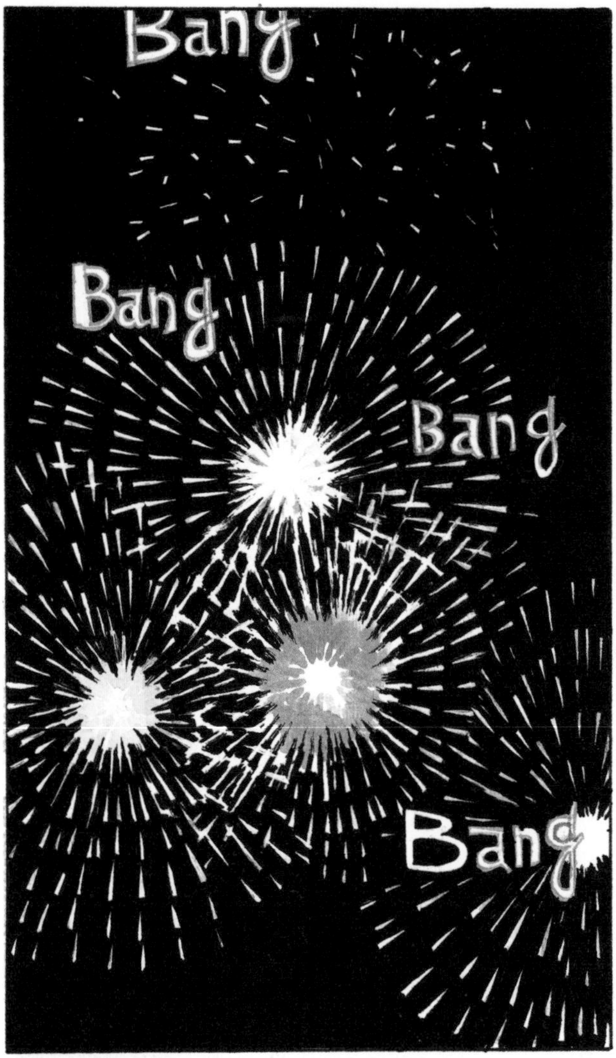
Bang
Bang
Bang
Bang

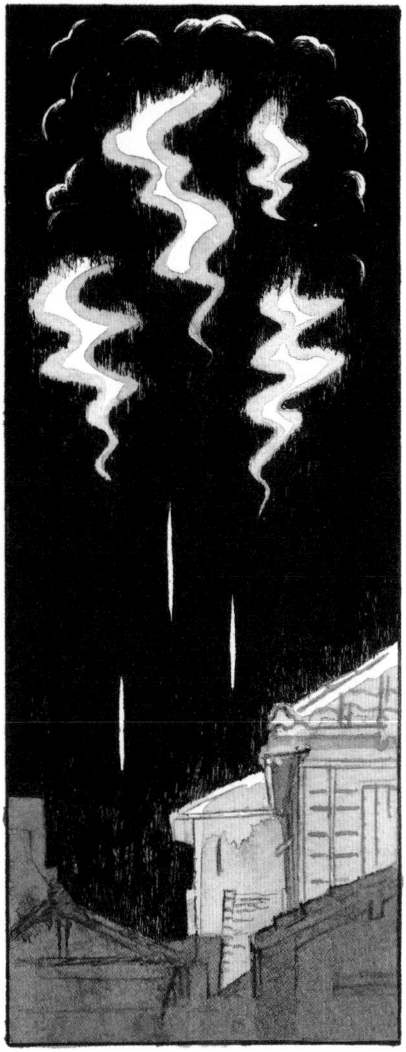

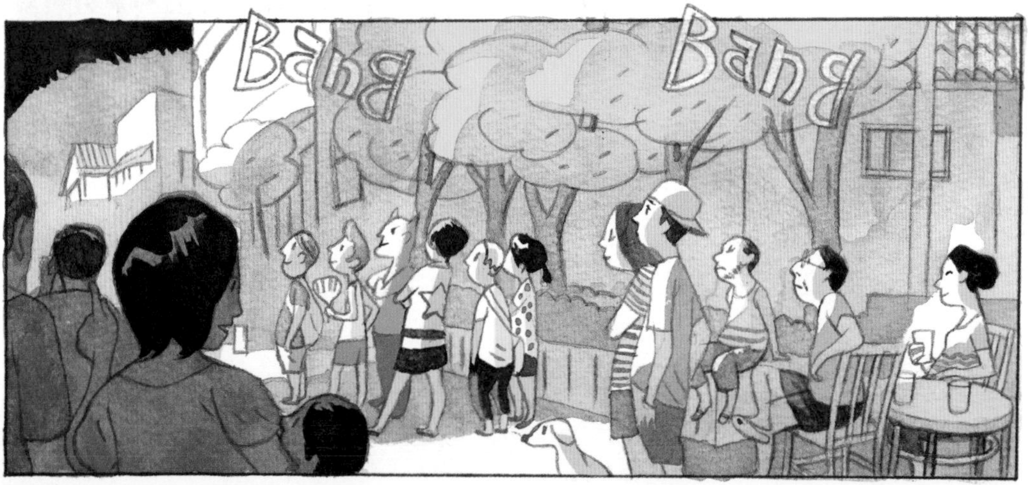
Bang
Bang

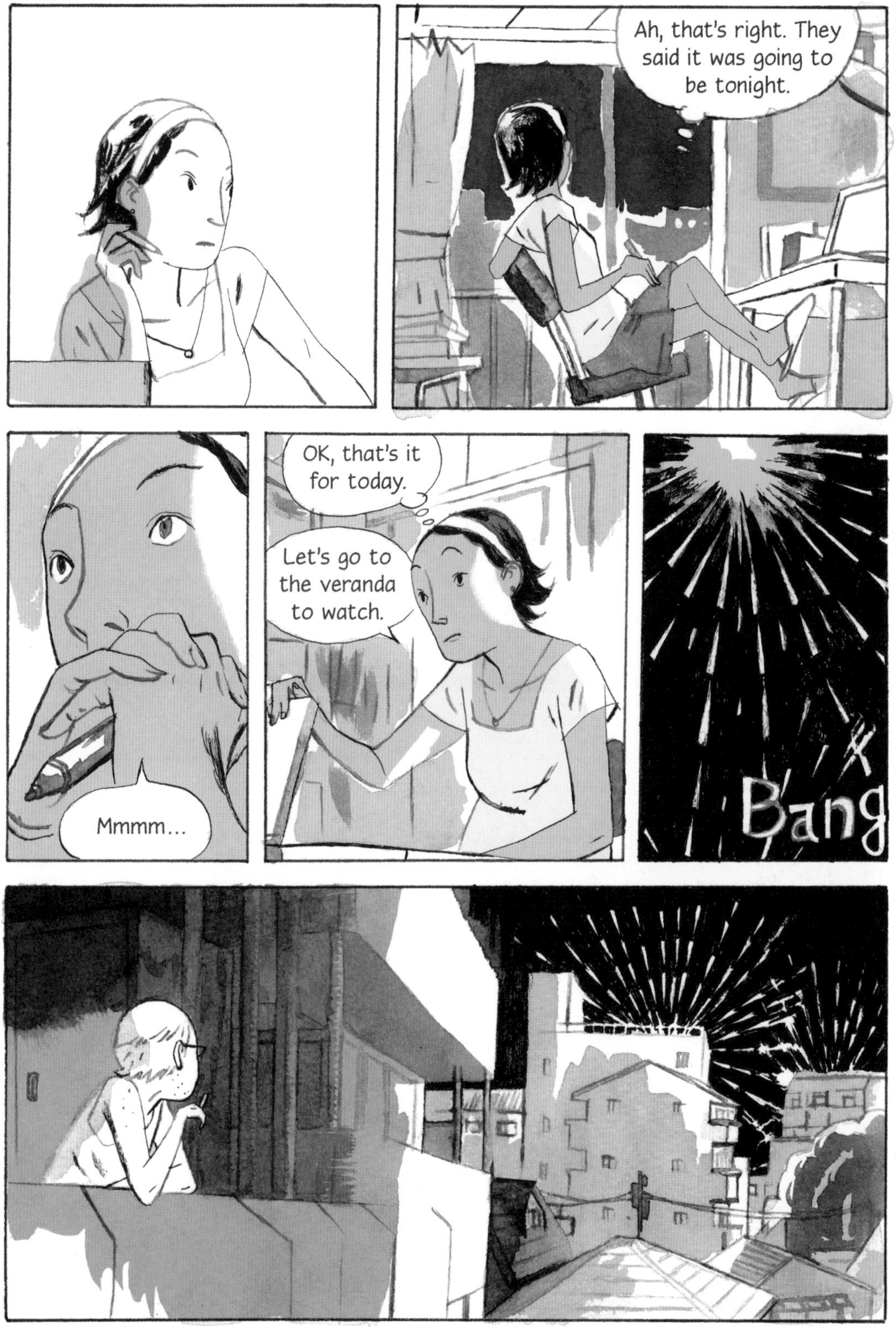
Ah, that's right. They said it was going to be tonight.
Mmmm...
OK, that's it for today.
Let's go to the veranda to watch.
Bang

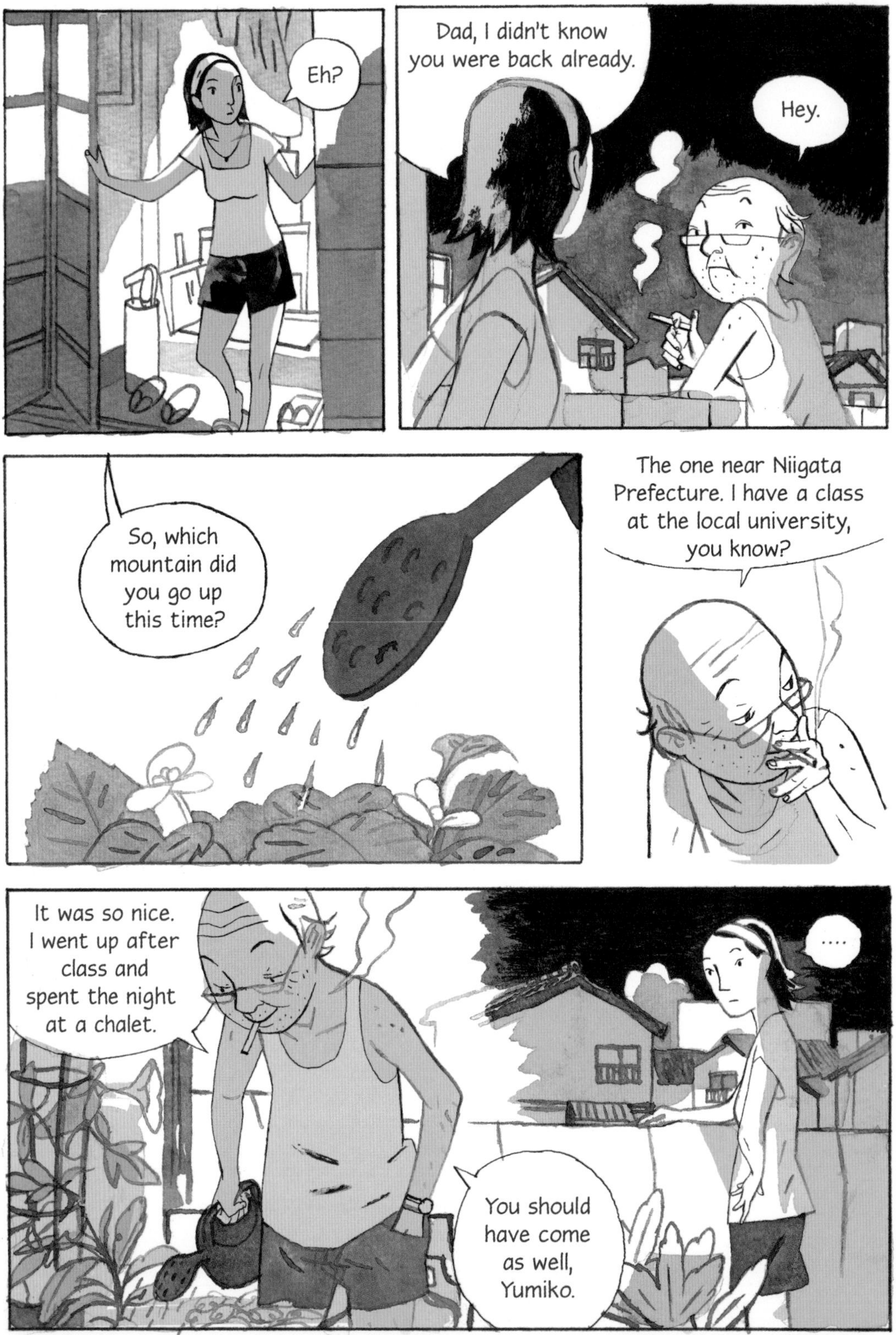
Eh?
Dad, I didn't know you were back already.
Hey.
So, which mountain did you go up this time?
The one near Niigata Prefecture. I have a class at the local university, you know?
It was so nice. I went up after class and spent the night at a chalet.
....
You should have come as well, Yumiko.

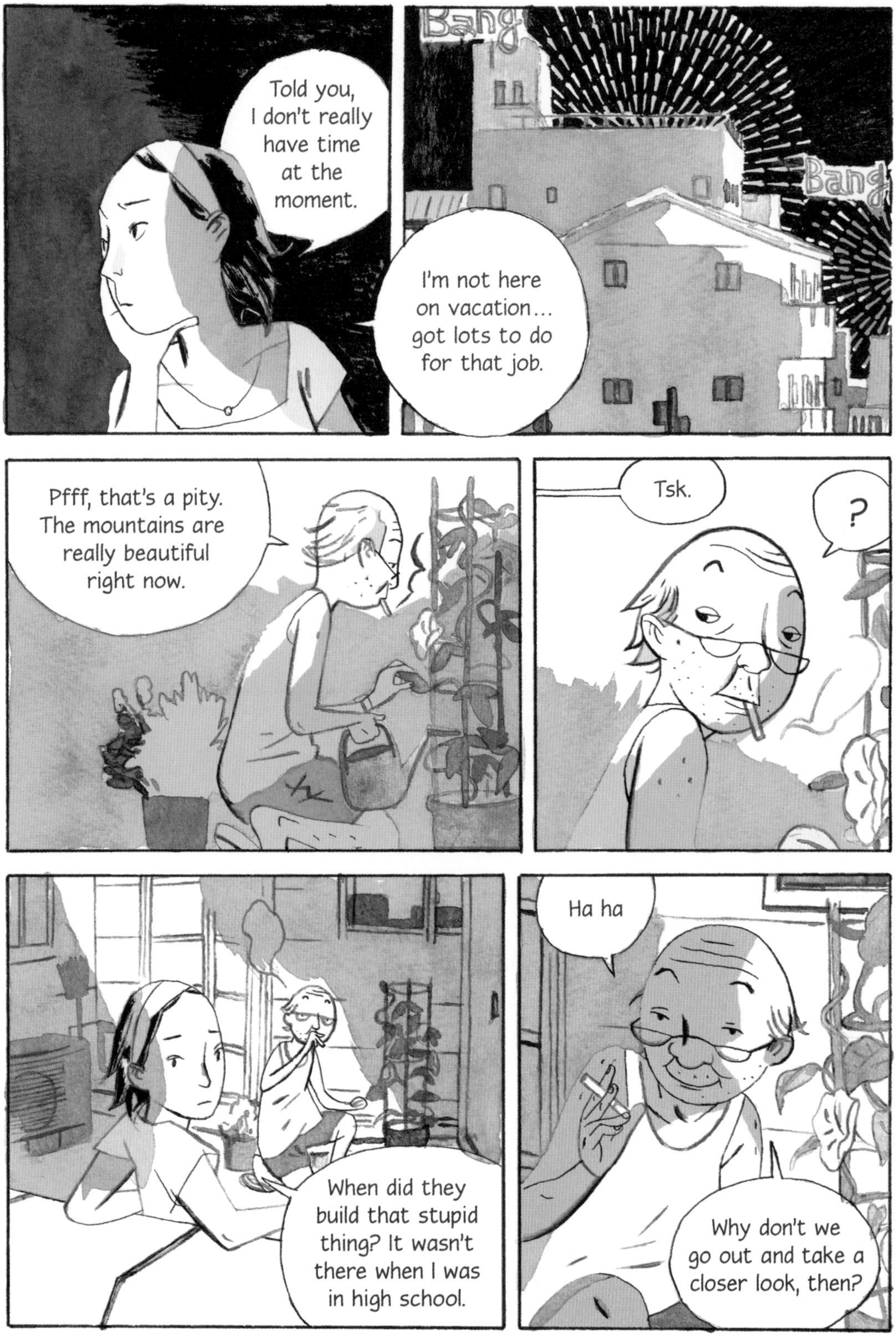
Told you, I don't really have time at the moment.
Bang
Bang
I'm not here on vacation... got lots to do for that job.
Pfff, that's a pity. The mountains are really beautiful right now.
Tsk.
?
When did they build that stupid thing? It wasn't there when I was in high school.
Ha ha
Why don't we go out and take a closer look, then?

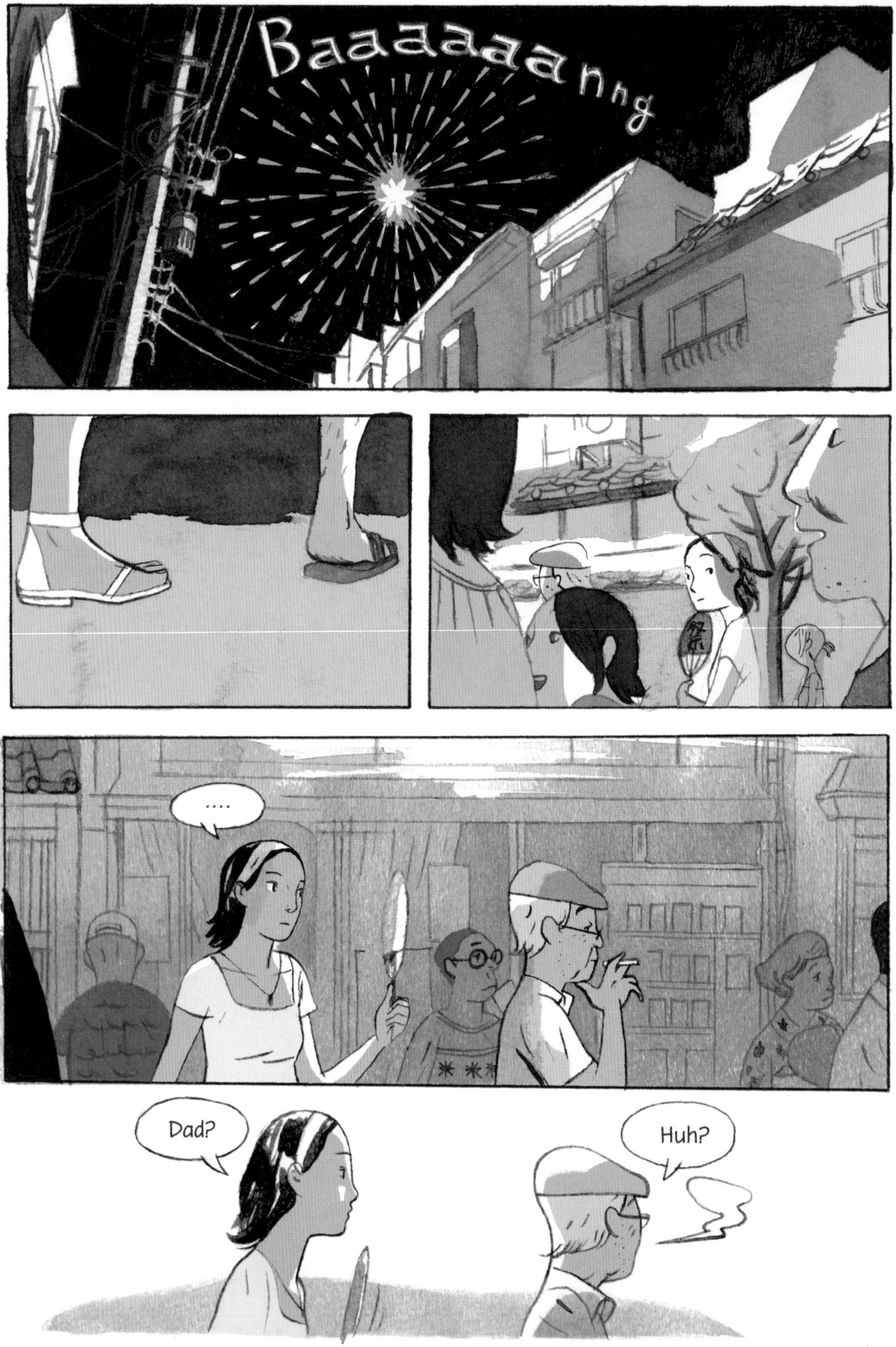
Baaaaaaanng
....
Dad?
Huh?

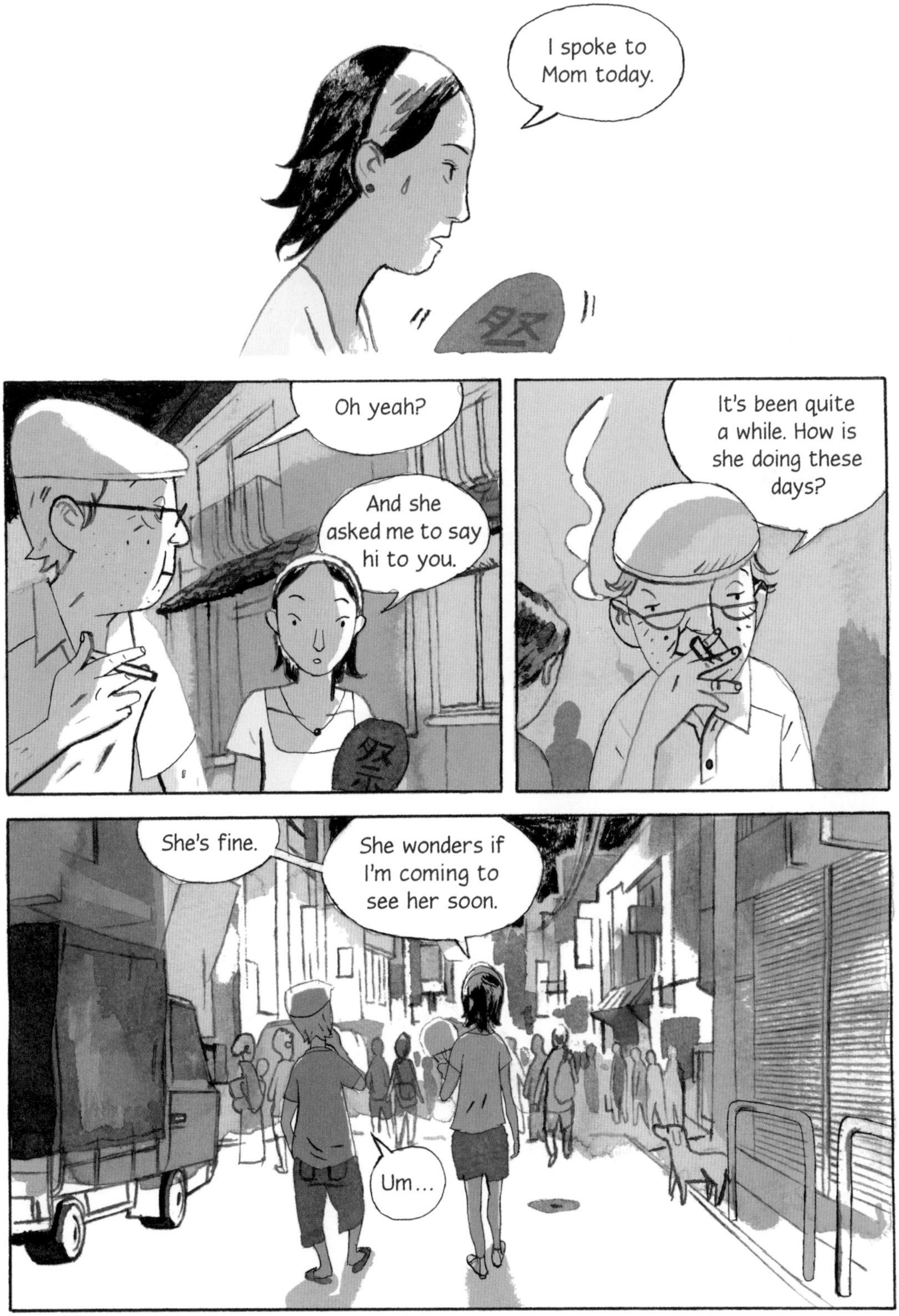
I spoke to Mom today.
Oh yeah?
And she asked me to say hi to you.
It's been quite a while. How is she doing these days?
She's fine.
She wonders if I'm coming to see her soon.
Um...

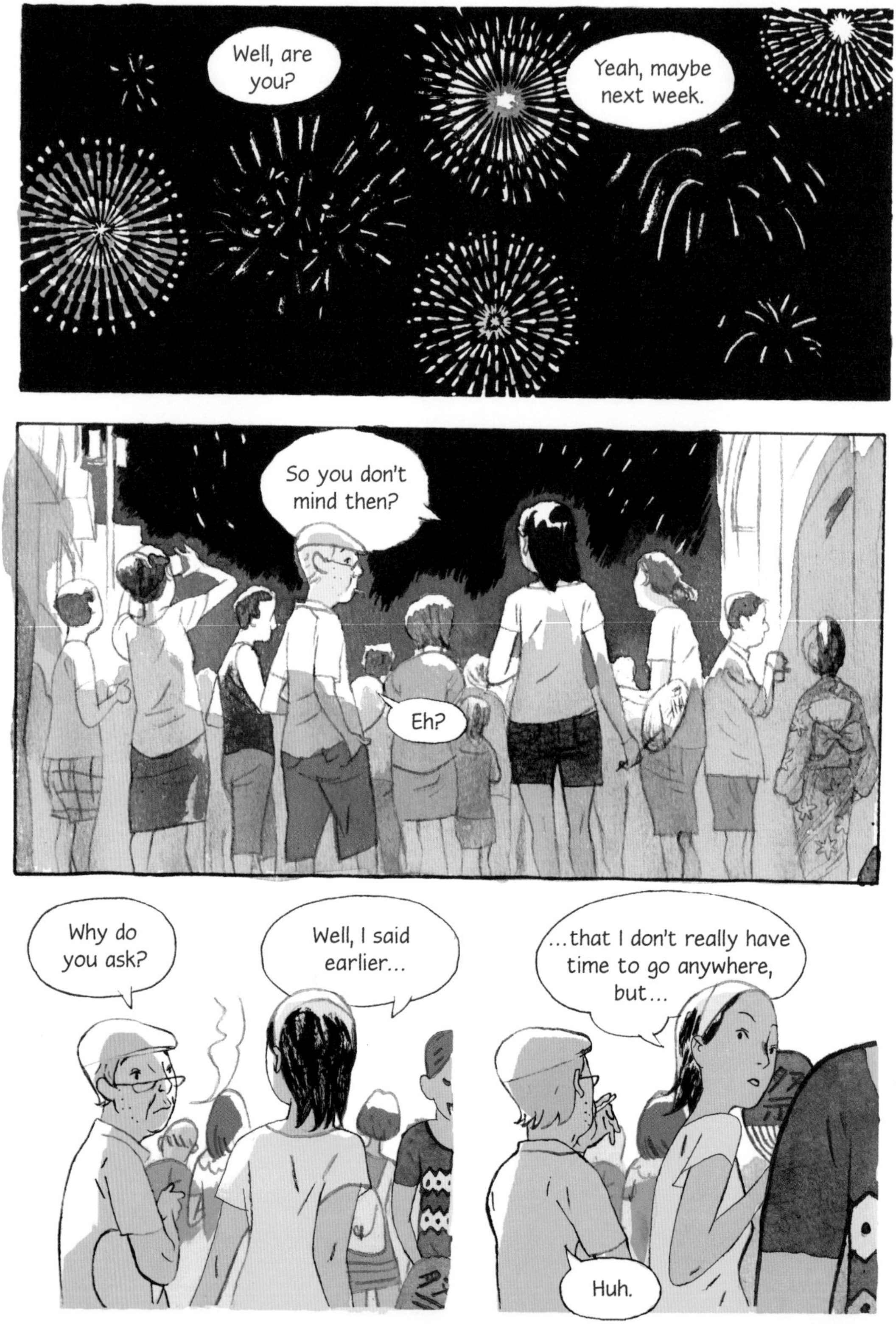
Well, are you?
Yeah, maybe next week.
So you don't mind then?
Eh?
Why do you ask?
Well, I said earlier...
...that I don't really have time to go anywhere, but...
Huh.

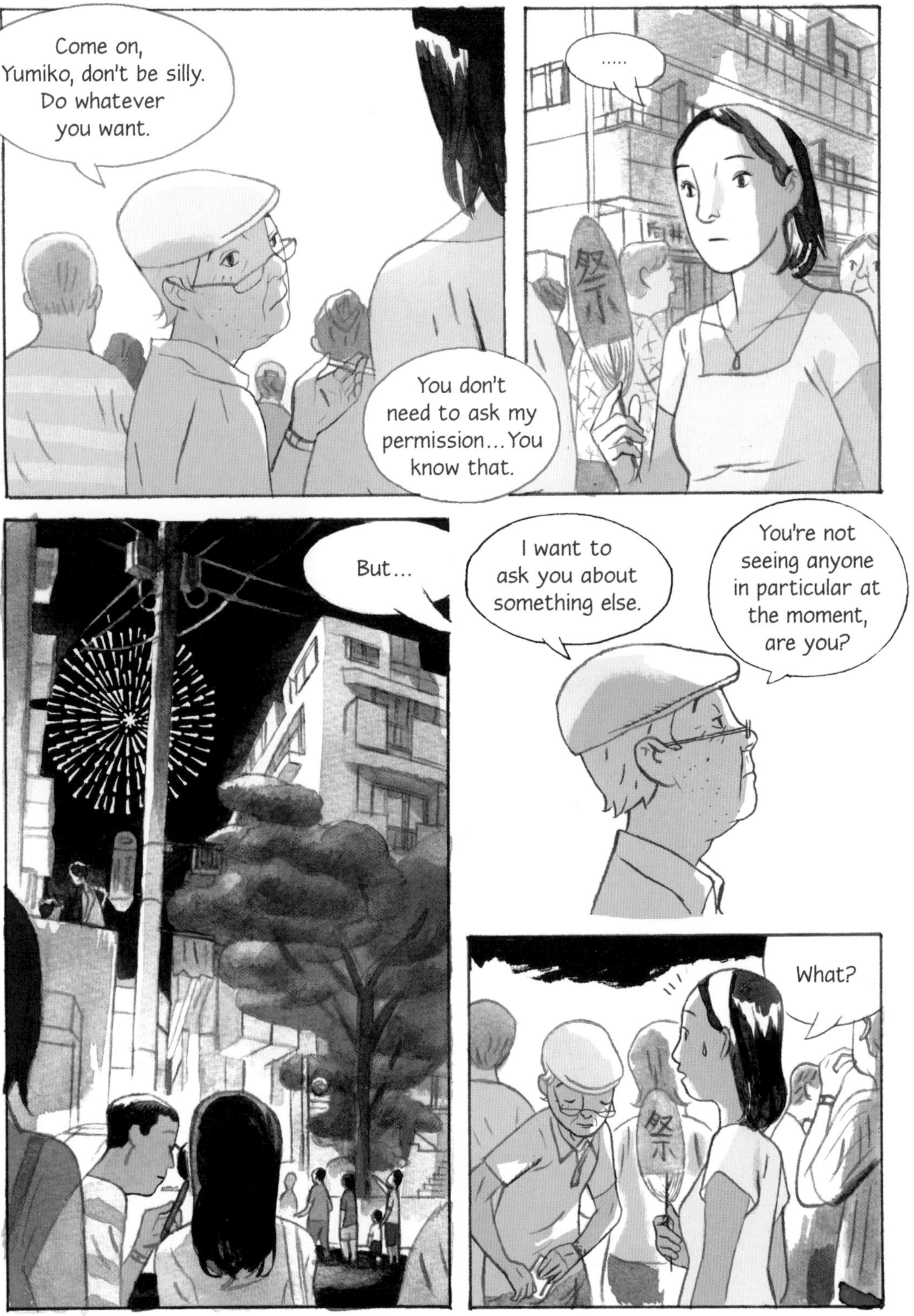
Come on, Yumiko, don't be silly. Do whatever you want.
.....
You don't need to ask my permission... You know that.
But...
I want to ask you about something else.
You're not seeing anyone in particular at the moment, are you?
What?

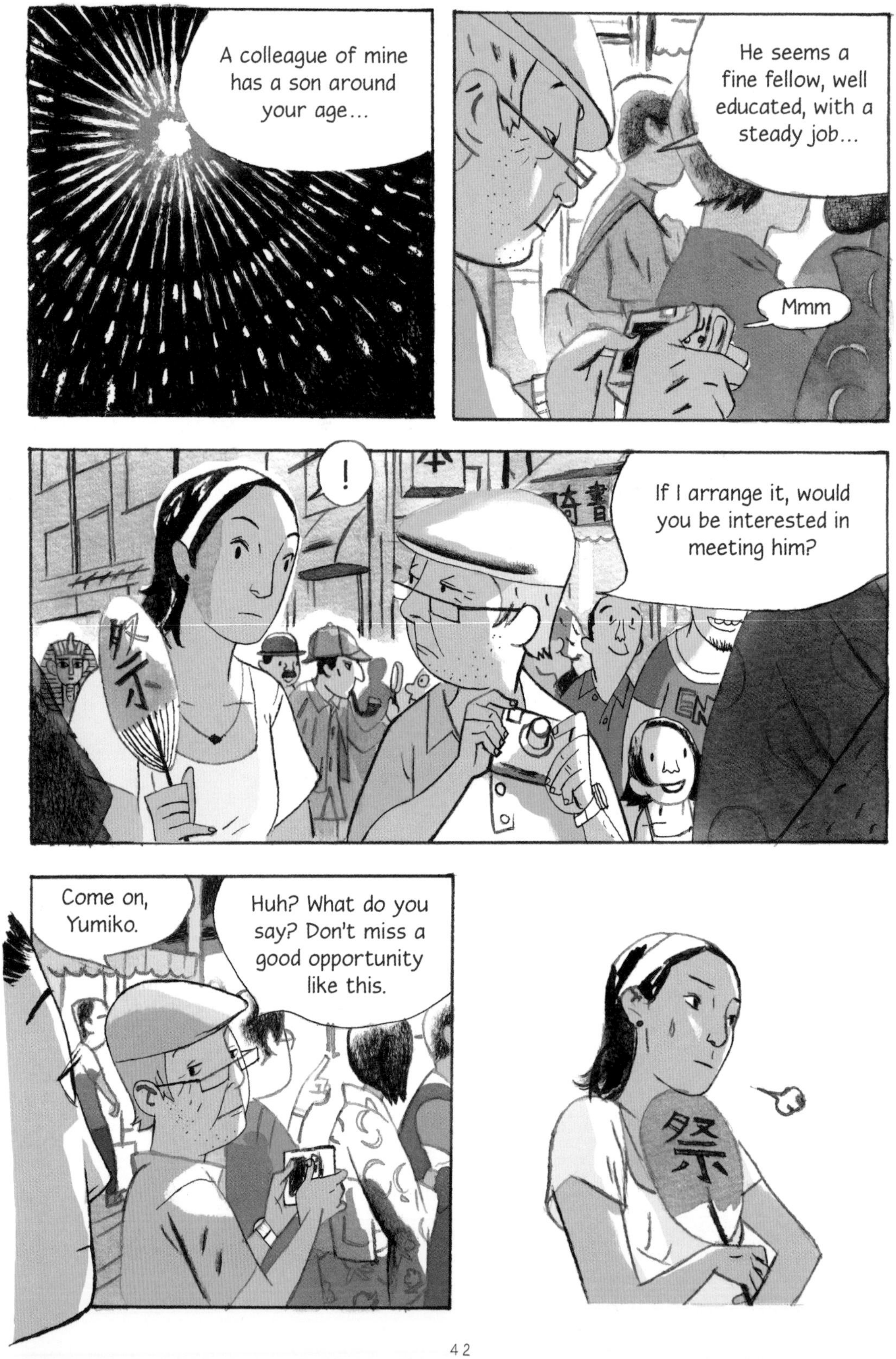
A colleague of mine has a son around your age...
He seems a fine fellow, well educated, with a steady job...
Mmm
!
If I arrange it, would you be interested in meeting him?
Come on, Yumiko.
Huh? What do you say? Don't miss a good opportunity like this.

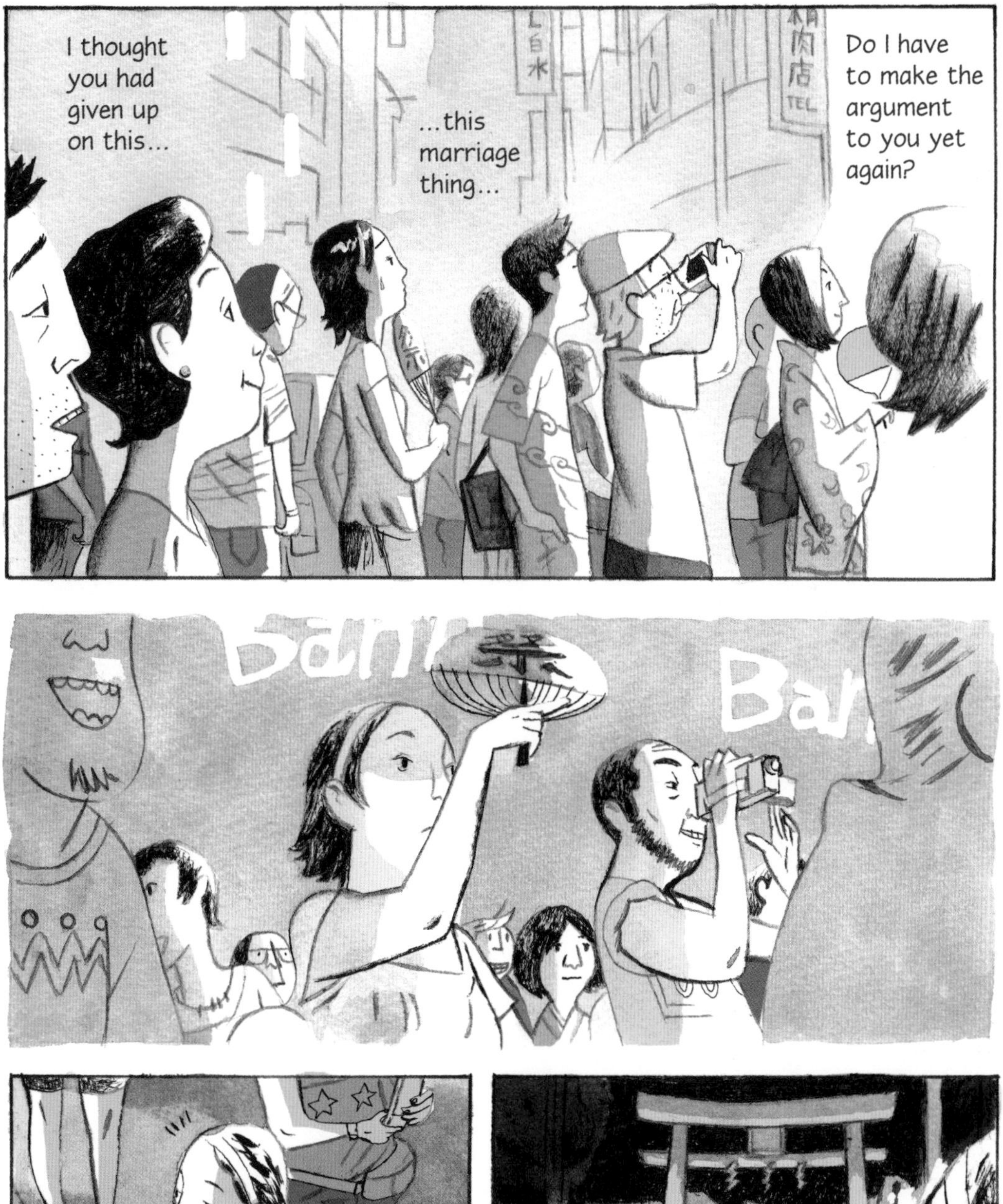
I thought you had given up on this...
...this marriage thing...
Do I have to make the argument to you yet again?

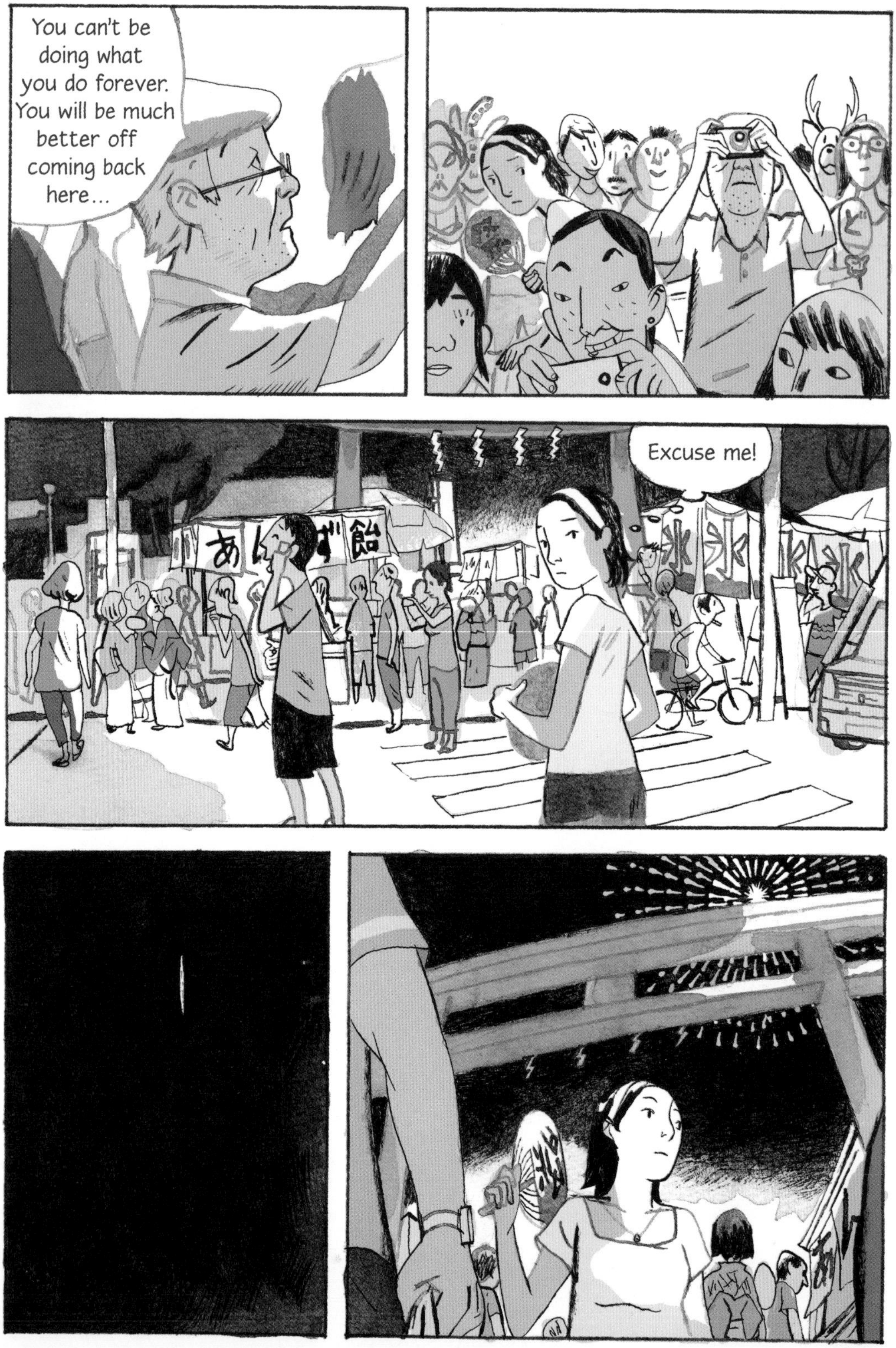
You can't be doing what you do forever. You will be much better off coming back here...
Excuse me!

To avoid the conversation, I walked into
the local Shinto shrine
where I played as
a child.

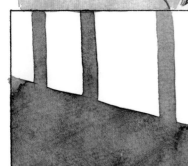 It was a
pleasant
surprise to
see it had
changed only
a little since
then...

...and how
calm it was inside...

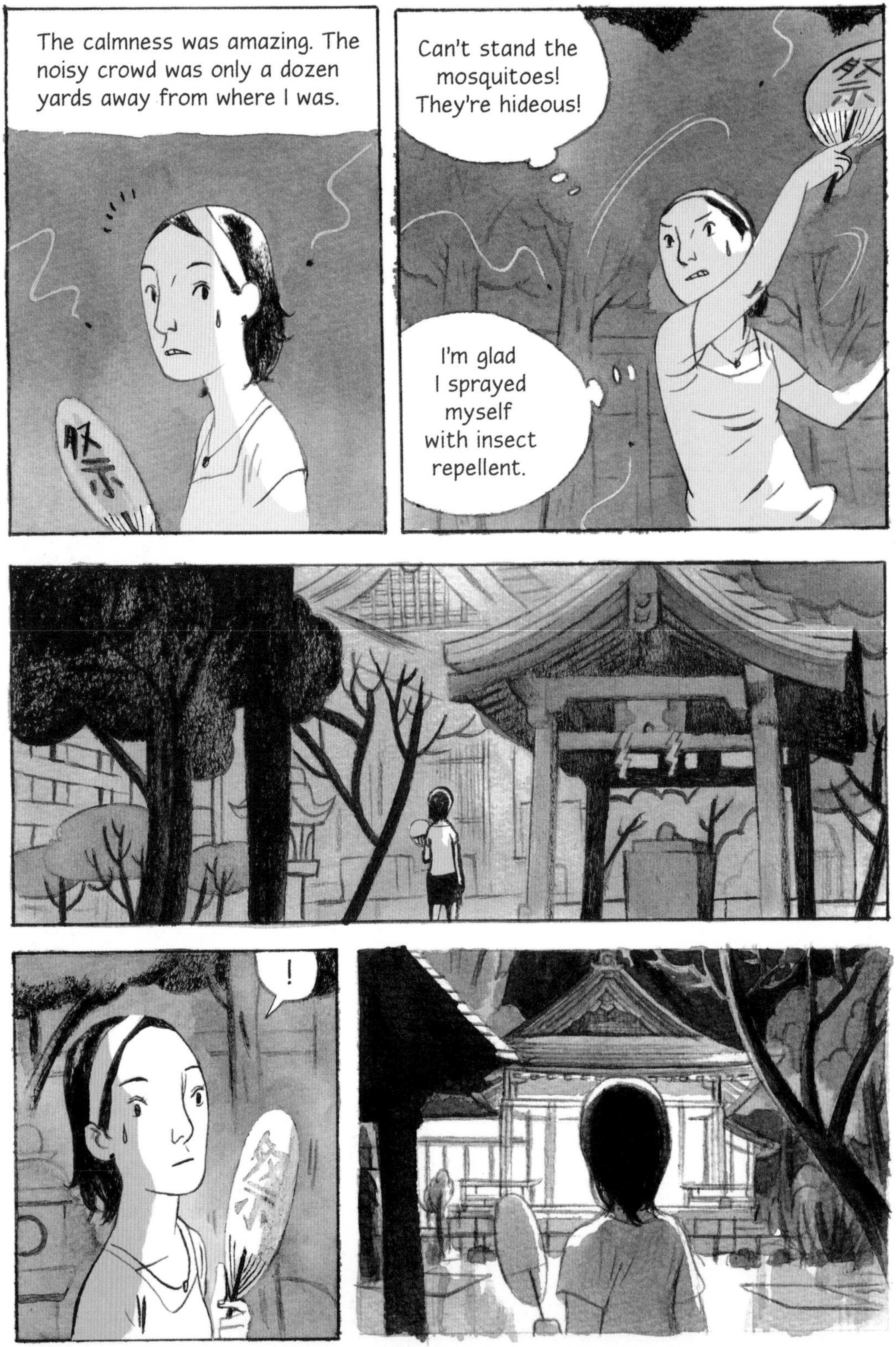
The calmness was amazing. The noisy crowd was only a dozen yards away from where I was.
祭
Can't stand the mosquitoes! They're hideous!
祭
I'm glad I sprayed myself with insect repellent.
!
祭

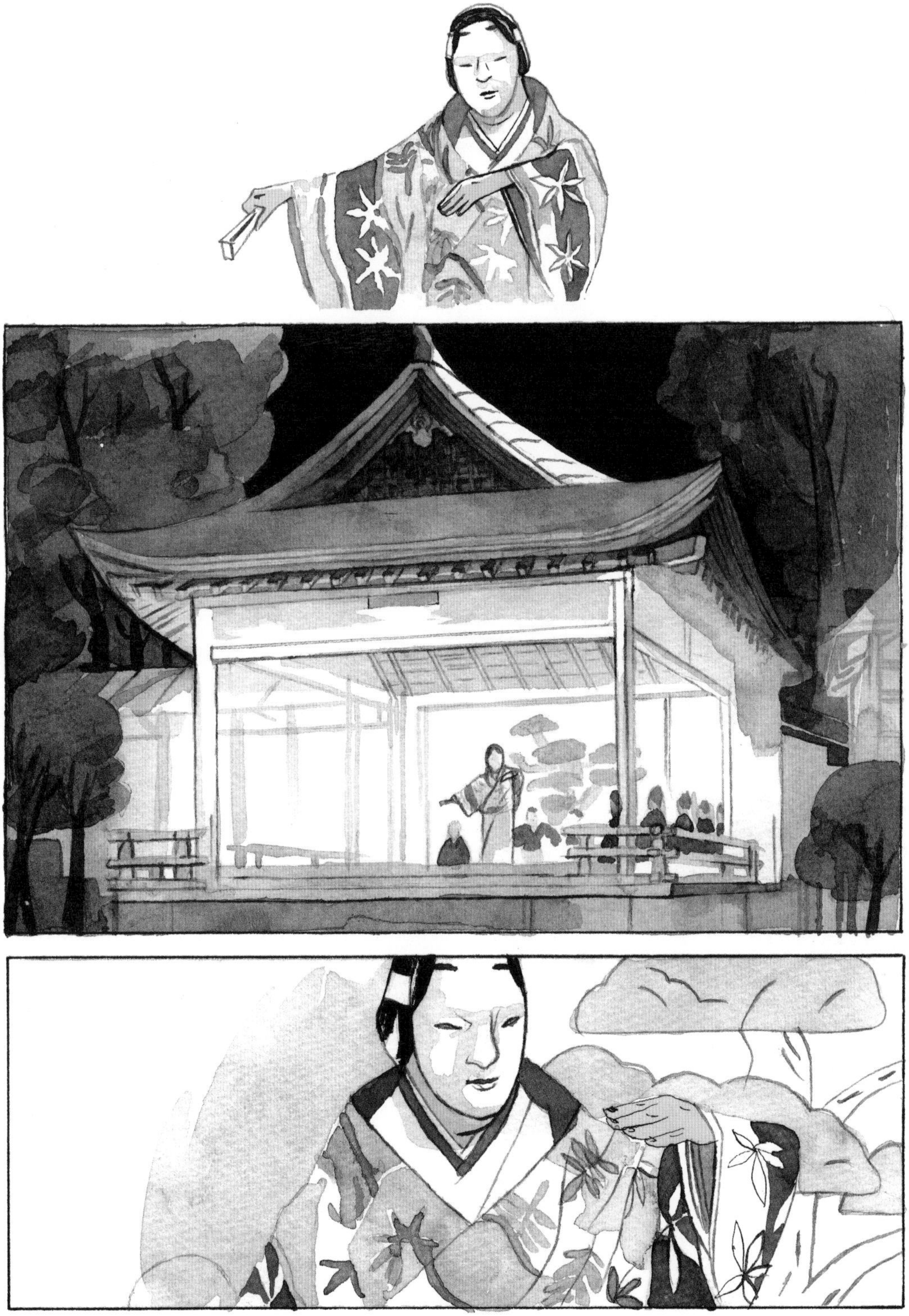

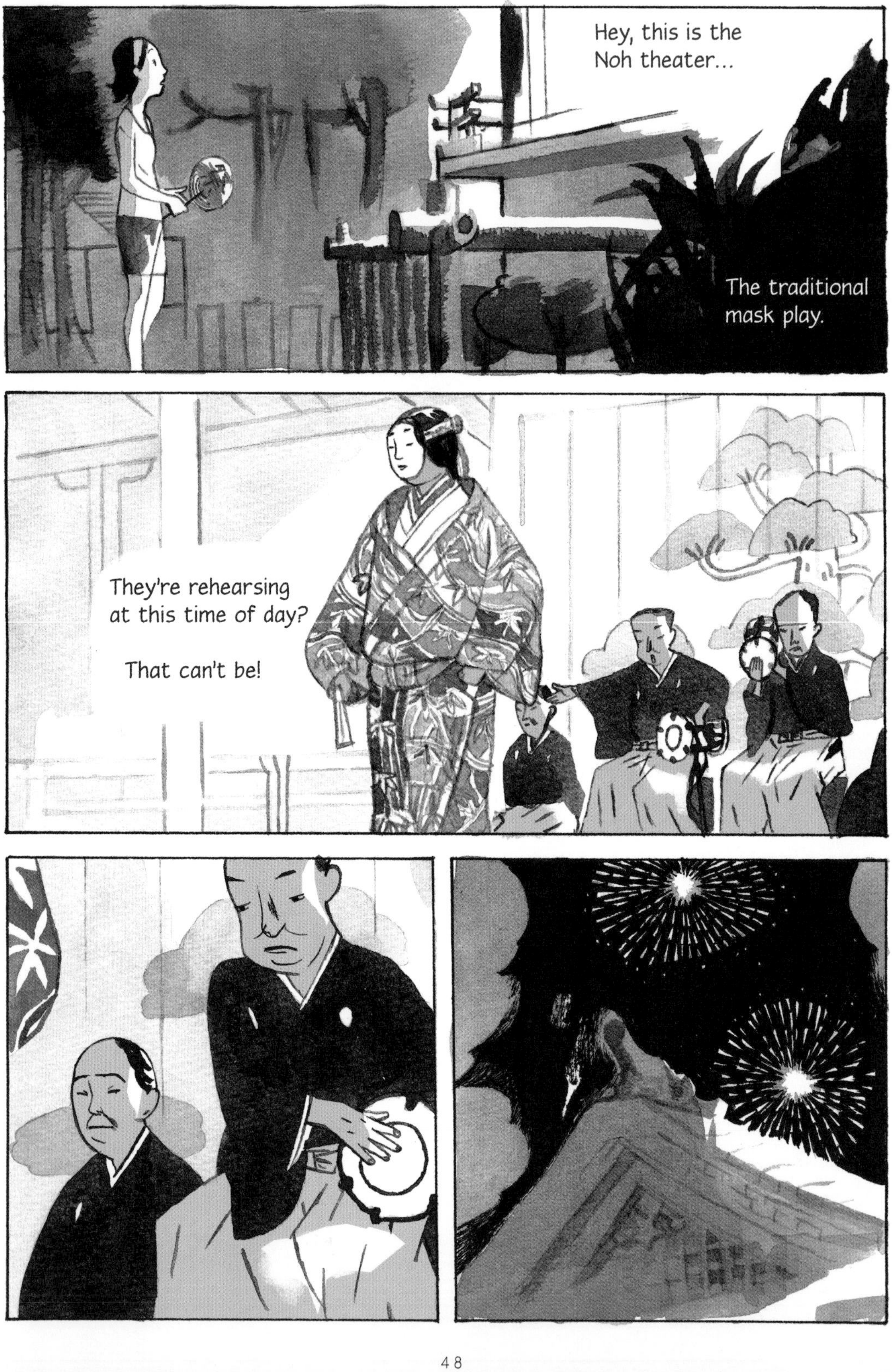
Hey, this is the Noh theater...
The traditional mask play.
They're rehearsing at this time of day?
That can't be!

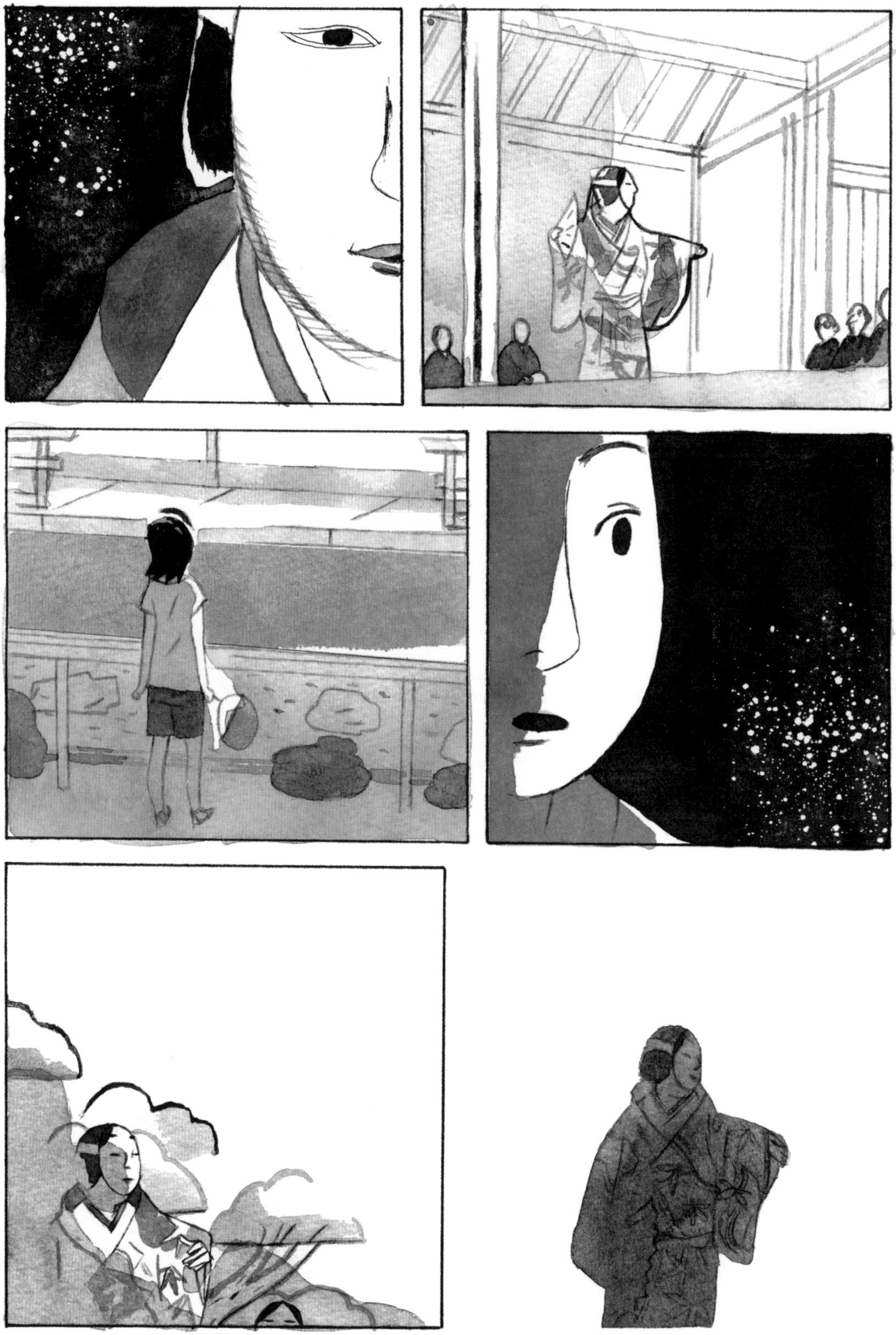

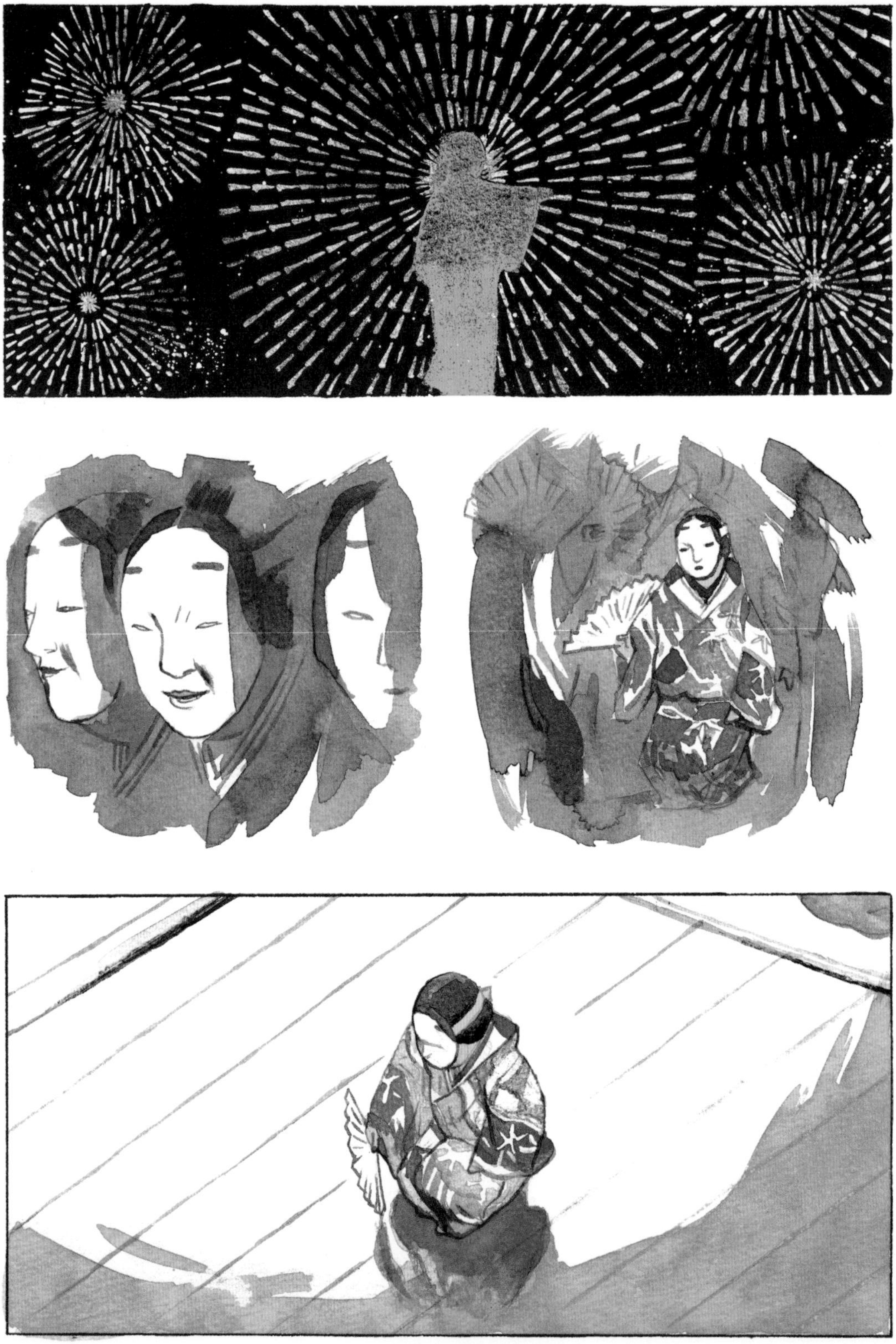

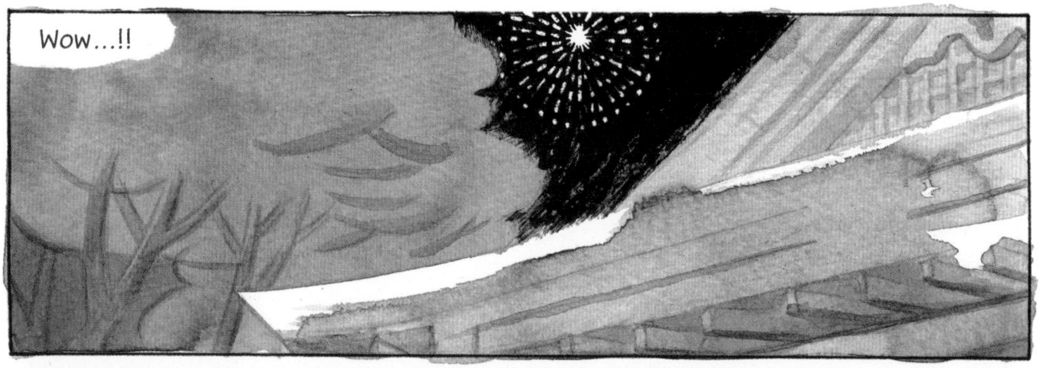
Wow...!!

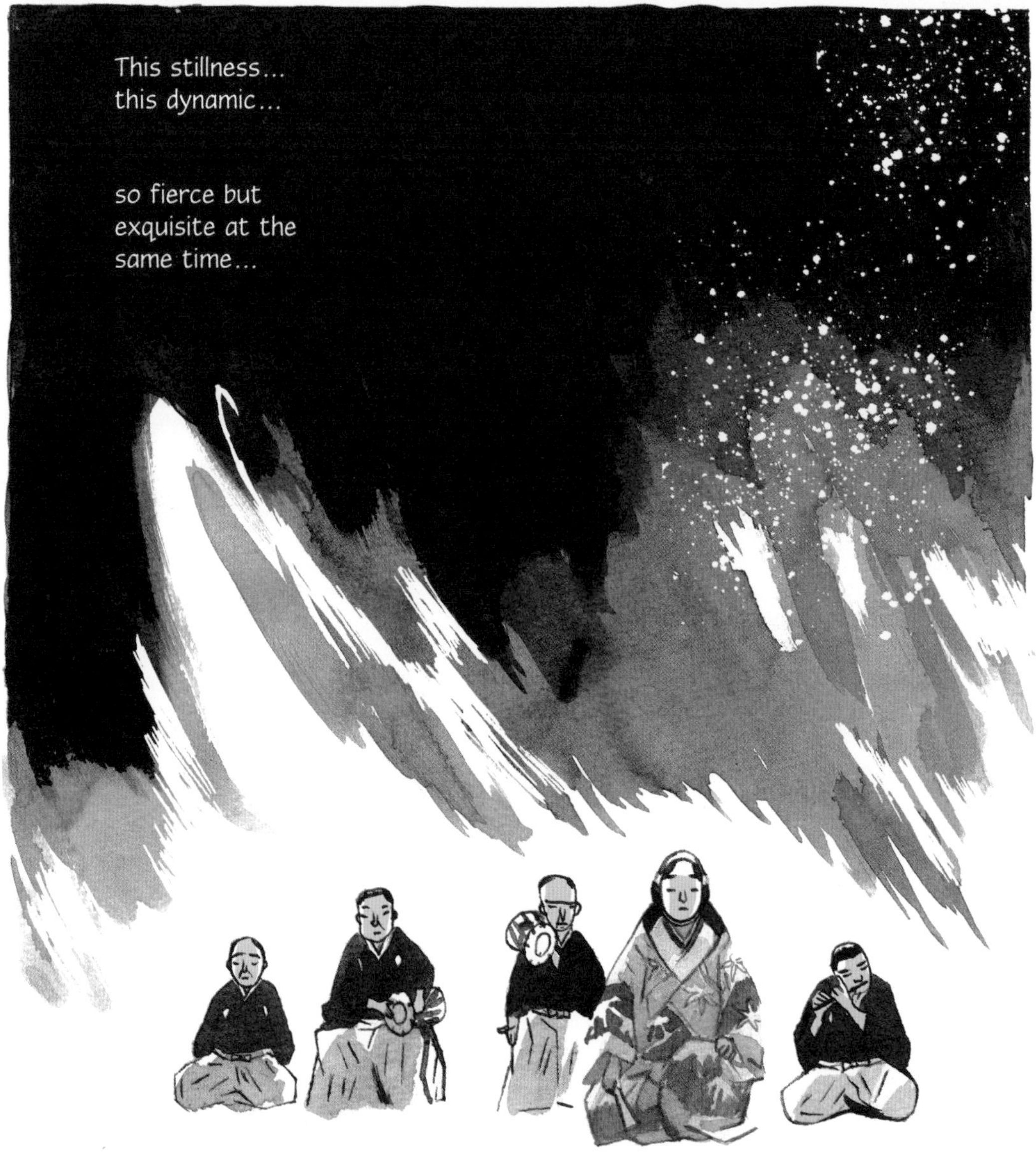
This stillness...
this dynamic...
so fierce but
exquisite at the
same time...

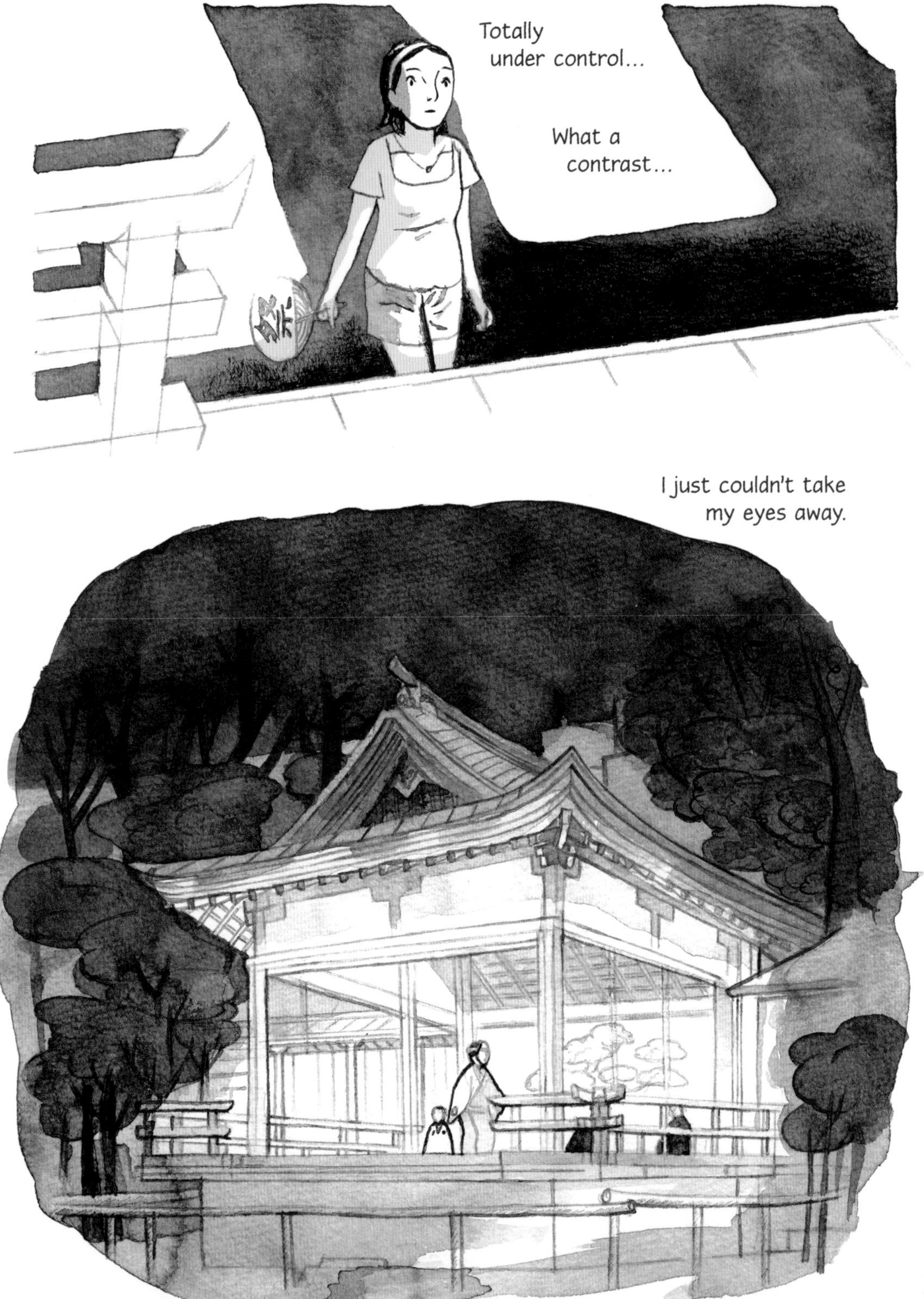
Totally under control...
What a contrast...
I just couldn't take my eyes away.

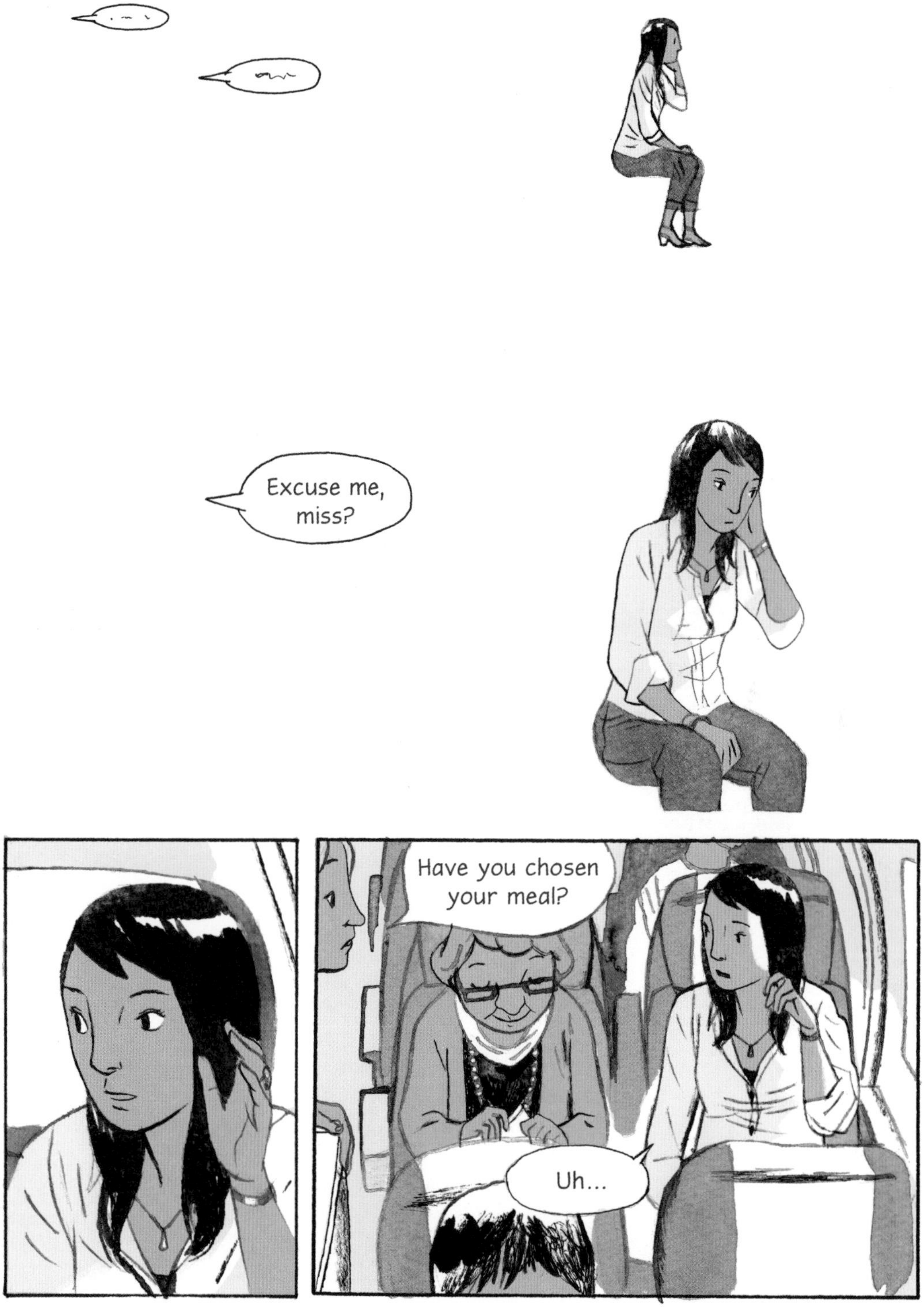
Excuse me, miss?
Have you chosen your meal?
Uh...

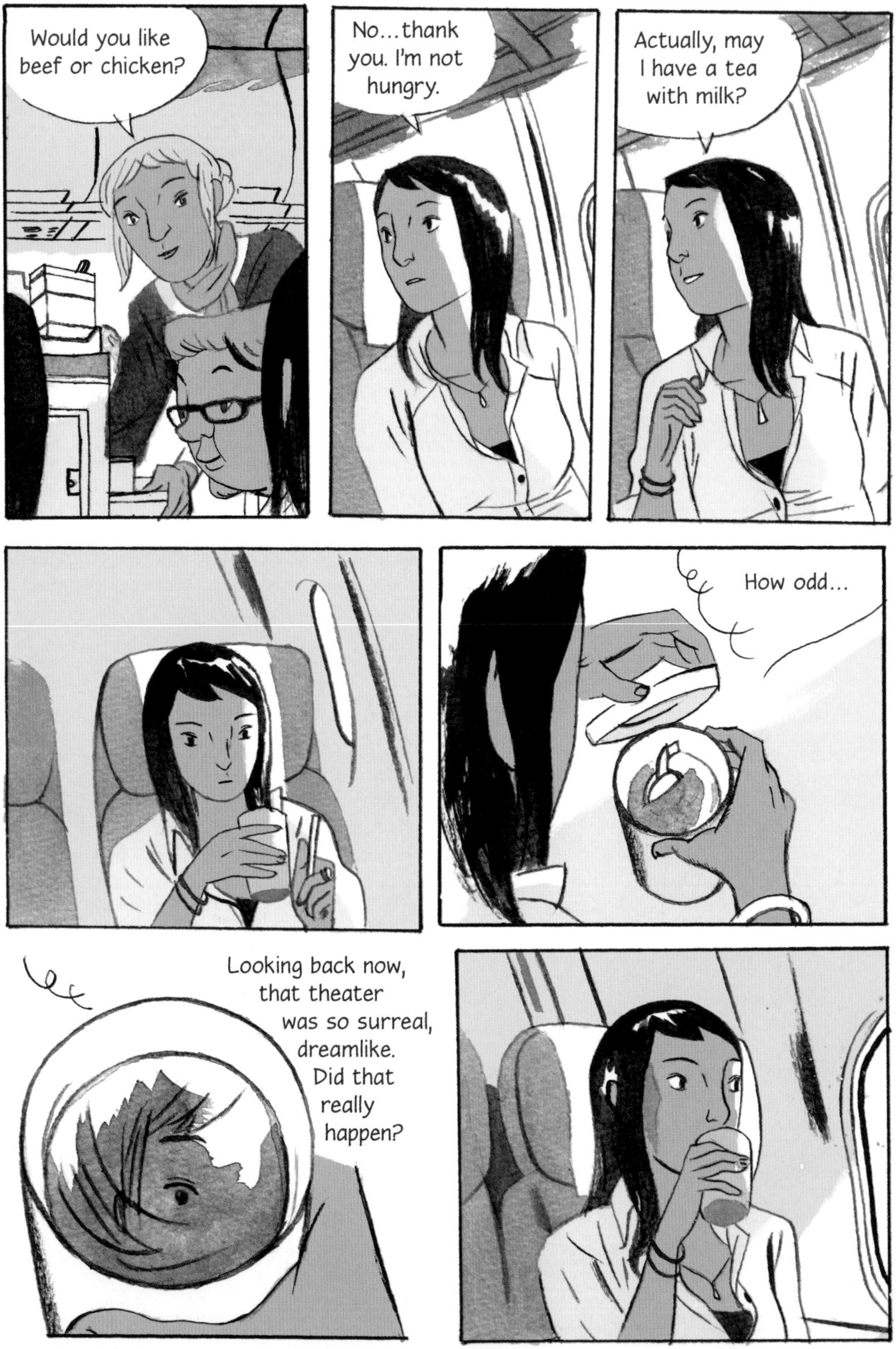

Would you like beef or chicken?
No...thank you. I'm not hungry.
Actually, may I have a tea with milk?
How odd...
Looking back now, that theater was so surreal, dreamlike. Did that really happen?

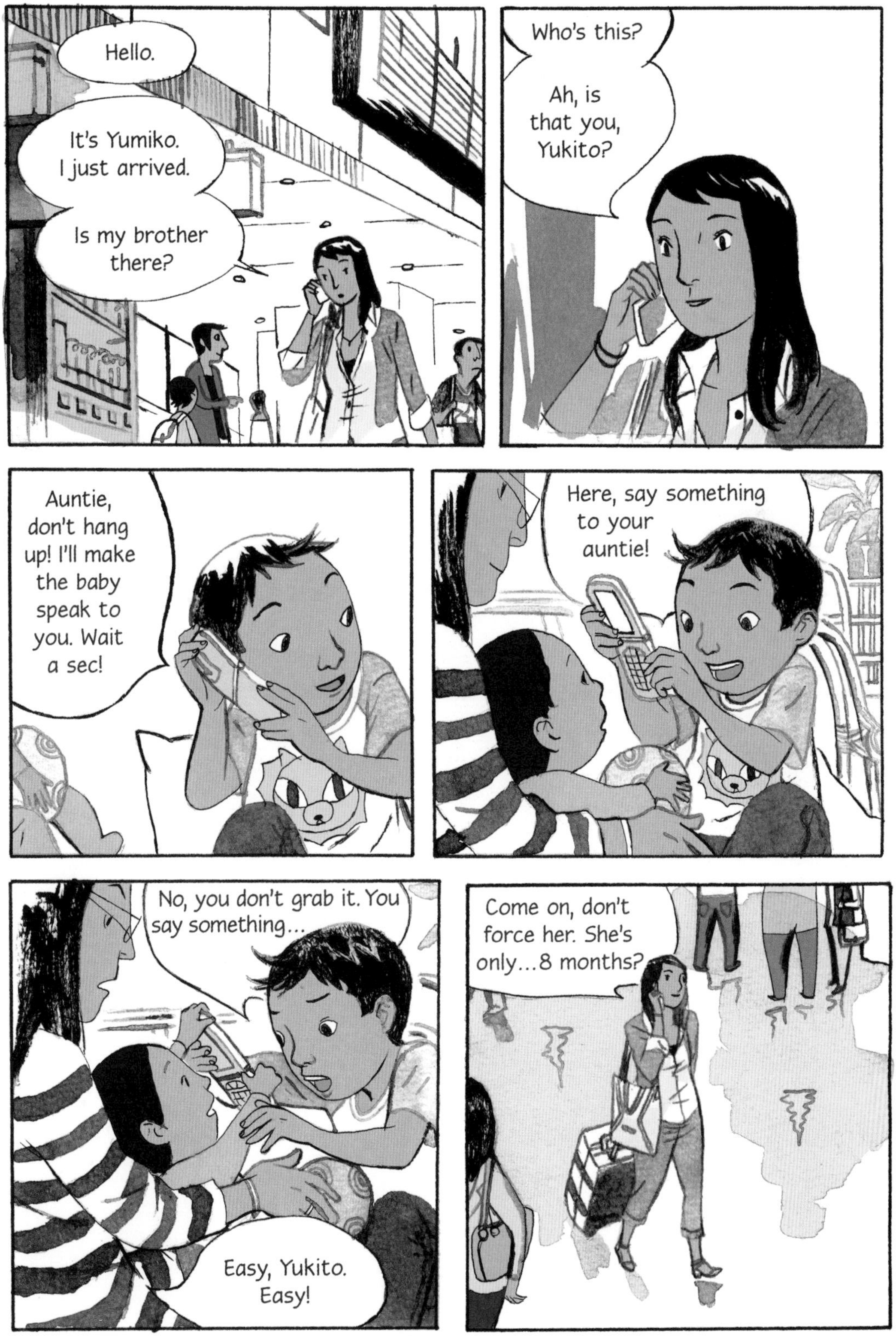

Hello.
It's Yumiko. I just arrived.
Is my brother there?
Who's this?
Ah, is that you, Yukito?
Auntie, don't hang up! I'll make the baby speak to you. Wait a sec!
Here, say something to your auntie!
No, you don't grab it. You say something...
Easy, Yukito. Easy!
Come on, don't force her. She's only...8 months?

Yawn...

The jet lag was coming on, and it was already feeling just like any other return trip...

My mind hadn't caught up yet.

II

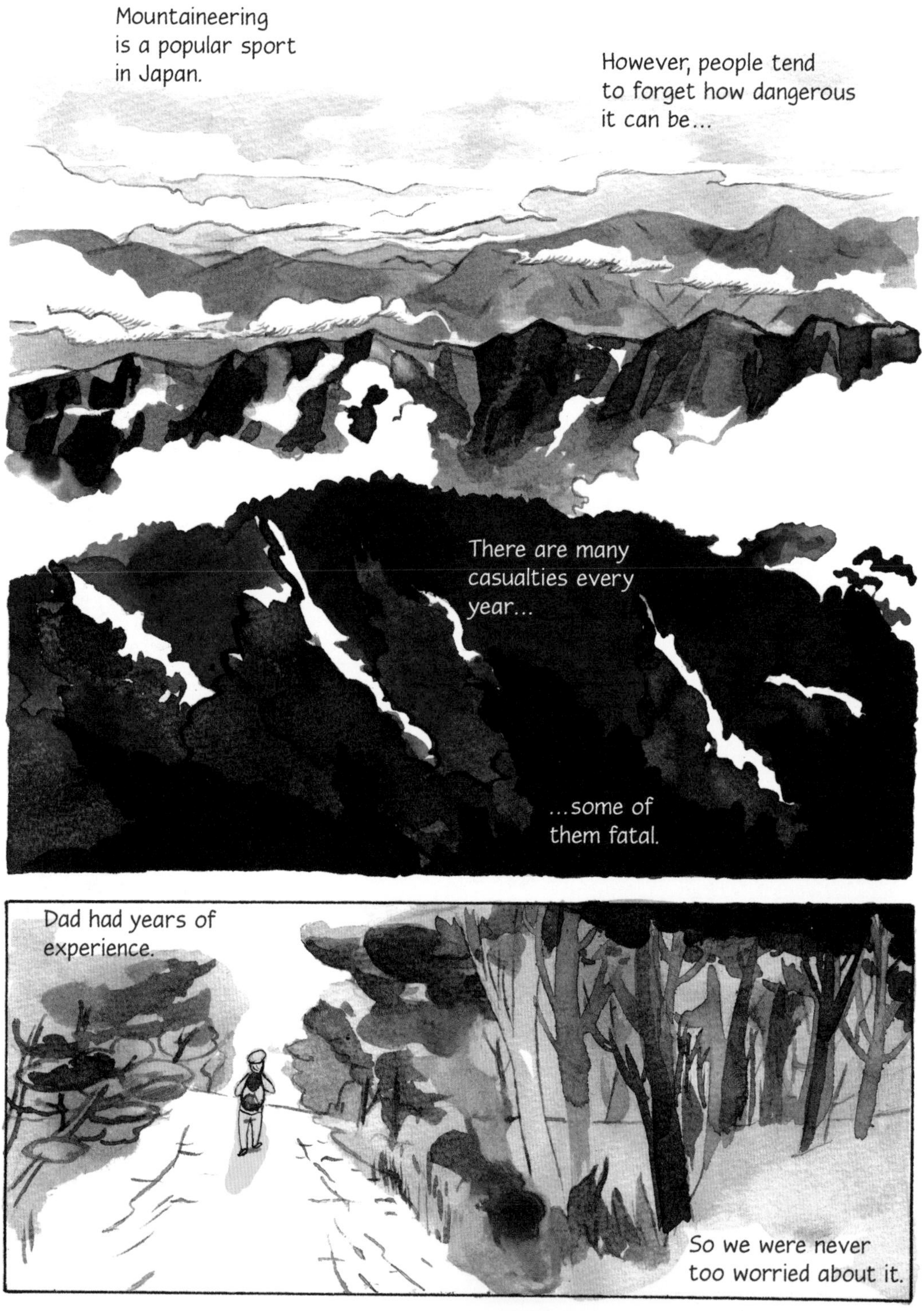
Mountaineering is a popular sport in Japan.
However, people tend to forget how dangerous it can be...
There are many casualties every year...
...some of them fatal.
Dad had years of experience.
So we were never too worried about it.

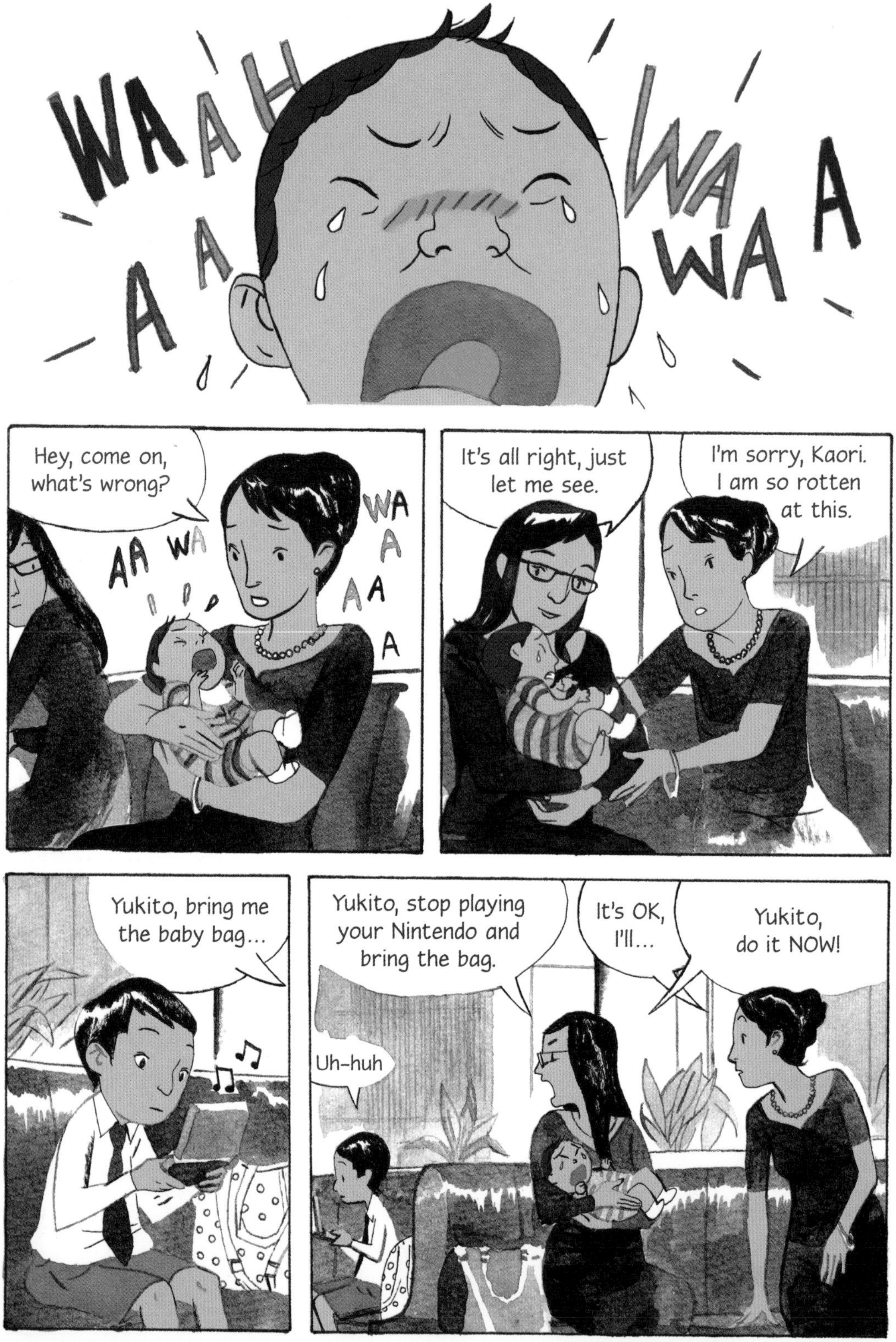
WAAAAH
AA
WAWAWA
A
Hey, come on, what's wrong?
AA WA
WA A A A A
It's all right, just let me see.
I'm sorry, Kaori. I am so rotten at this.
Yukito, bring me the baby bag…
Yukito, stop playing your Nintendo and bring the bag.
Uh-huh
It's OK, I'll…
Yukito, do it NOW!

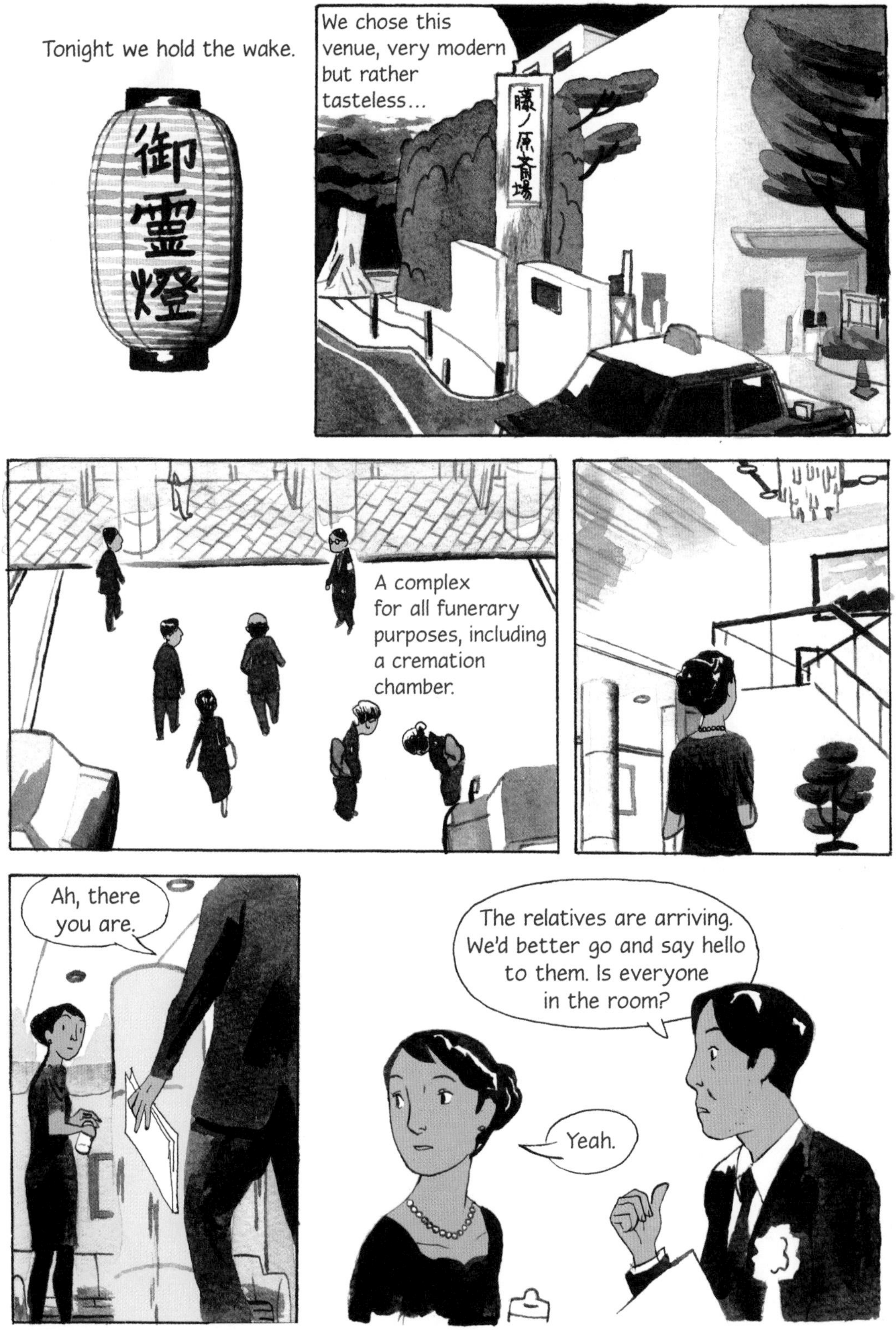
Tonight we hold the wake.
御霊燈
We chose this venue, very modern but rather tasteless...
A complex for all funerary purposes, including a cremation chamber.
Ah, there you are.
The relatives are arriving. We'd better go and say hello to them. Is everyone in the room?
Yeah.

64

v. good   good   average

But over time, various ranks were created and the family can pay for a name with higher status...

But what difference does it make?

So with this package, Kaimyō isn't included?

I'm afraid not.

To honor the dead is understandable.

But buying it seems wrong to me.

It's all for the sake of saving face...

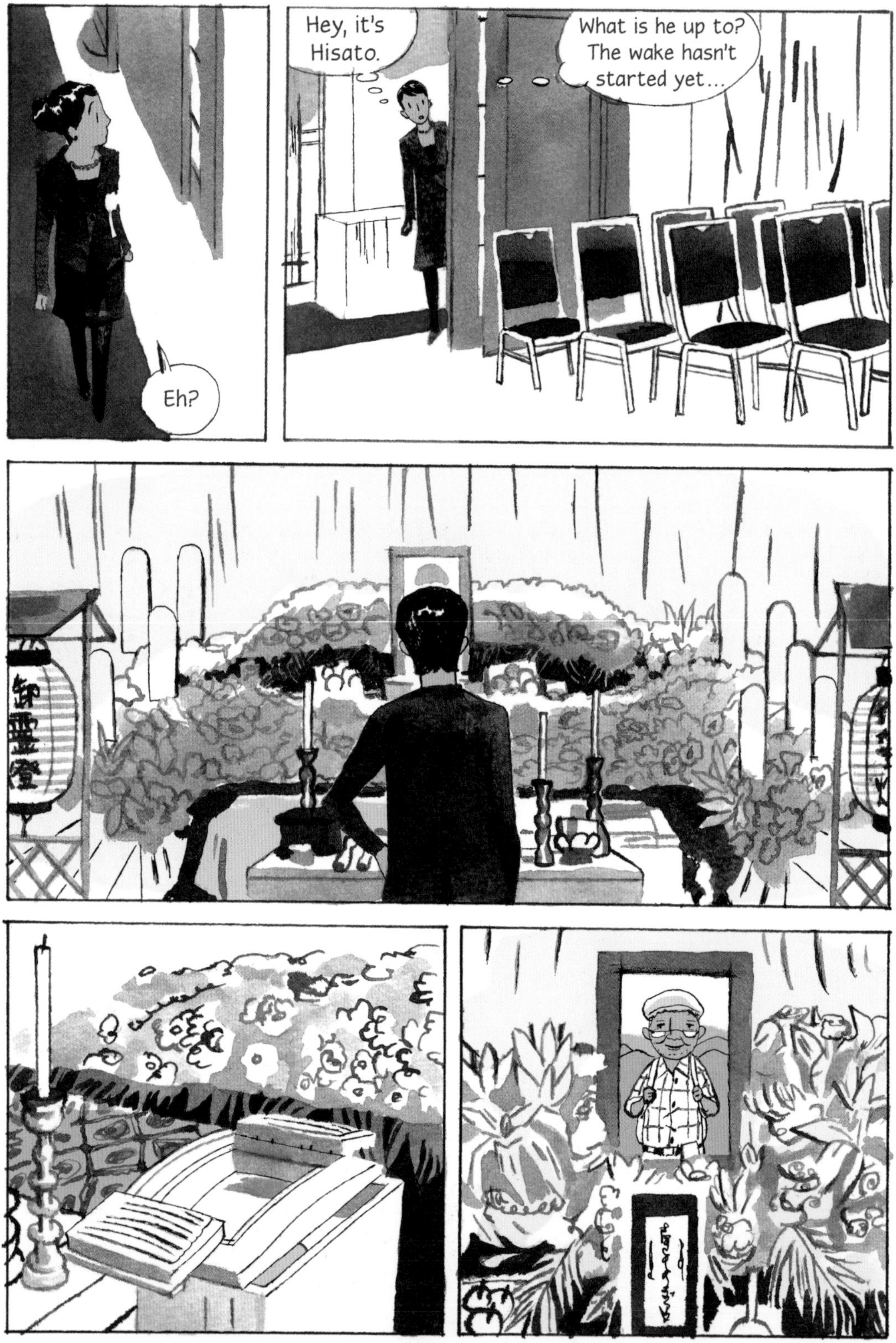
Eh?
Hey, it's Hisato.
What is he up to? The wake hasn't started yet…

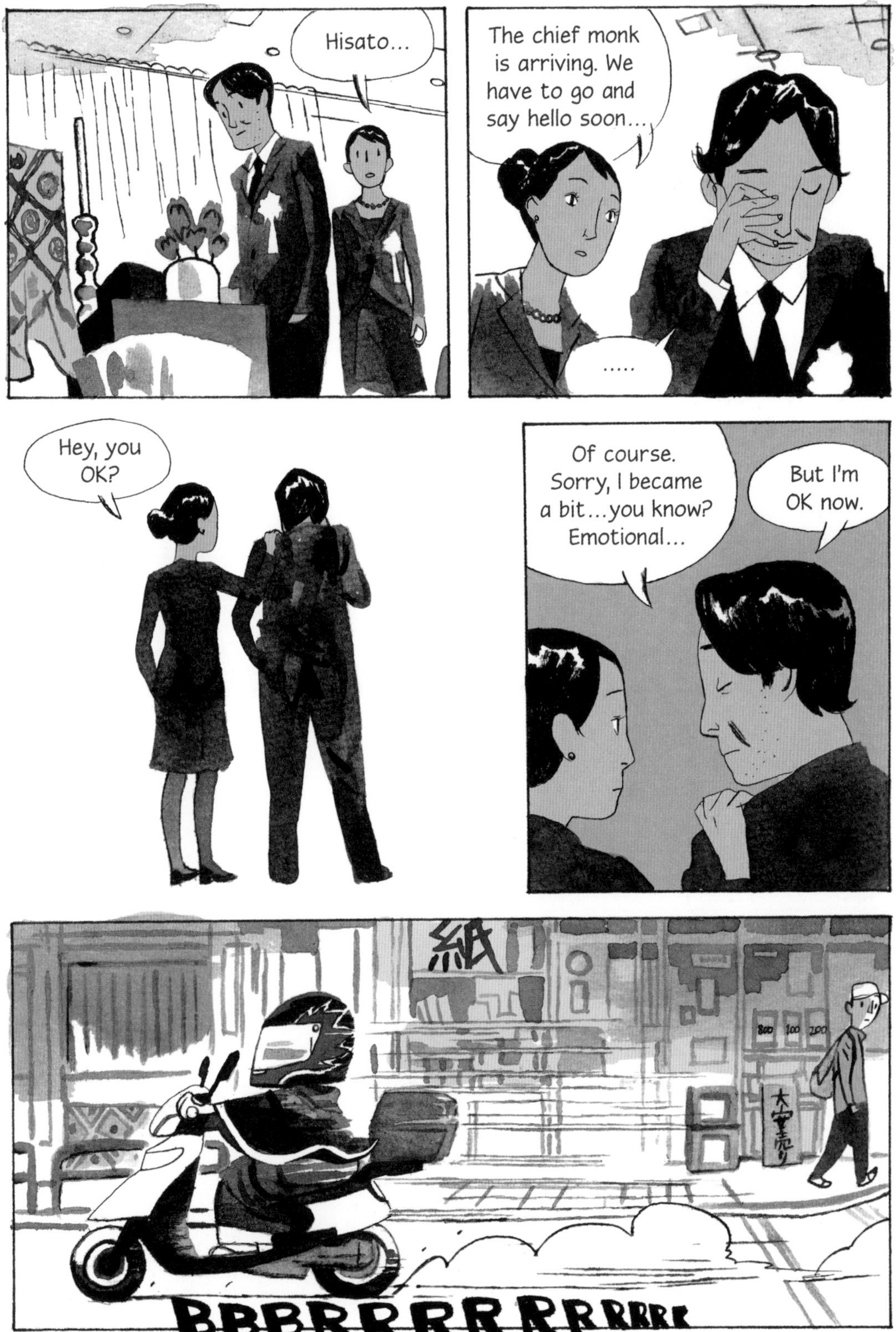
Hisato...
The chief monk is arriving. We have to go and say hello soon...
.....
Hey, you OK?
Of course. Sorry, I became a bit...you know? Emotional...
But I'm OK now.
BBBRRRRRRRRRR

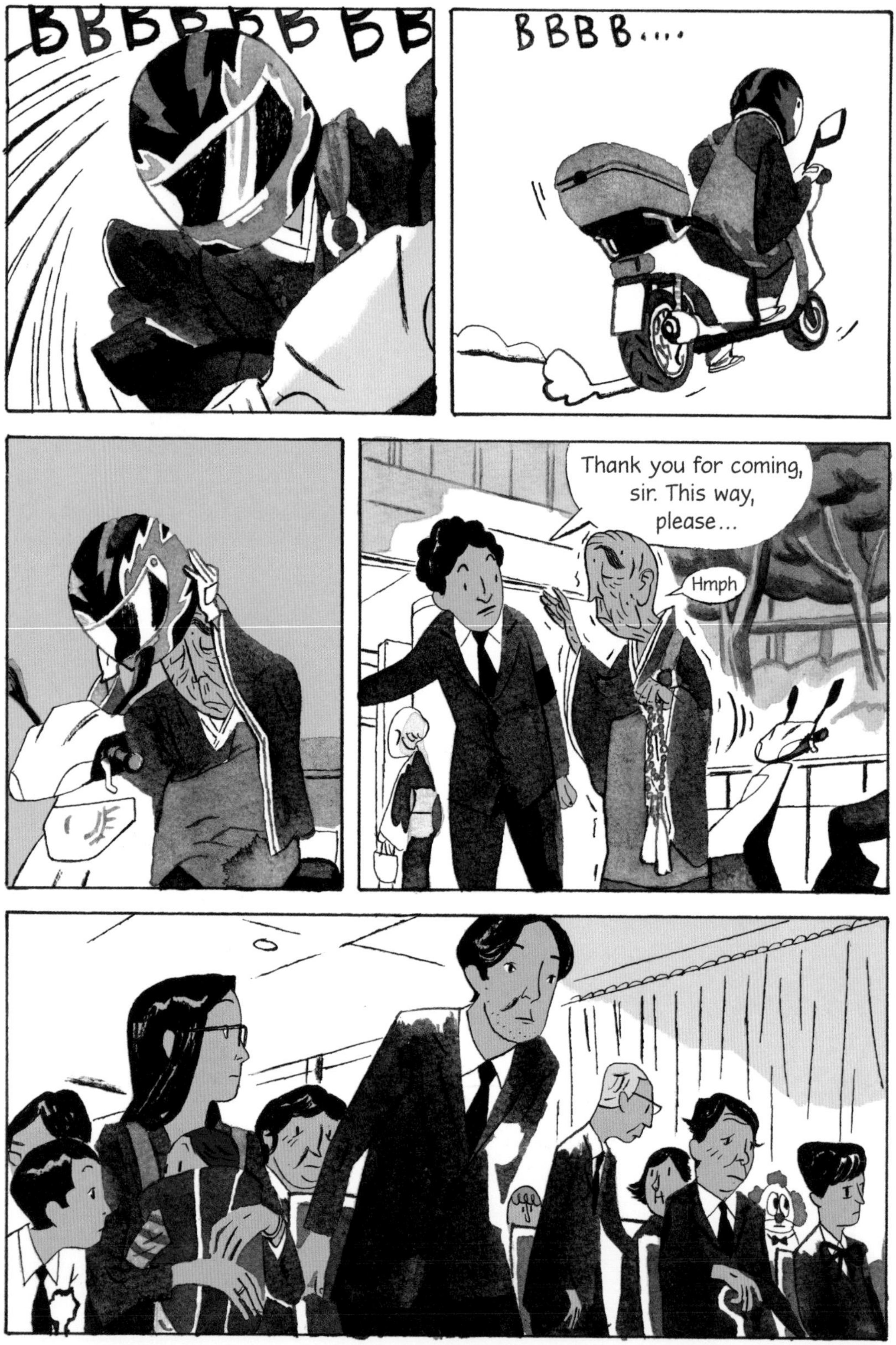
BBBBBBBBB
BBBB....
Thank you for coming, sir. This way, please...
Hmph

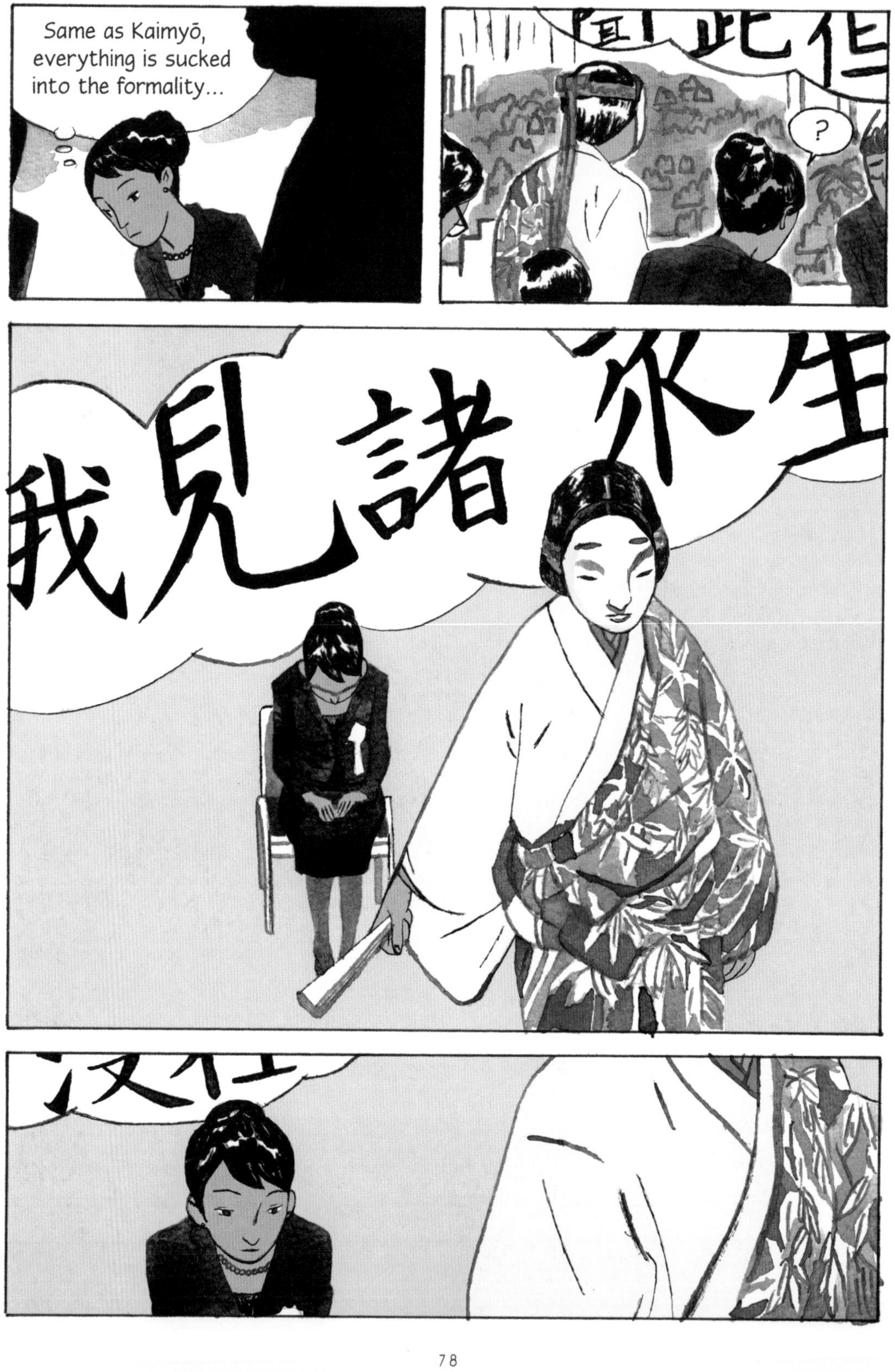
Same as Kaimyō, everything is sucked into the formality...
?
我見諸

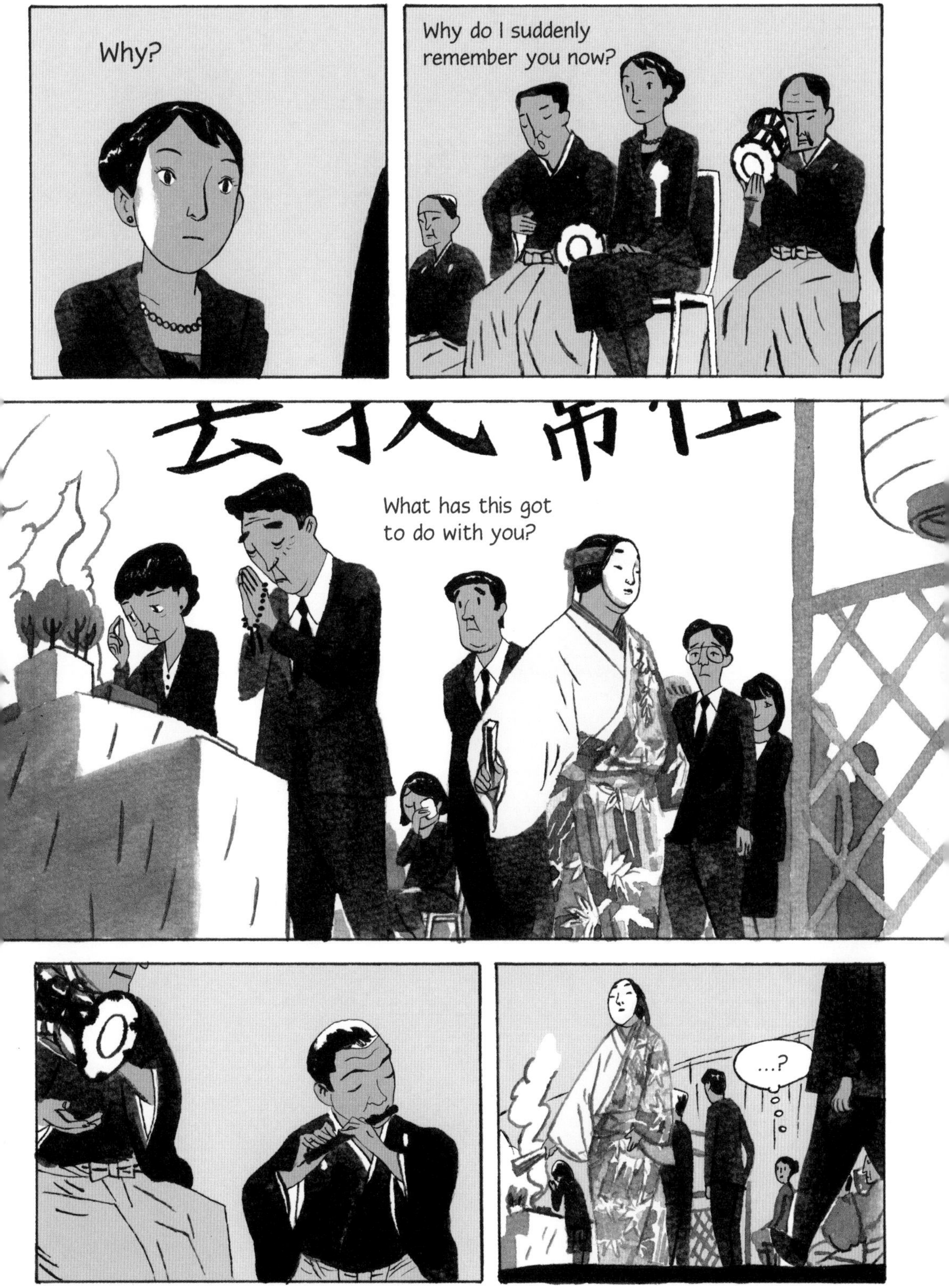
Why?
Why do I suddenly remember you now?
What has this got to do with you?
...?

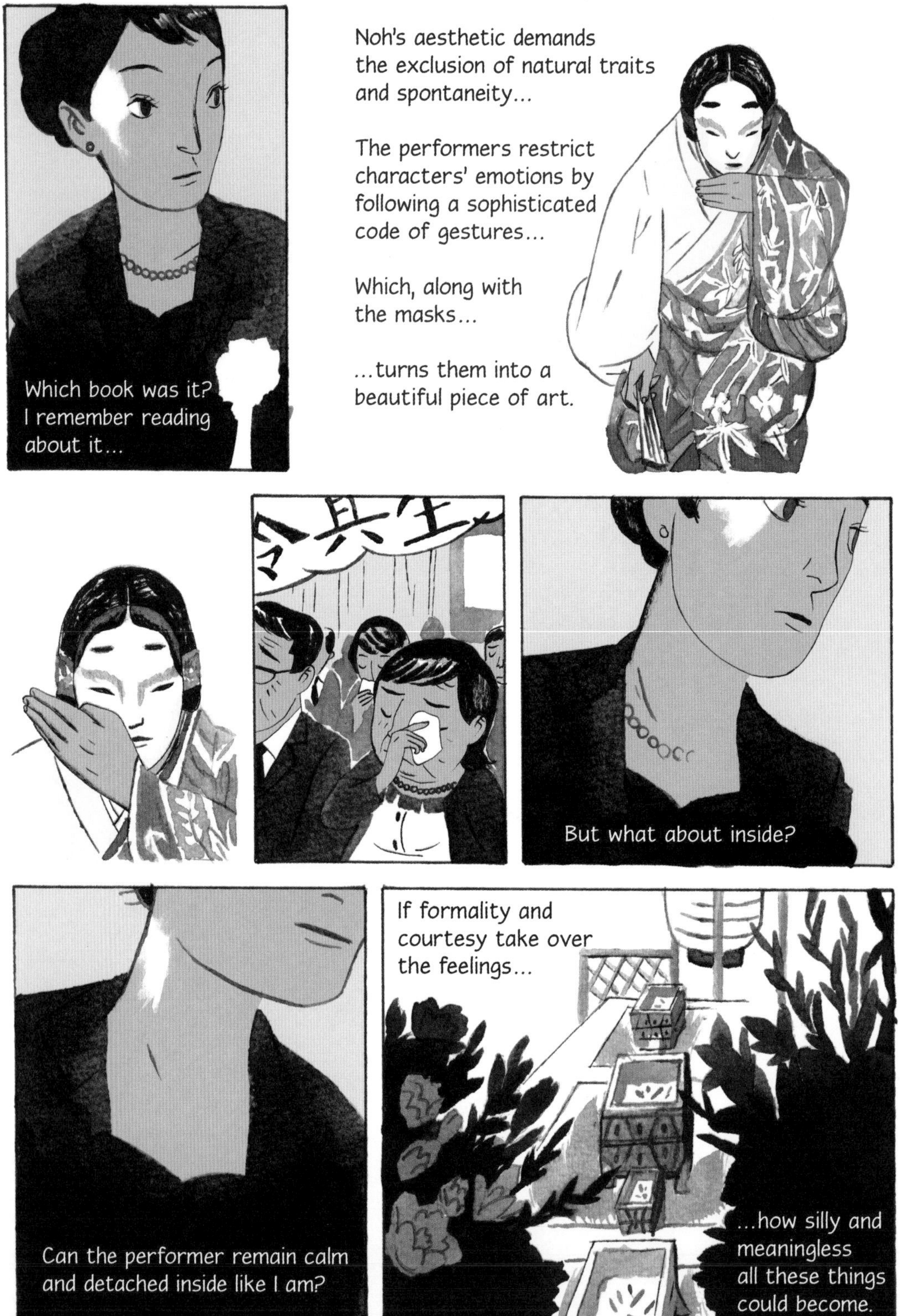

Which book was it? I remember reading about it...
Noh's aesthetic demands the exclusion of natural traits and spontaneity...
The performers restrict characters' emotions by following a sophisticated code of gestures...
Which, along with the masks...
...turns them into a beautiful piece of art.
But what about inside?
Can the performer remain calm and detached inside like I am?
If formality and courtesy take over the feelings...
...how silly and meaningless all these things could become.

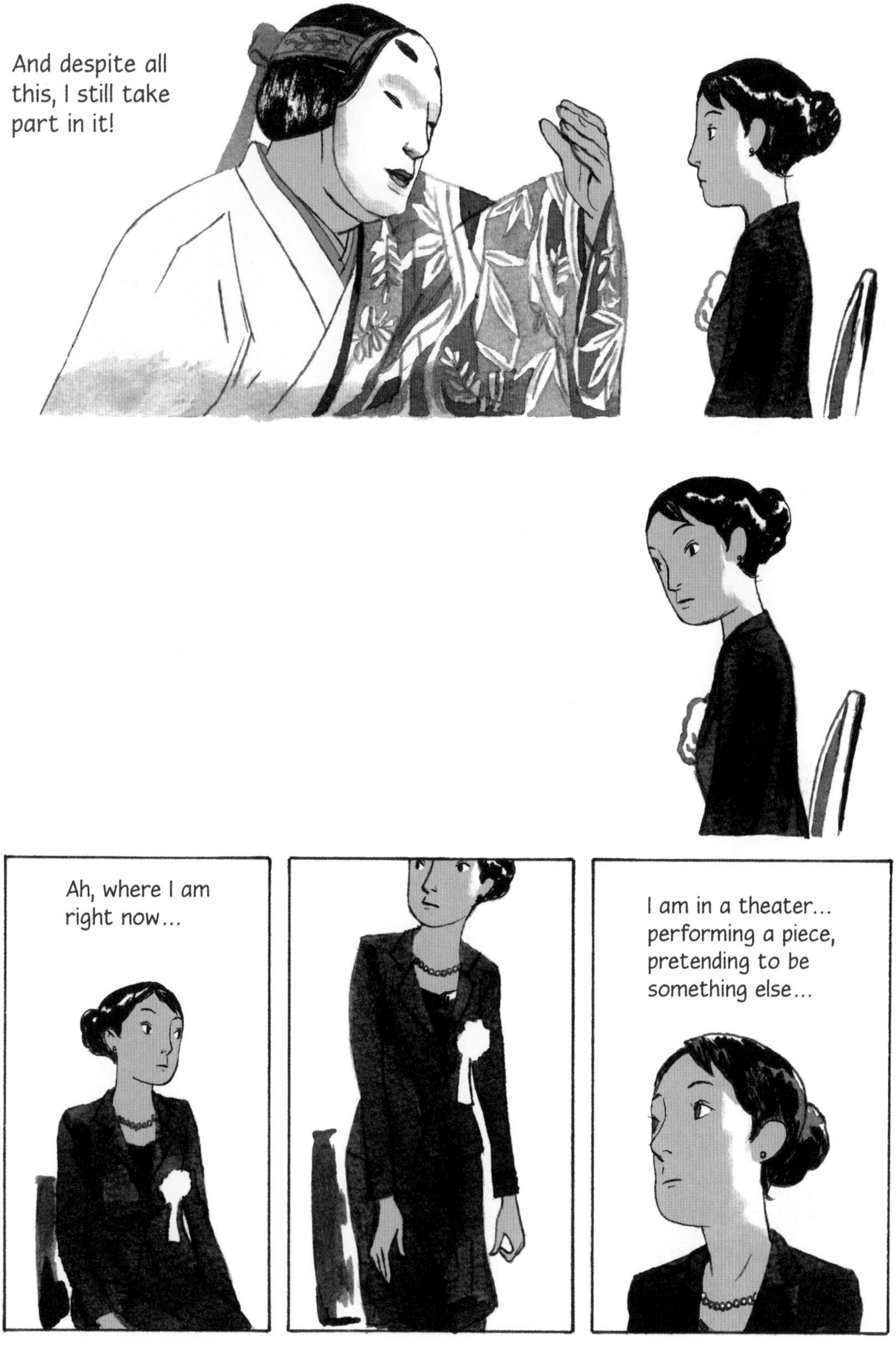
And despite all this, I still take part in it!
Ah, where I am right now...
I am in a theater... performing a piece, pretending to be something else...

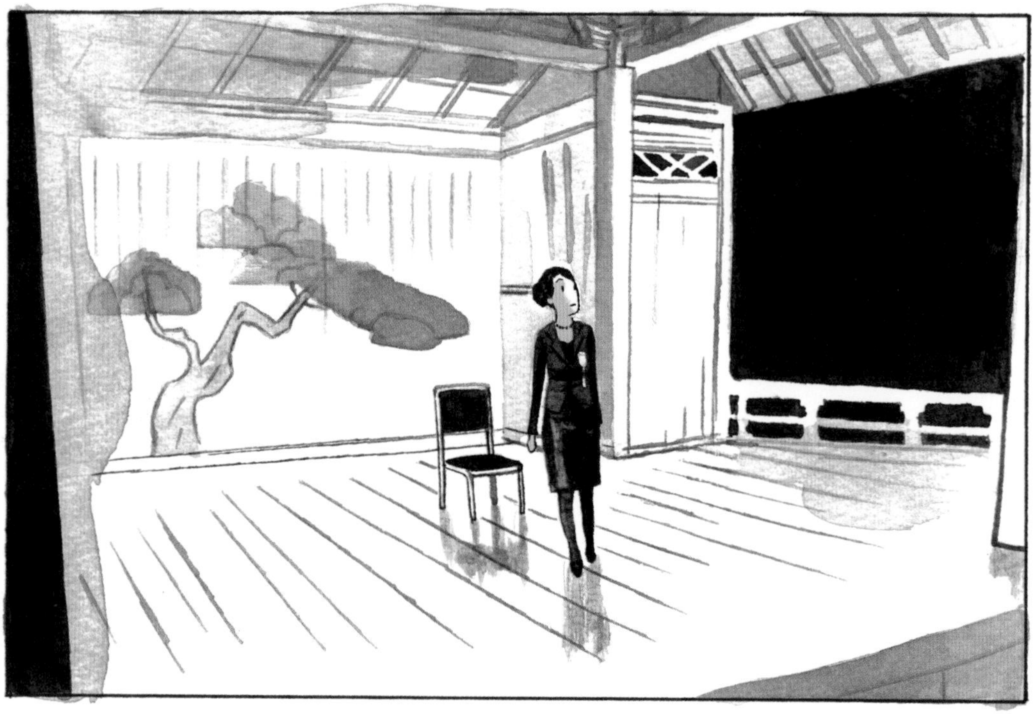

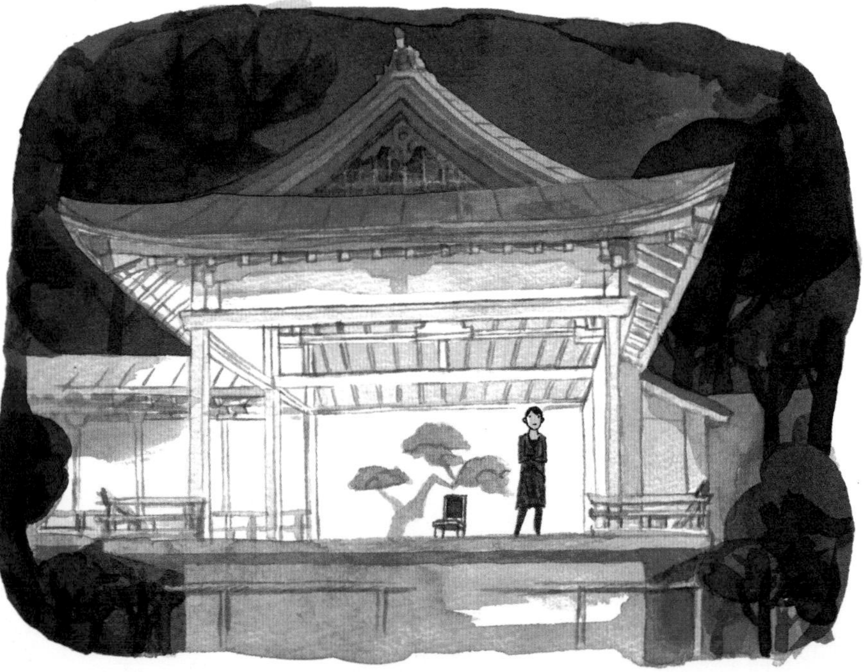

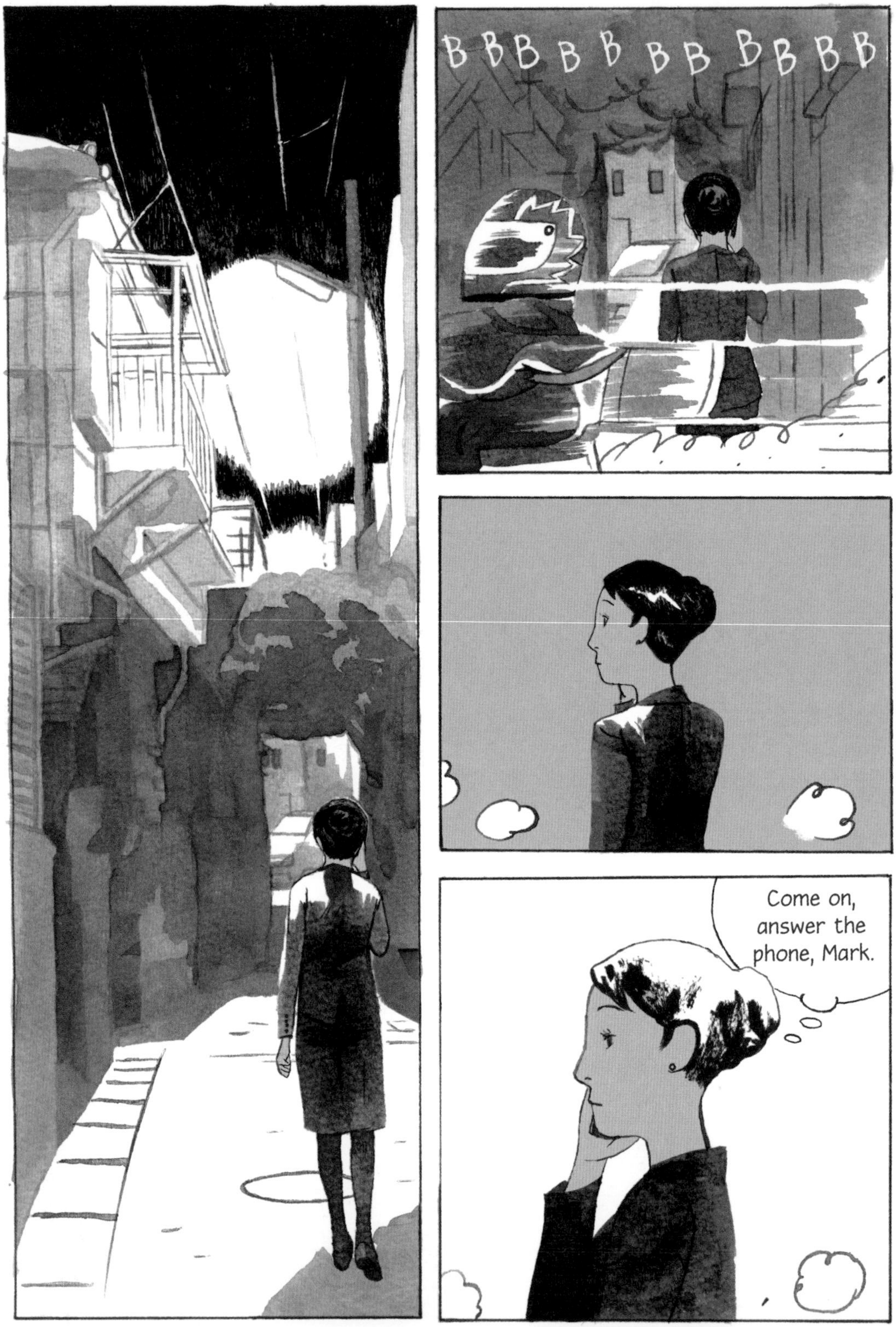
B B B B B B B B B B B
Come on, answer the phone, Mark.

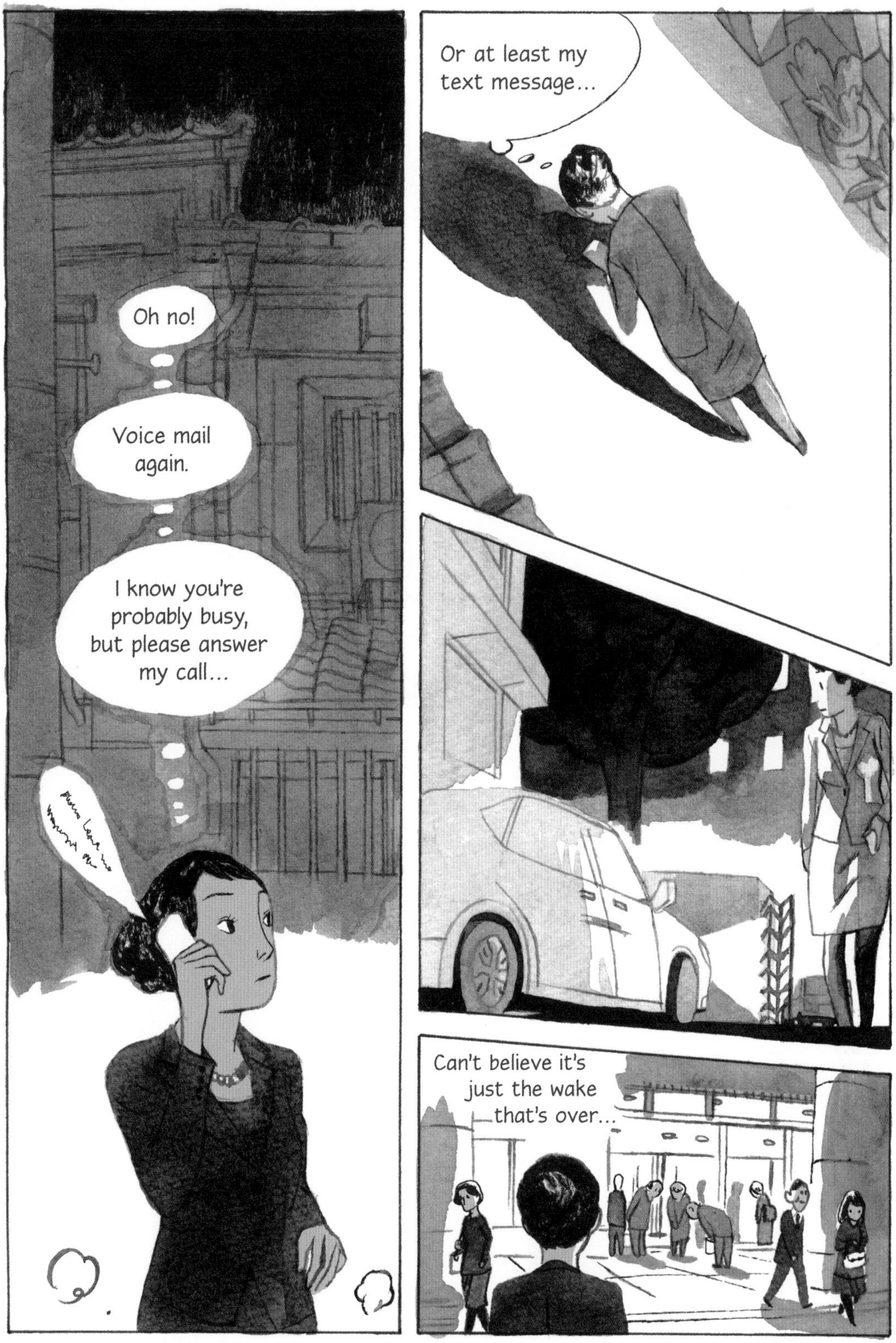
Oh no!
Voice mail again.
I know you're probably busy, but please answer my call...
Or at least my text message...
Can't believe it's just the wake that's over...

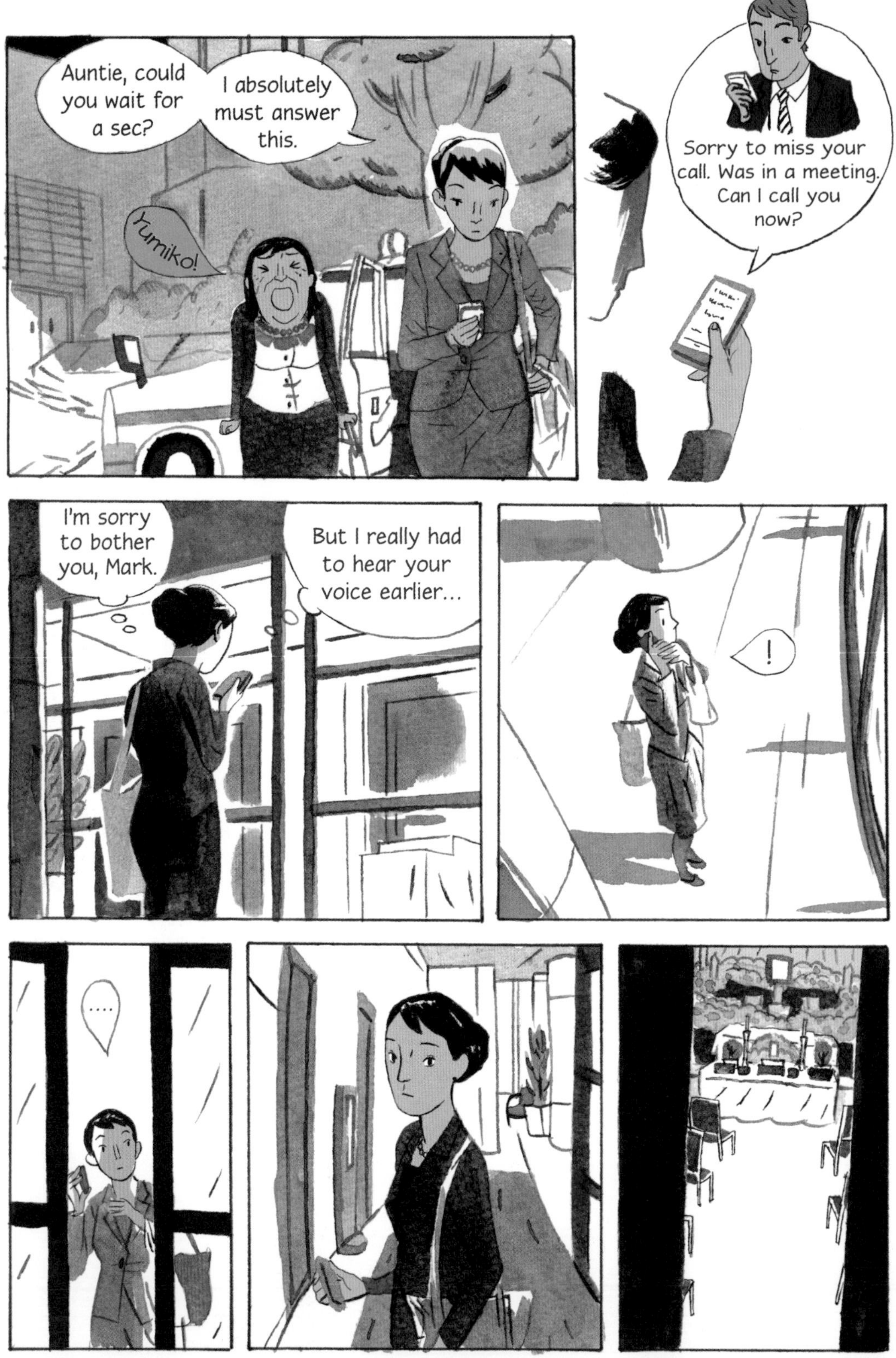
Auntie, could you wait for a sec?
I absolutely must answer this.
Yumiko!
Sorry to miss your call. Was in a meeting. Can I call you now?
I'm sorry to bother you, Mark.
But I really had to hear your voice earlier...
!
....

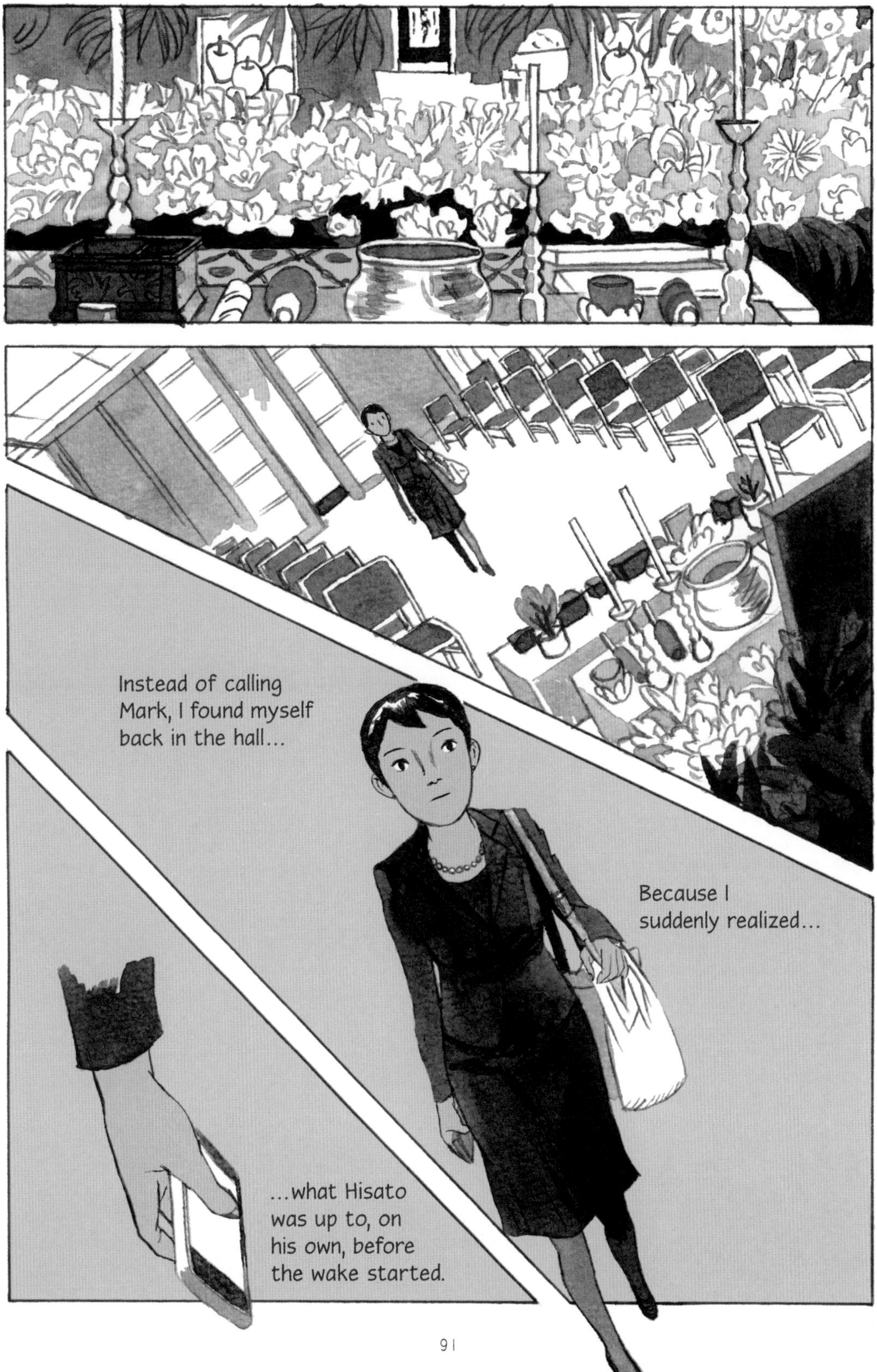
Instead of calling Mark, I found myself back in the hall...
Because I suddenly realized...
...what Hisato was up to, on his own, before the wake started.

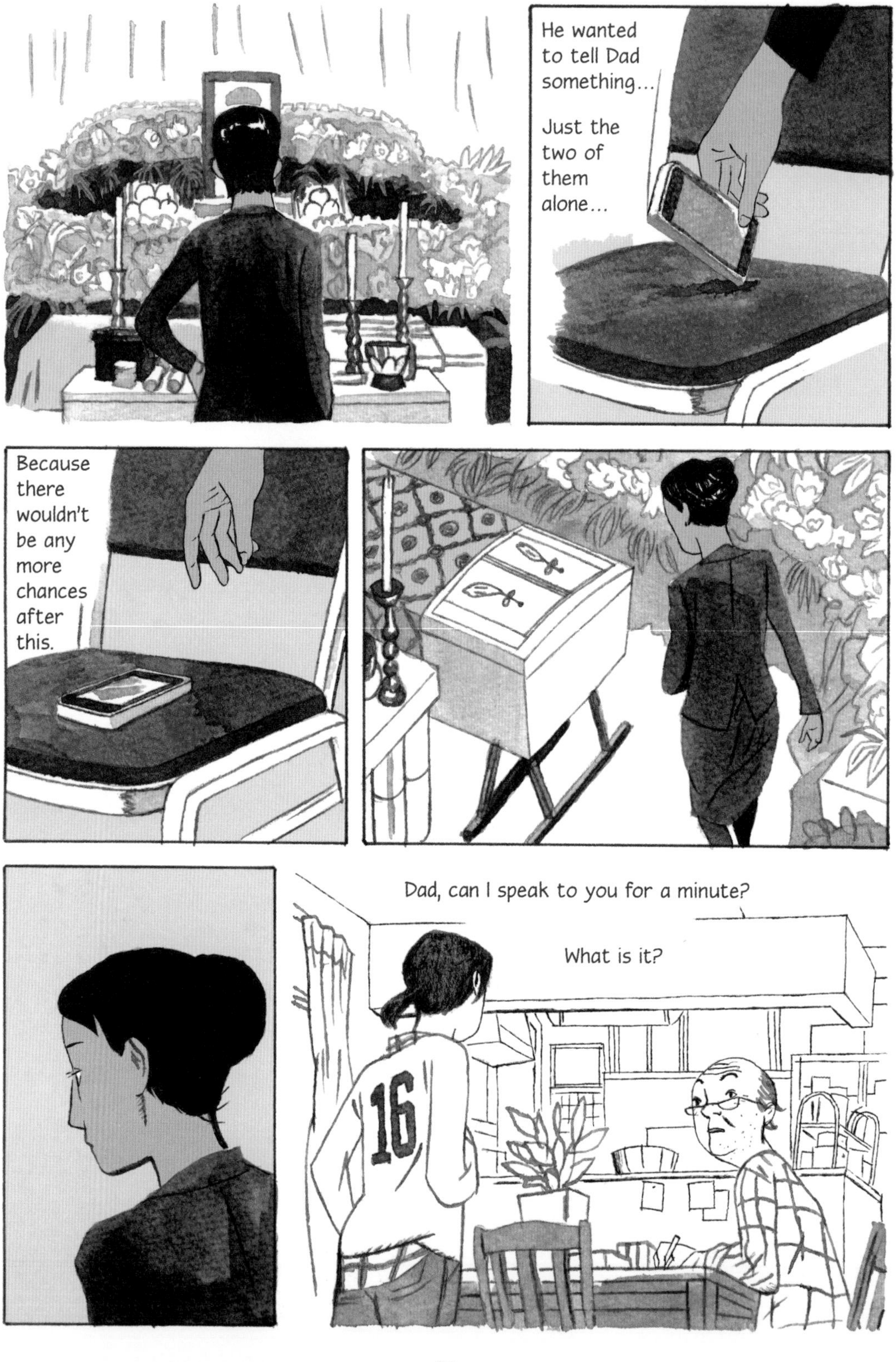
He wanted to tell Dad something...
Just the two of them alone...
Because there wouldn't be any more chances after this.
Dad, can I speak to you for a minute?
What is it?

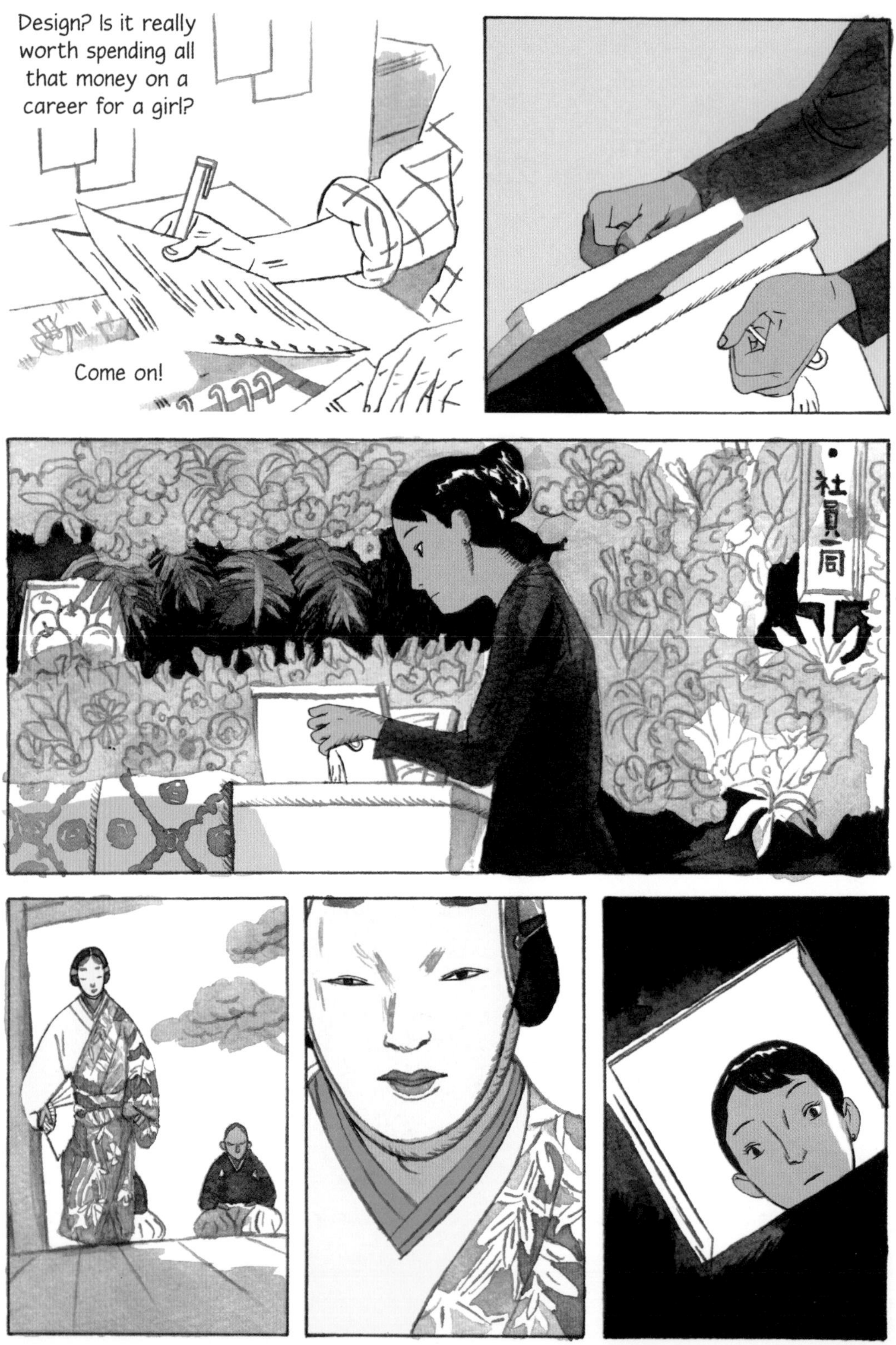
Design? Is it really worth spending all that money on a career for a girl?
Come on!
社員一同

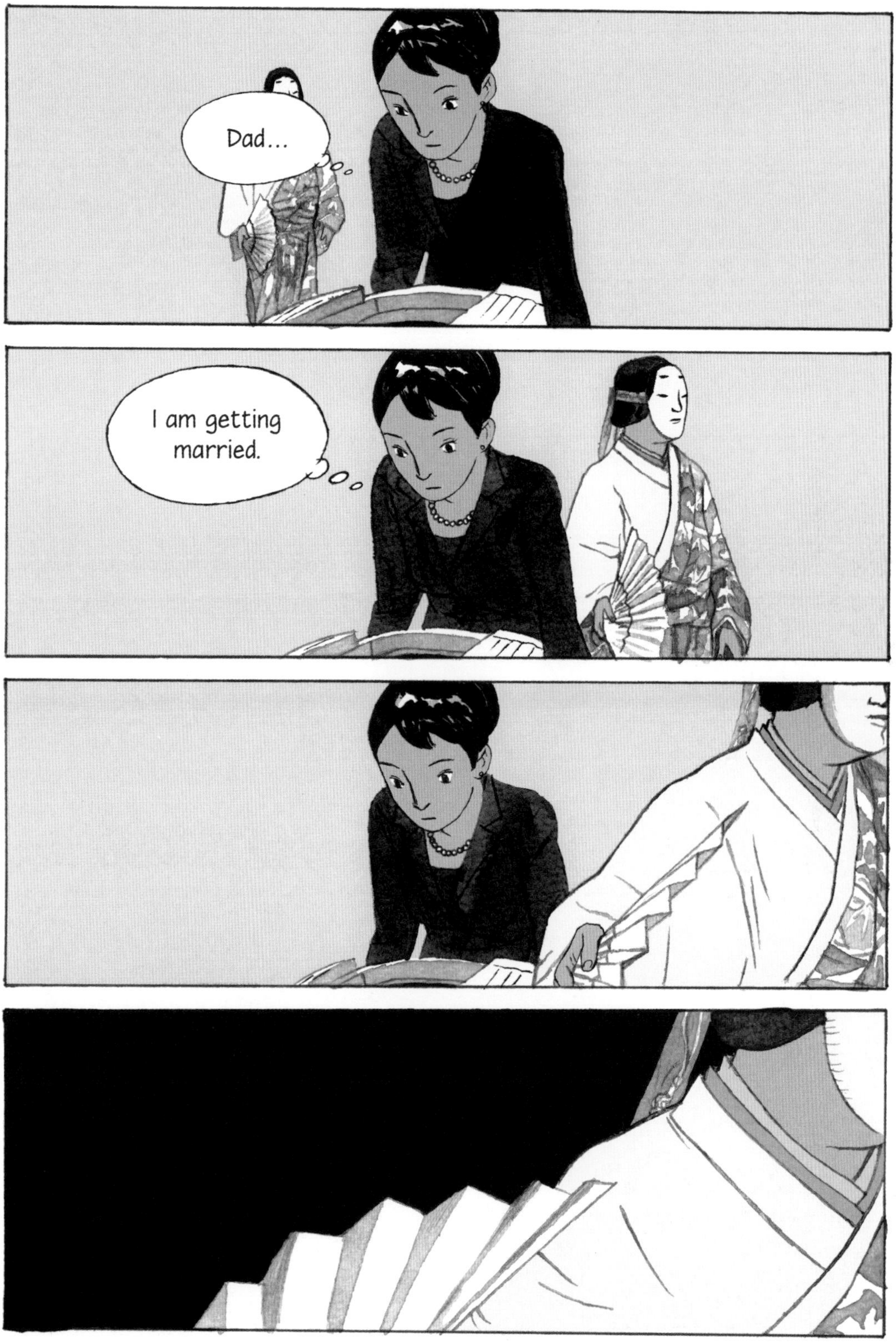
Dad...
I am getting married.

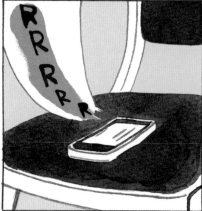

The next moment...

I was putting my
hand into his coffin...

Touching
his dead
flesh...

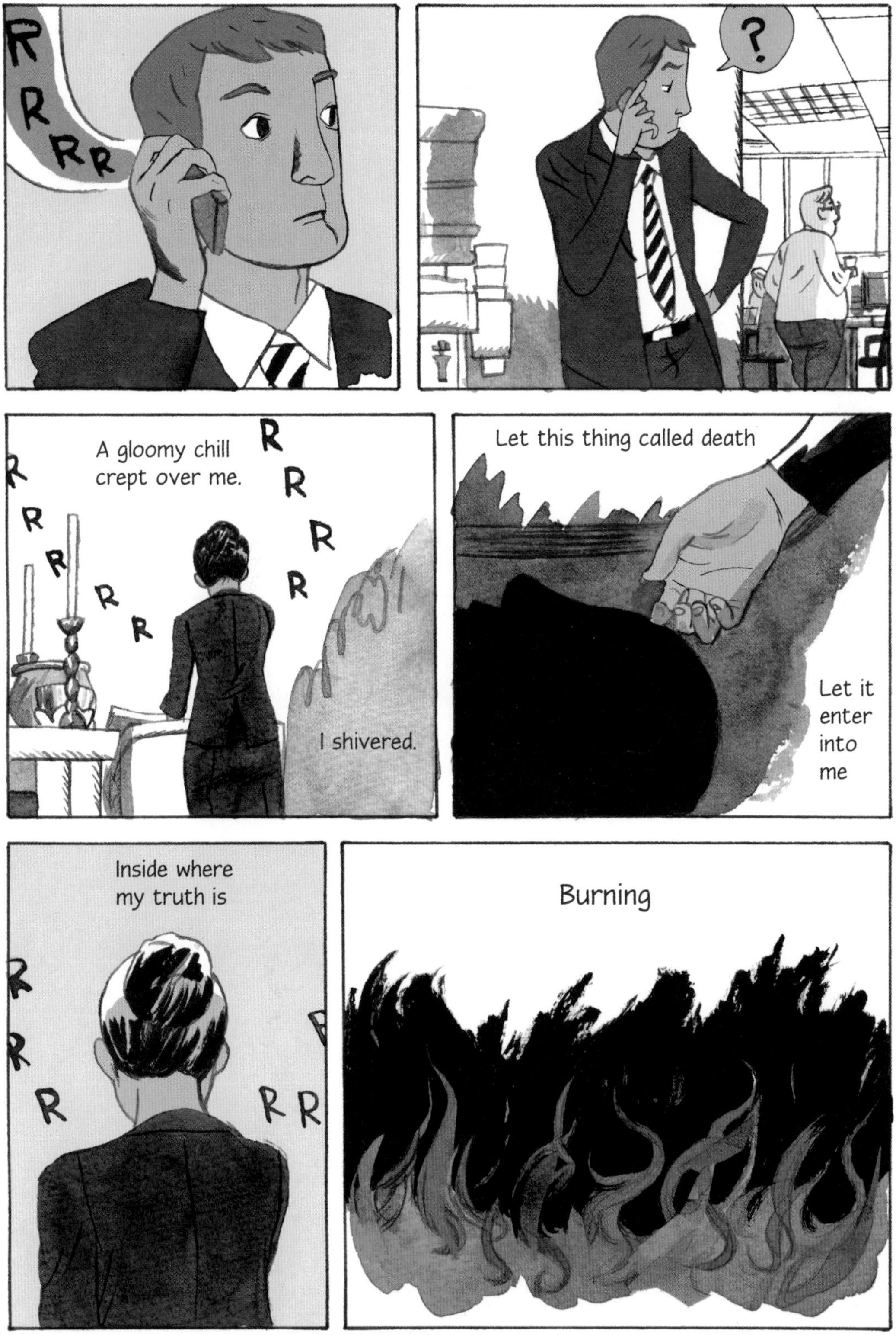
RRRRR
?
R R R R R R R R R R R R
A gloomy chill crept over me.
I shivered.
Let this thing called death
Let it enter into me
Inside where my truth is
R R R R R
Burning

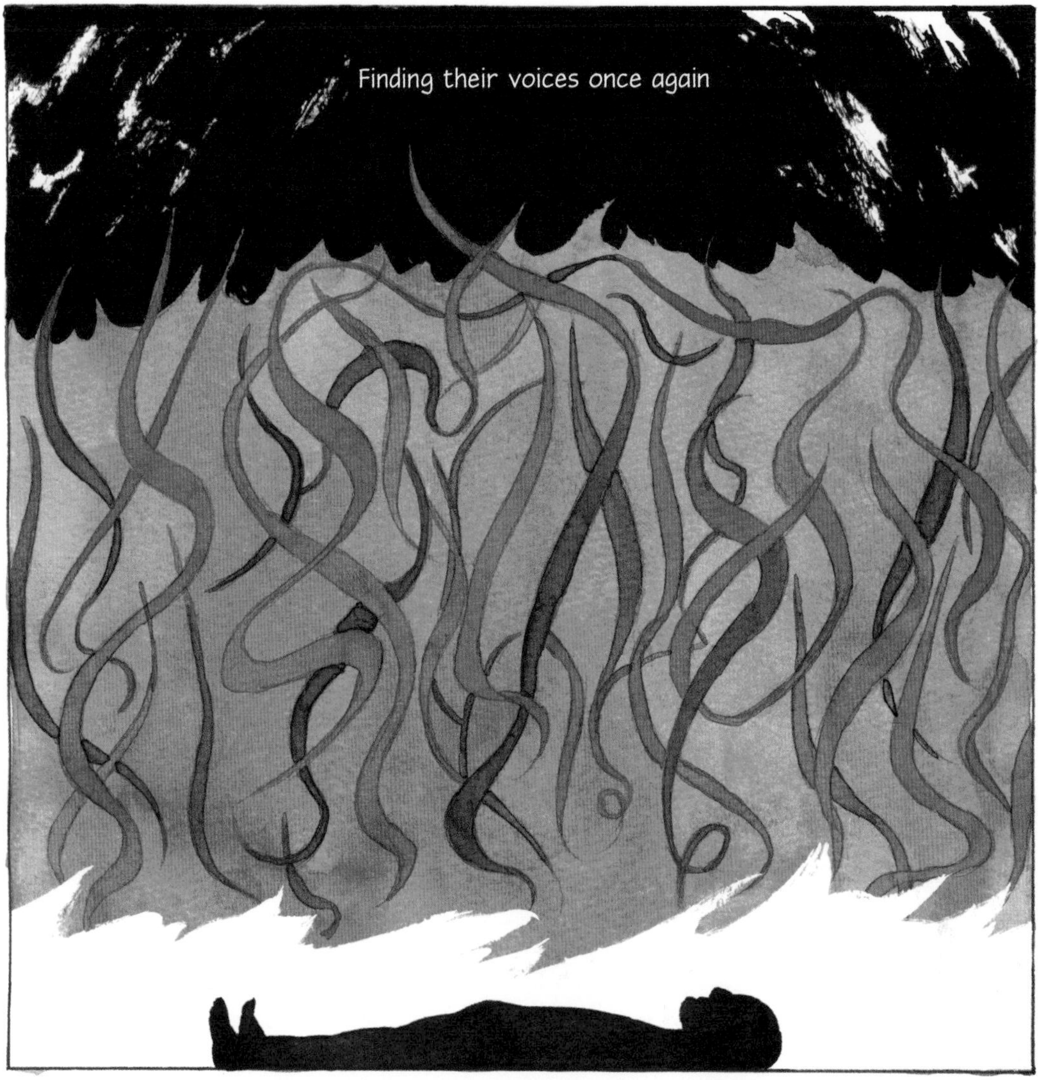
Finding their voices once again

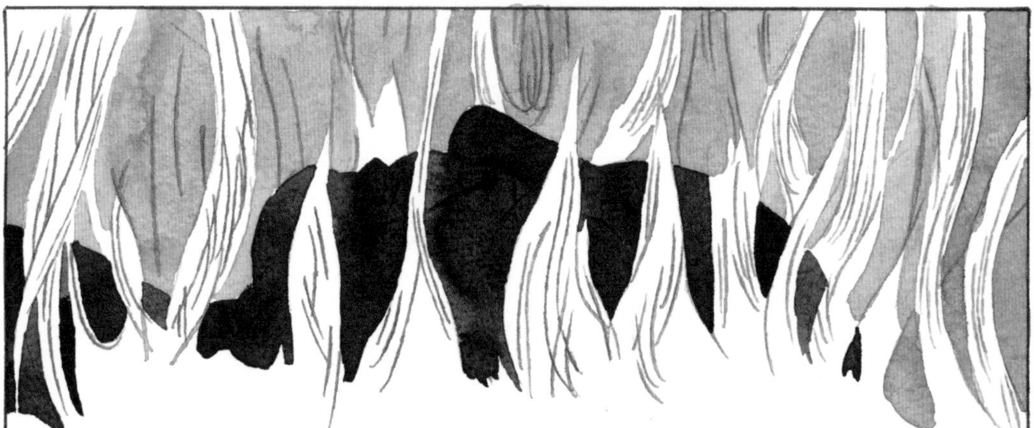

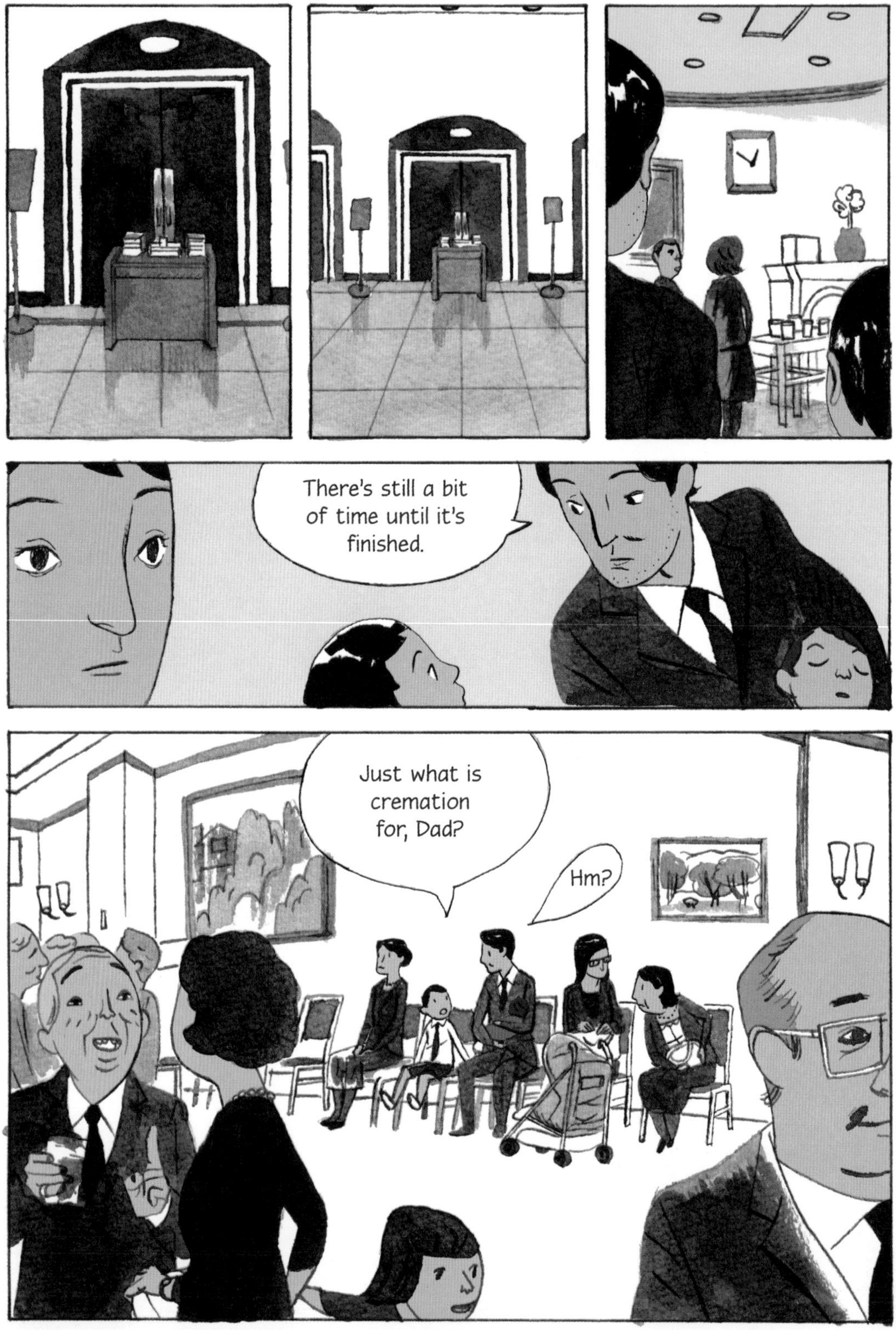
There's still a bit of time until it's finished.
Just what is cremation for, Dad?
Hm?

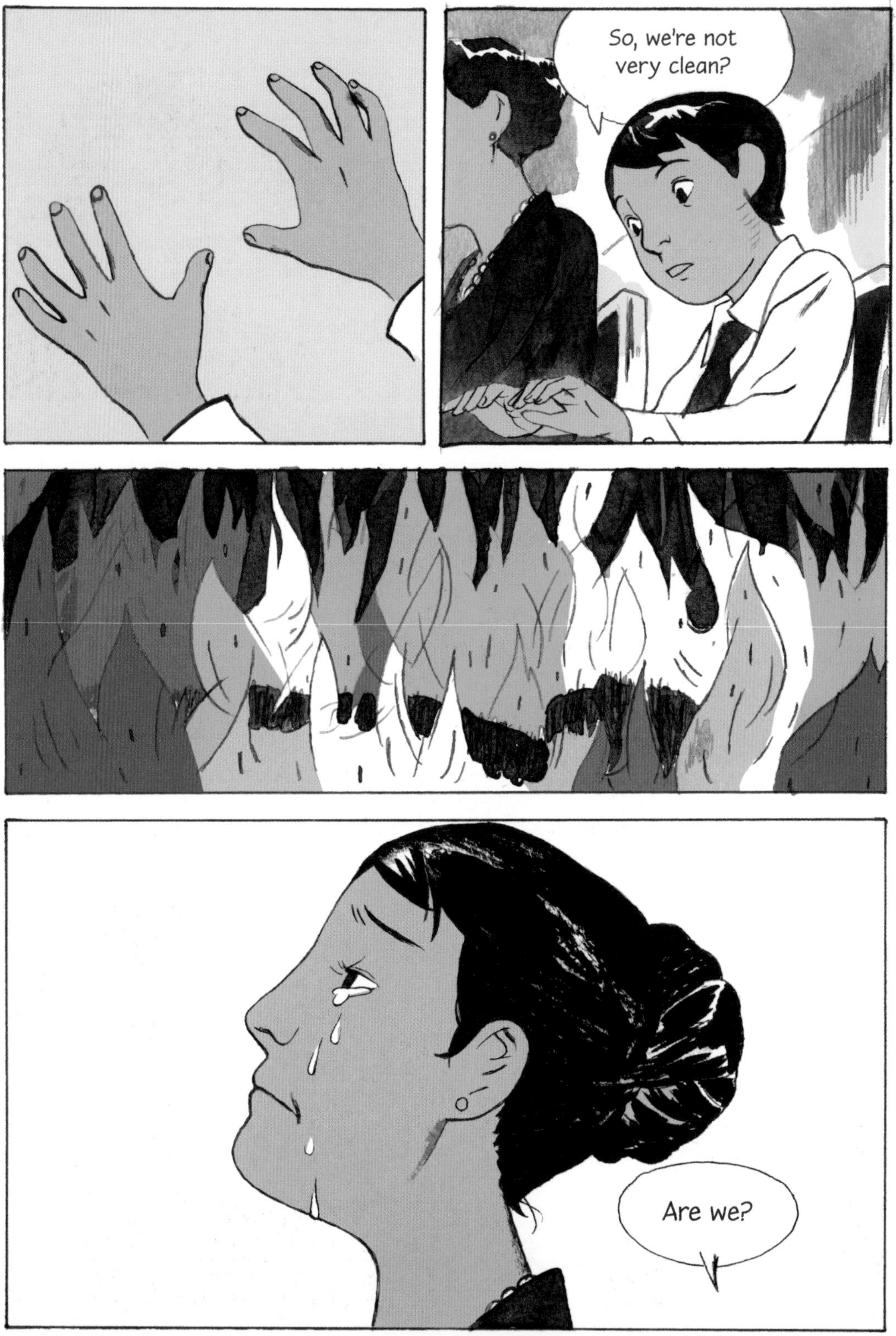
So, we're not very clean?
Are we?

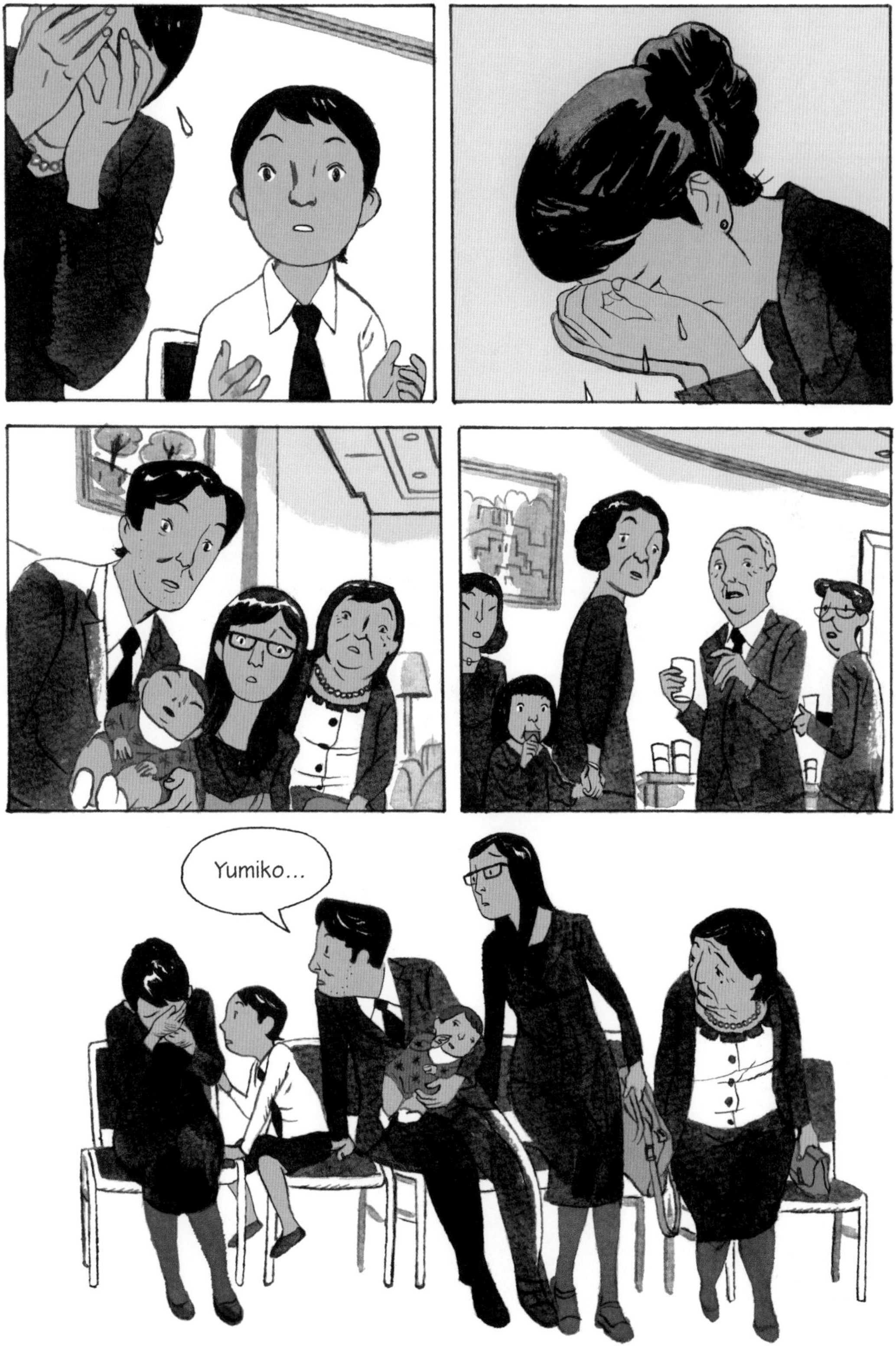
Yumiko...

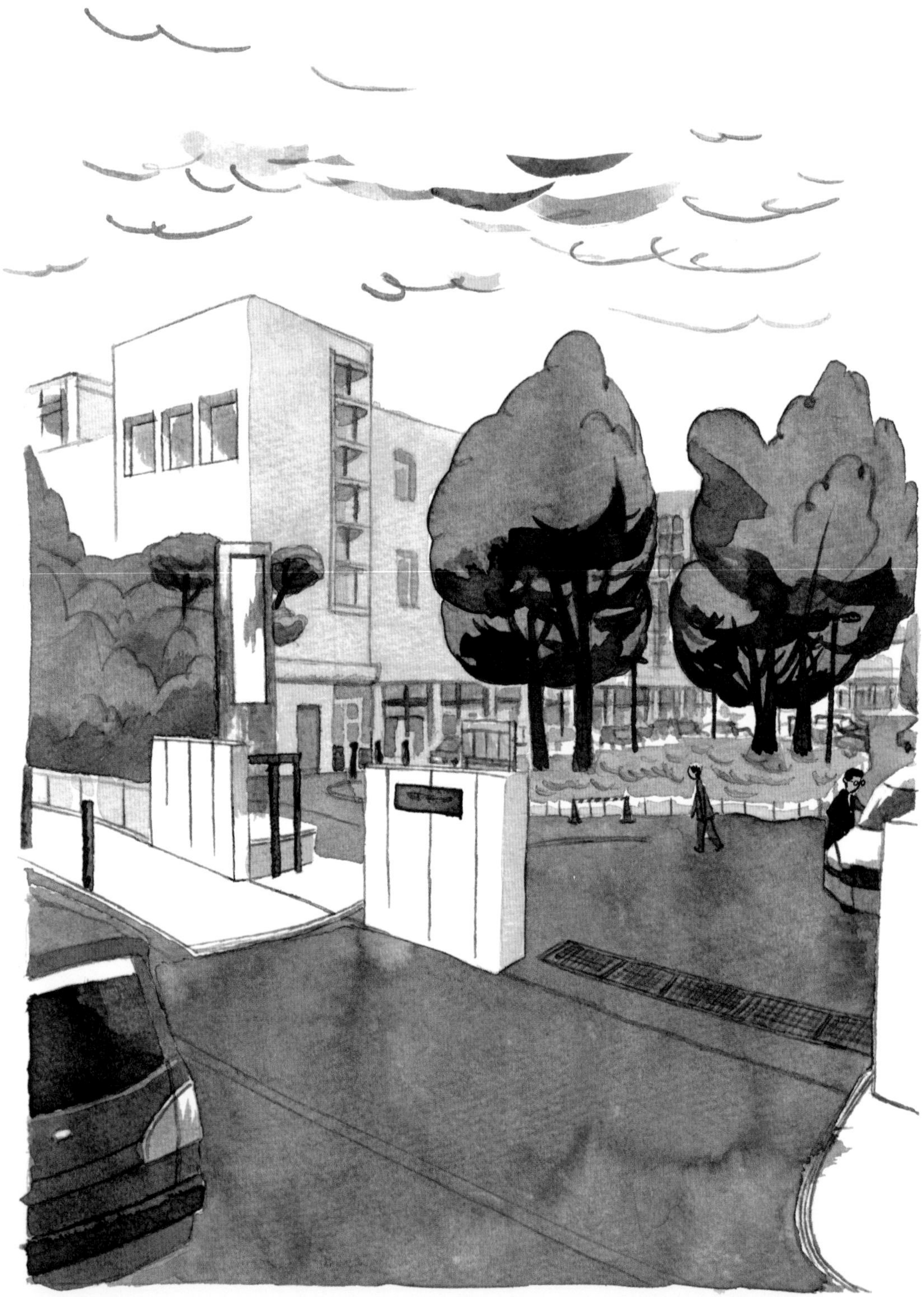

III

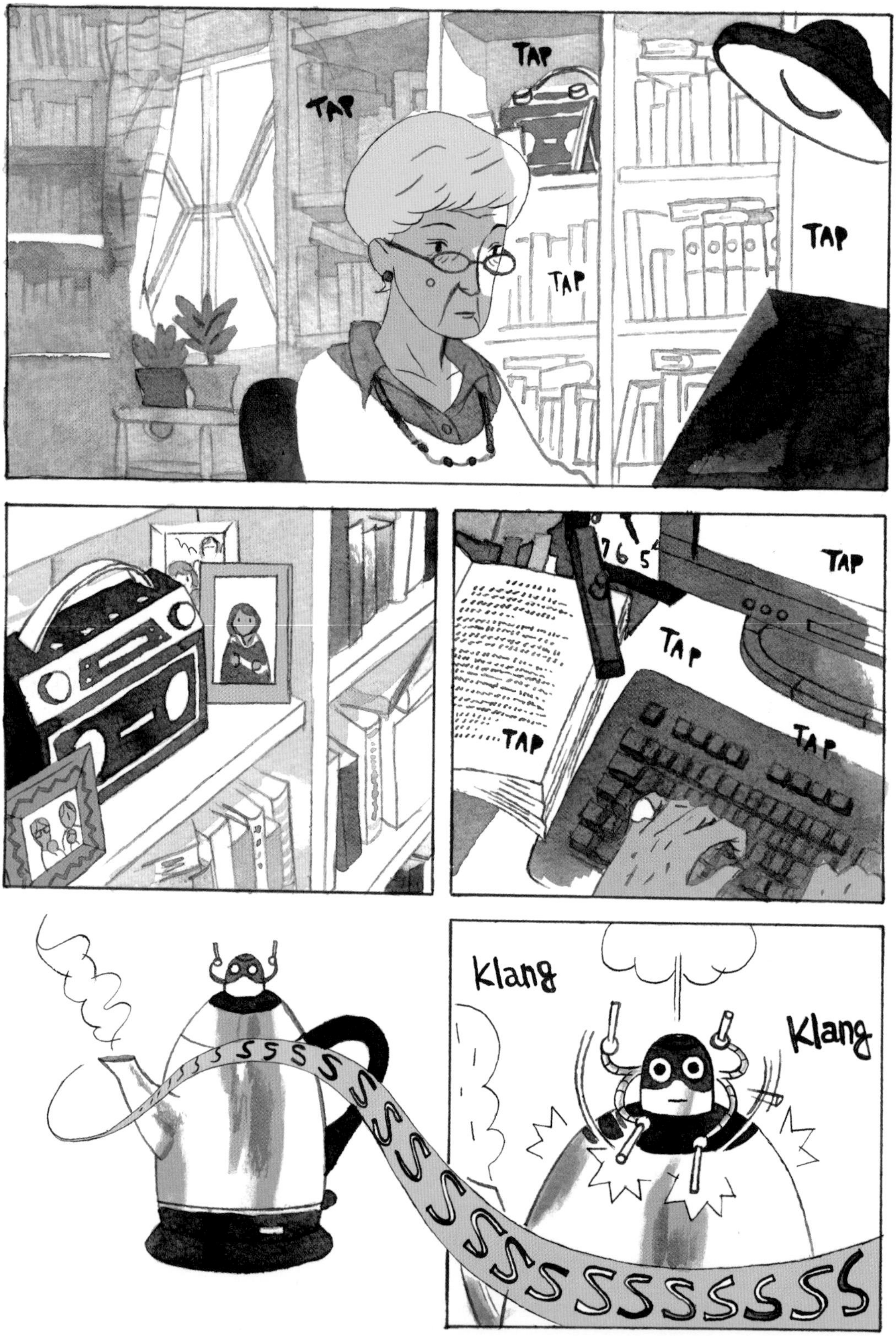
TAP
TAP
TAP
TAP
TAP
TAP
TAP
TAP
TAP
ssssSSSSSSSSSSSSSSSSSSS
Klang
Klang

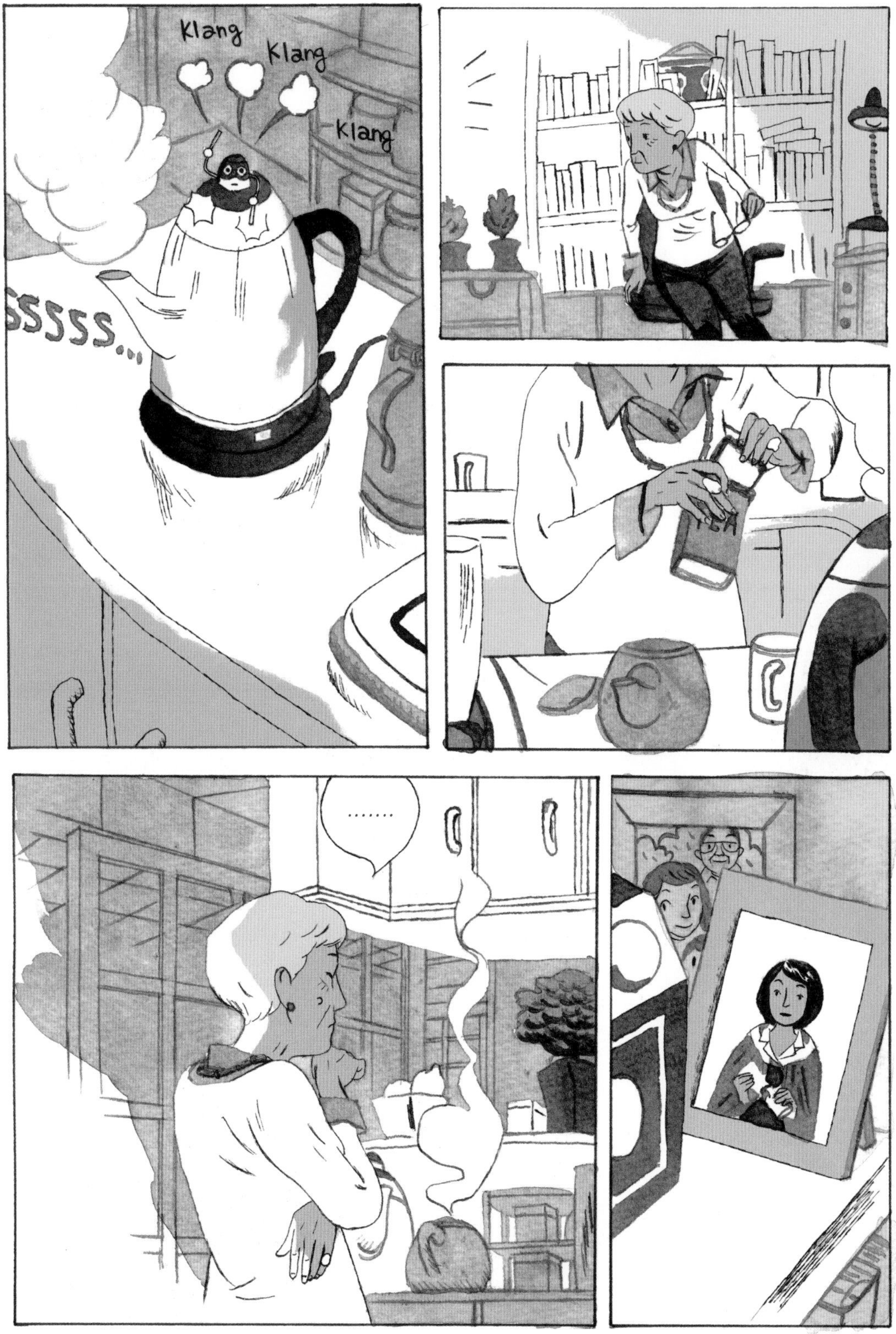
Klang
Klang
Klang
SSSSS...
TEA
....

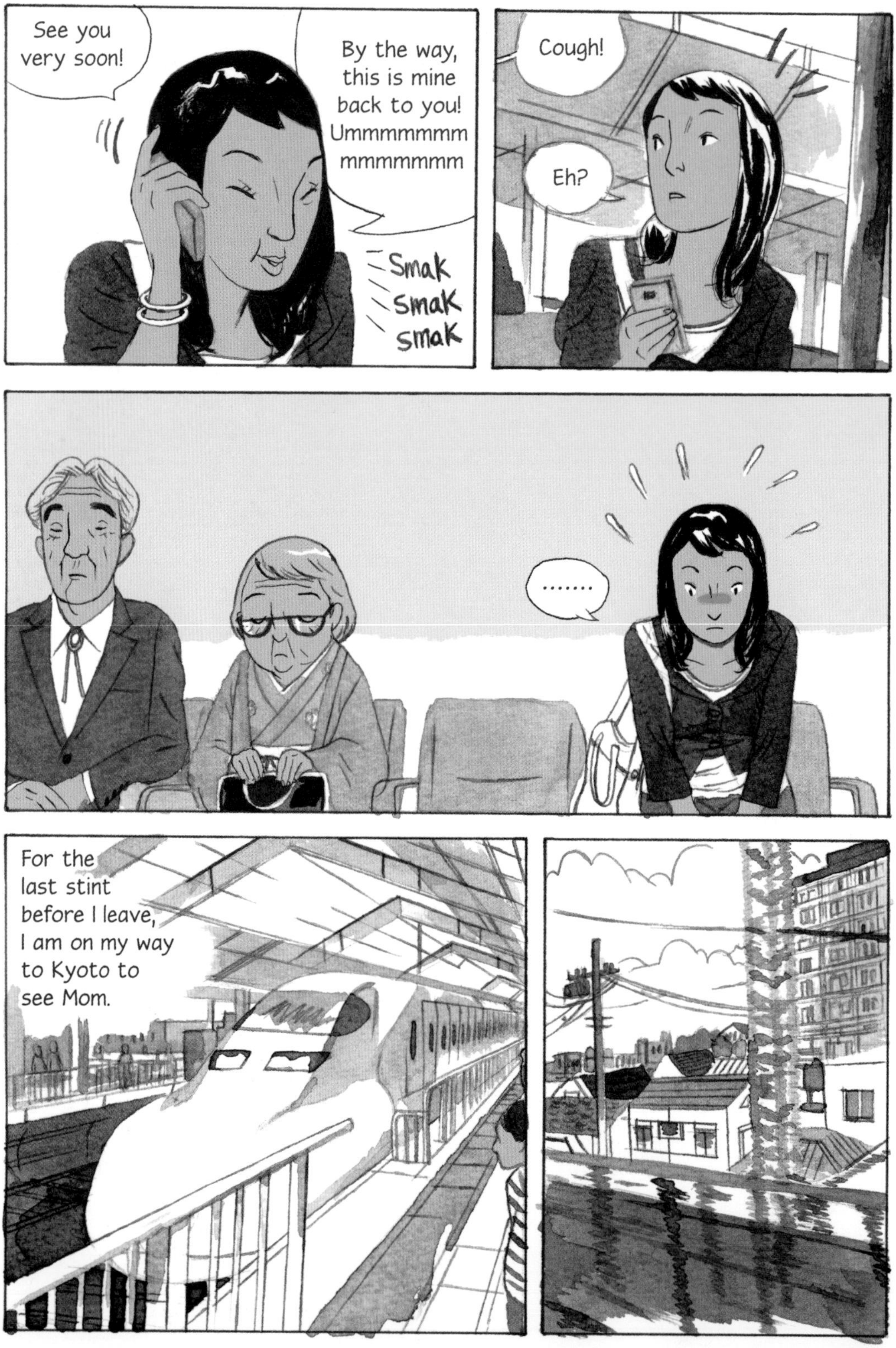
See you very soon!
By the way, this is mine back to you! Ummmmmmm mmmmmmm
Smak smak smak
Cough!
Eh?
....
For the last stint before I leave, I am on my way to Kyoto to see Mom.

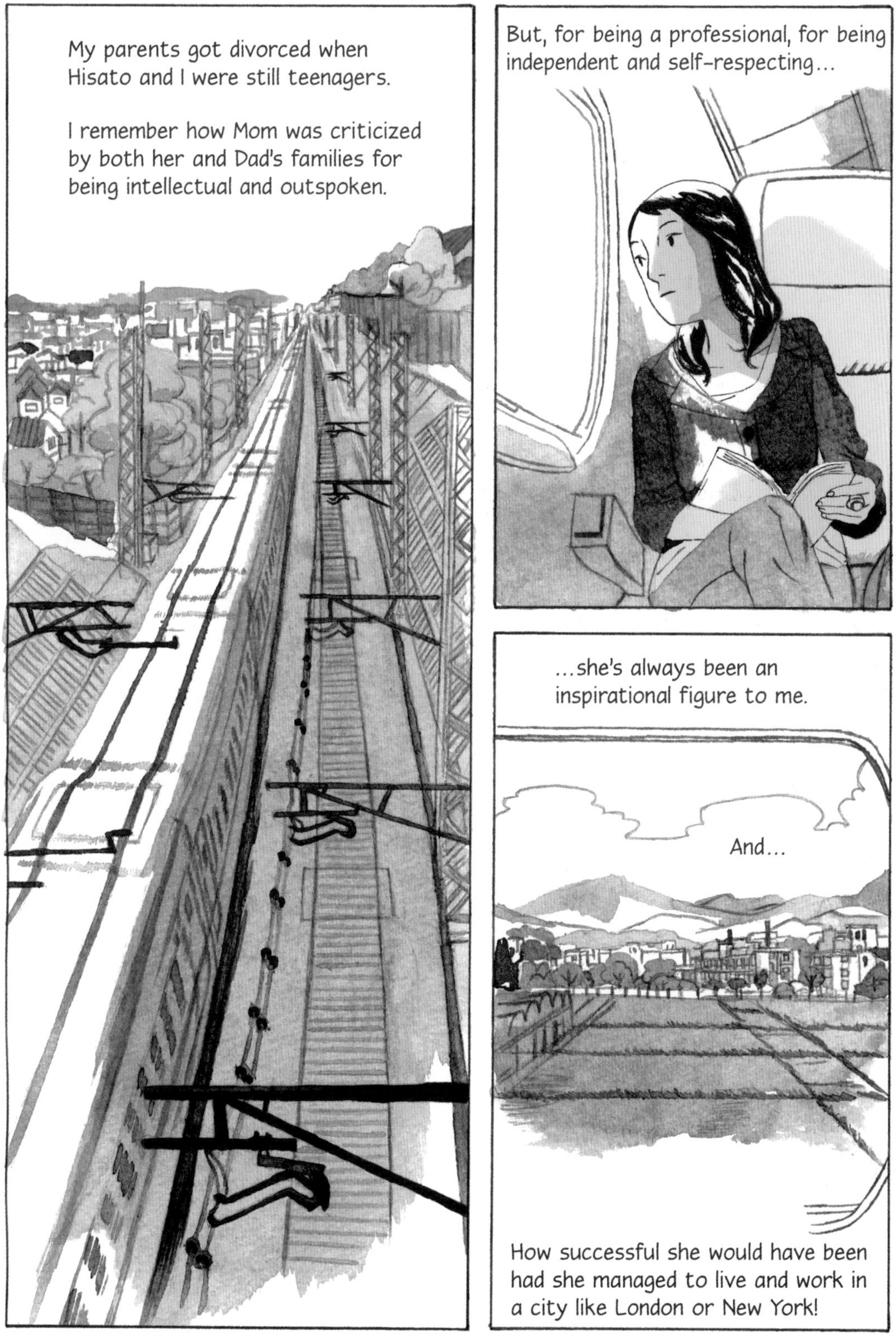
My parents got divorced when Hisato and I were still teenagers.
I remember how Mom was criticized by both her and Dad's families for being intellectual and outspoken.
But, for being a professional, for being independent and self-respecting...
...she's always been an inspirational figure to me.
And...
How successful she would have been had she managed to live and work in a city like London or New York!

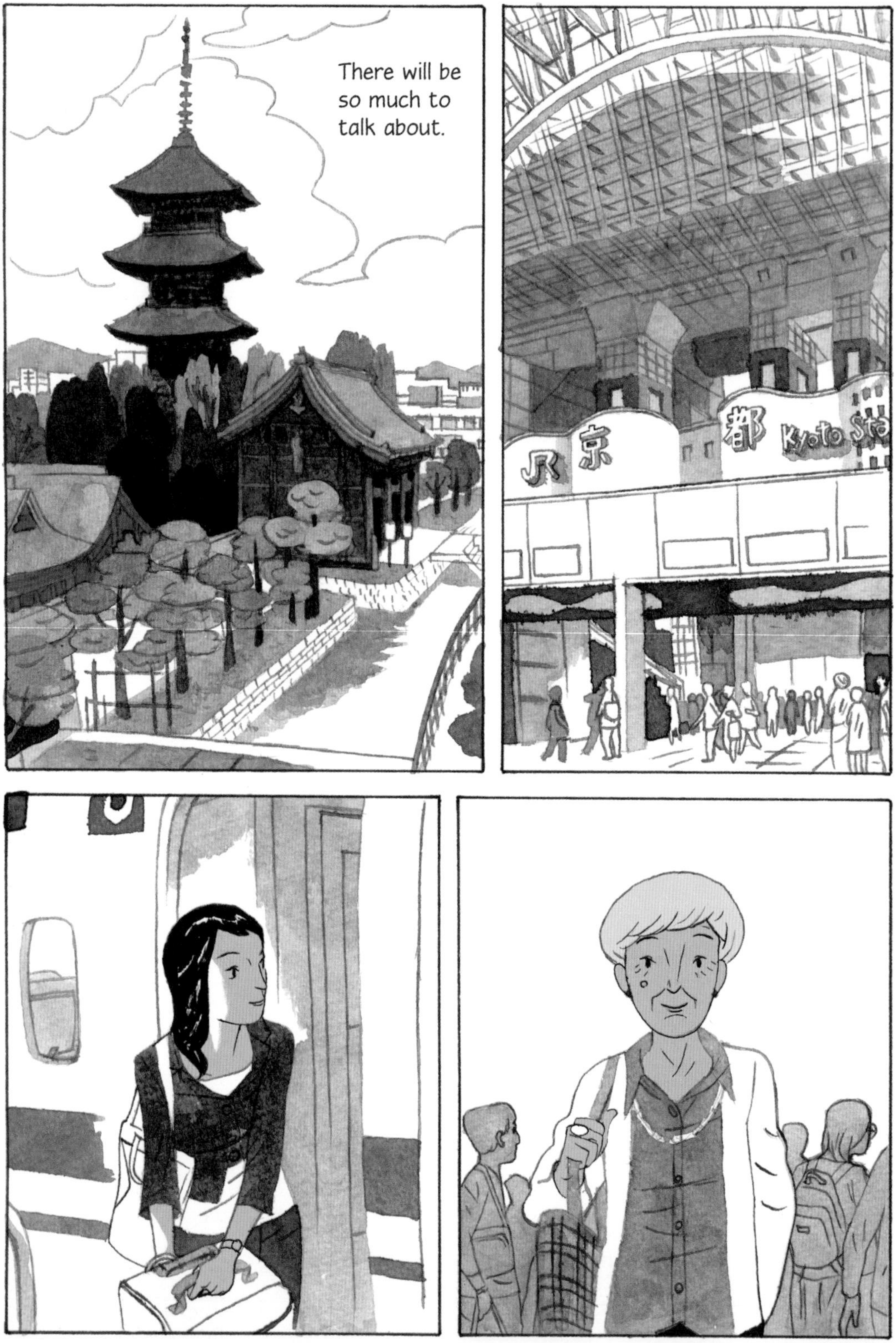
There will be so much to talk about.
京
都
Kyoto

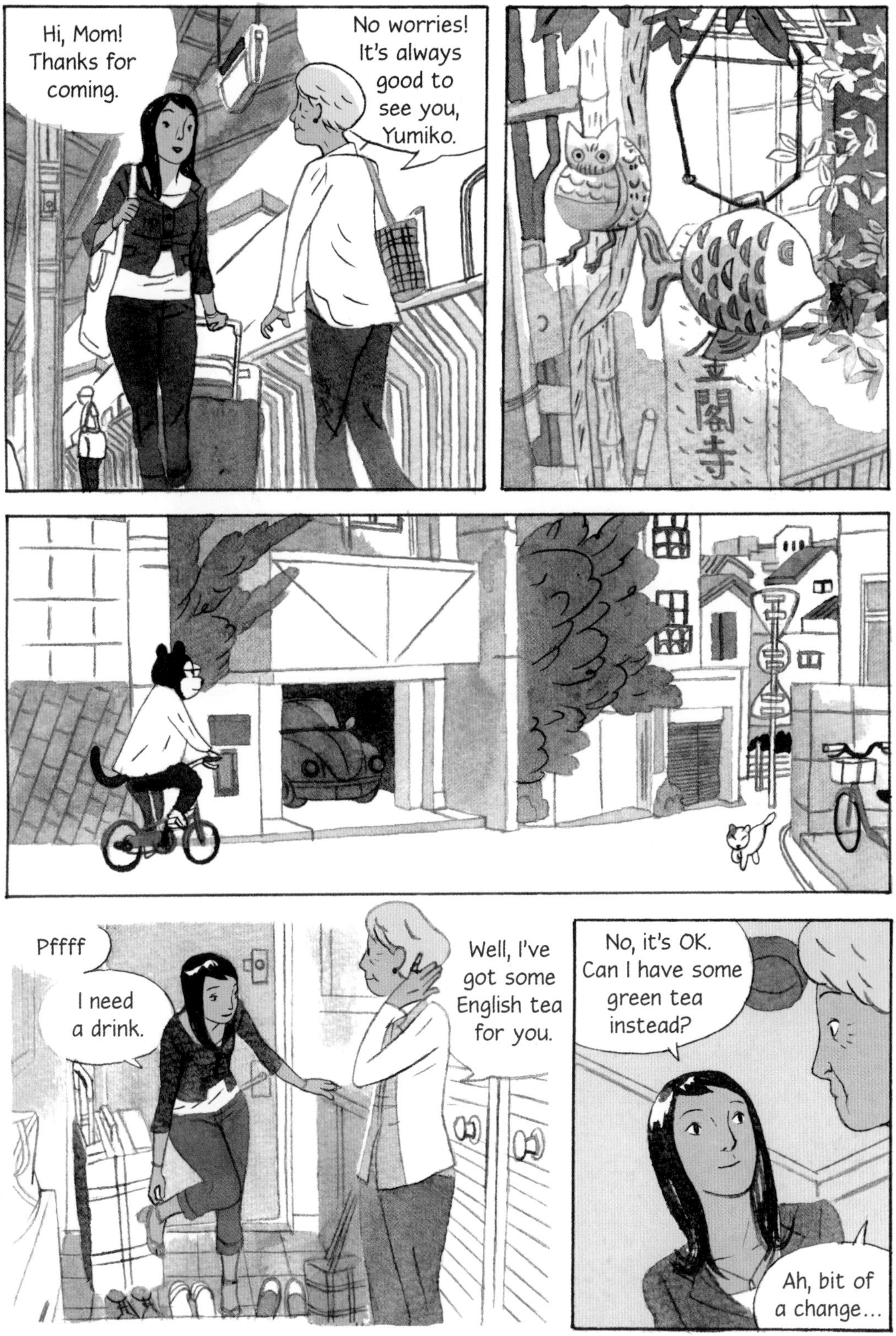
Hi, Mom! Thanks for coming.
No worries! It's always good to see you, Yumiko.
Pffff
I need a drink.
Well, I've got some English tea for you.
No, it's OK. Can I have some green tea instead?
Ah, bit of a change...

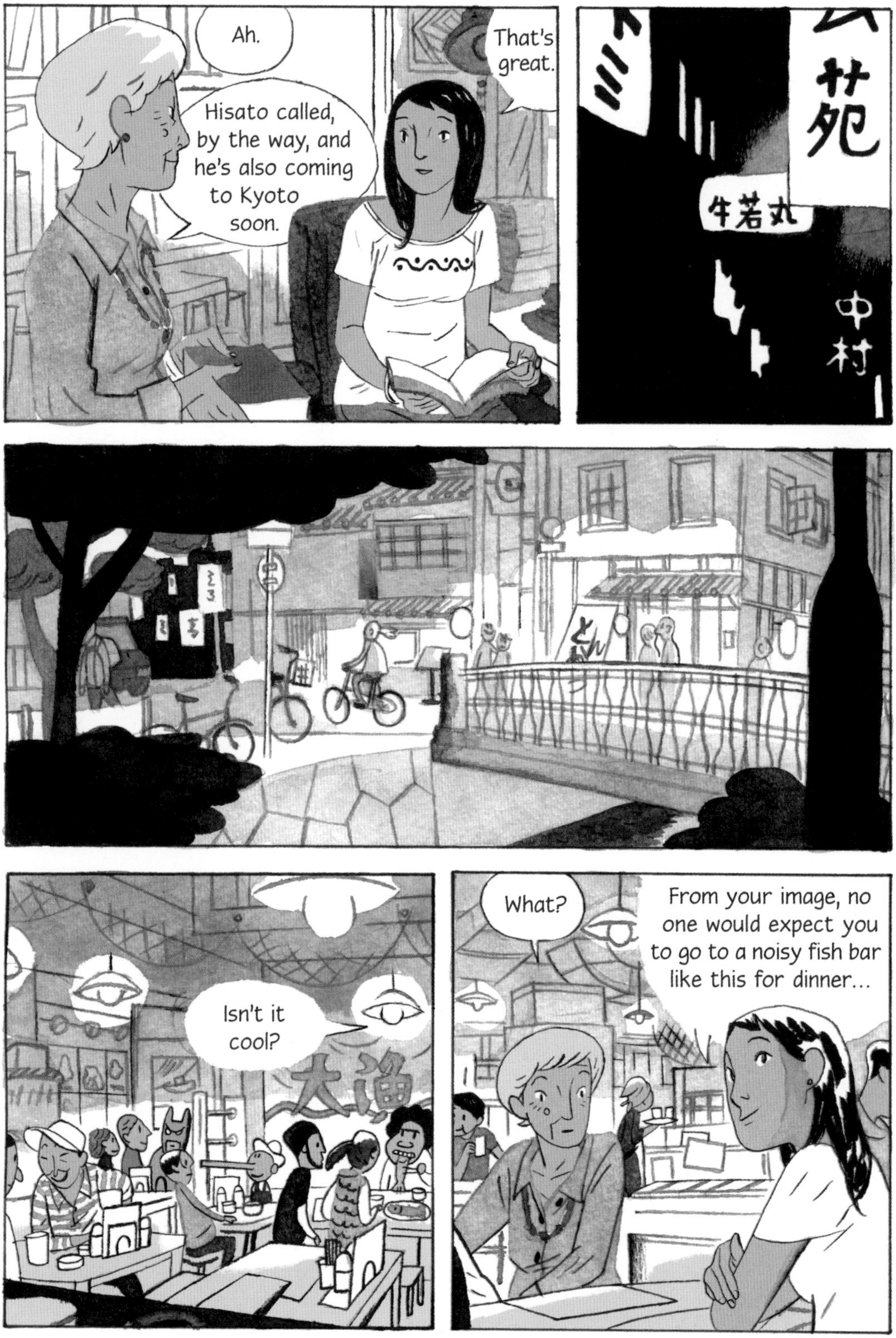
Ah.
That's great.
Hisato called, by the way, and he's also coming to Kyoto soon.
苑
牛若丸
中村
Isn't it cool?
What?
From your image, no one would expect you to go to a noisy fish bar like this for dinner...

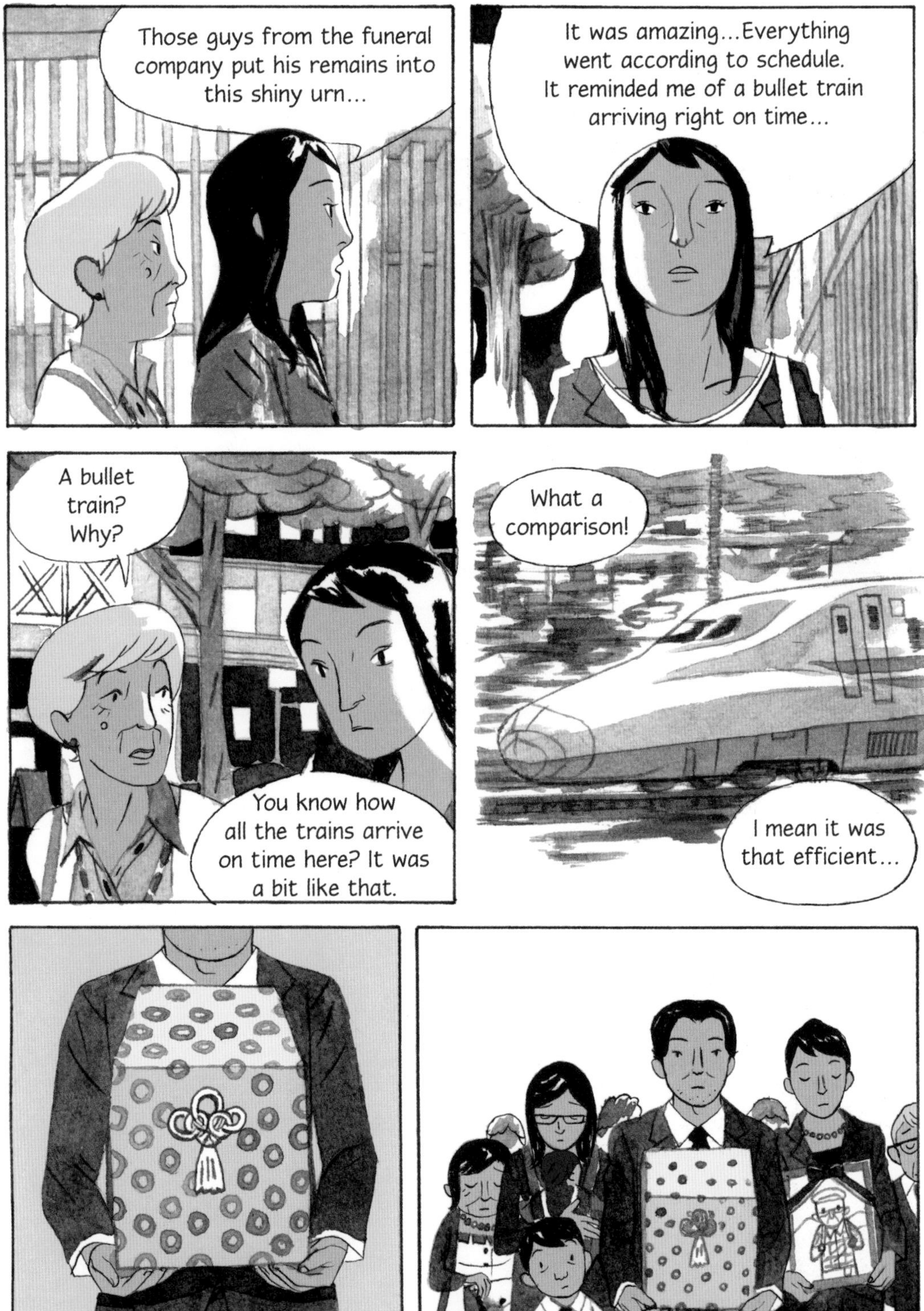
Those guys from the funeral company put his remains into this shiny urn...
It was amazing...Everything went according to schedule. It reminded me of a bullet train arriving right on time...
A bullet train? Why?
You know how all the trains arrive on time here? It was a bit like that.
What a comparison!
I mean it was that efficient...

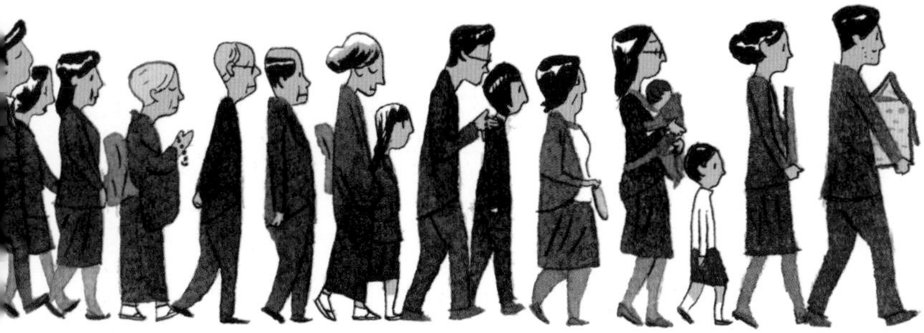

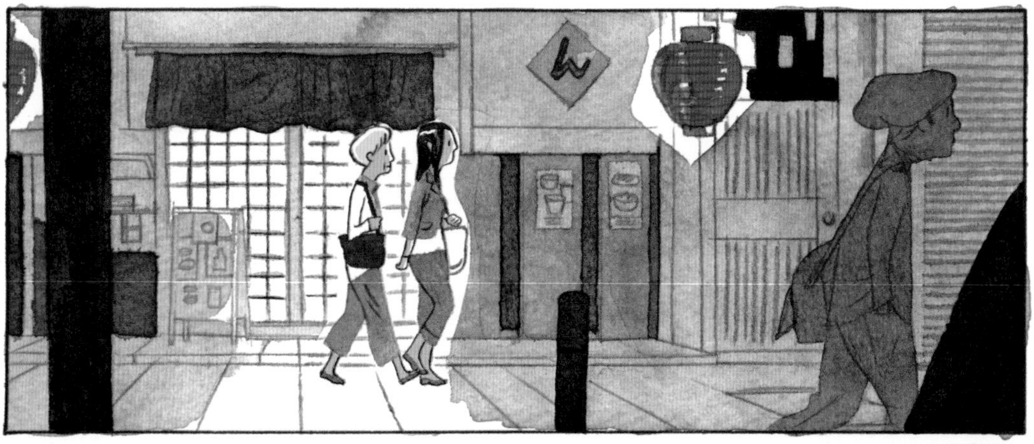

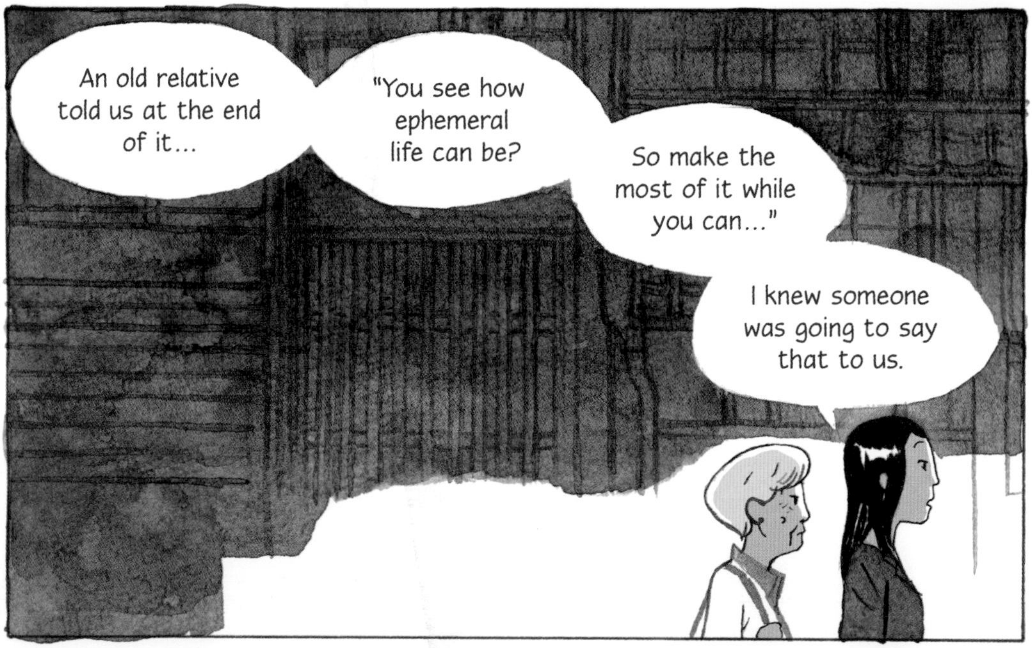

An old relative told us at the end of it...
"You see how ephemeral life can be?
So make the most of it while you can..."
I knew someone was going to say that to us.

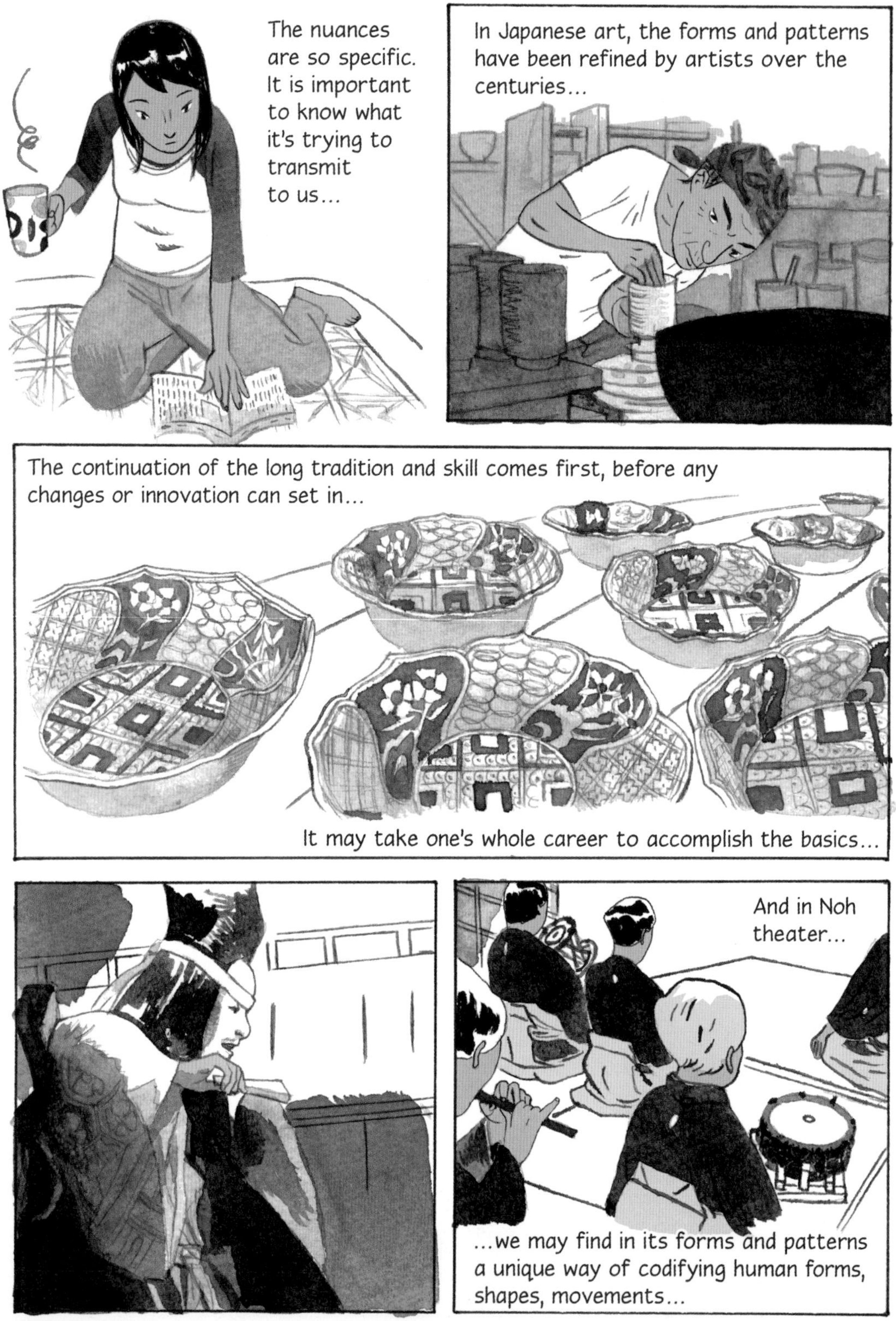
The nuances are so specific. It is important to know what it's trying to transmit to us...
In Japanese art, the forms and patterns have been refined by artists over the centuries...
The continuation of the long tradition and skill comes first, before any changes or innovation can set in...
It may take one's whole career to accomplish the basics...
And in Noh theater...
...we may find in its forms and patterns a unique way of codifying human forms, shapes, movements...

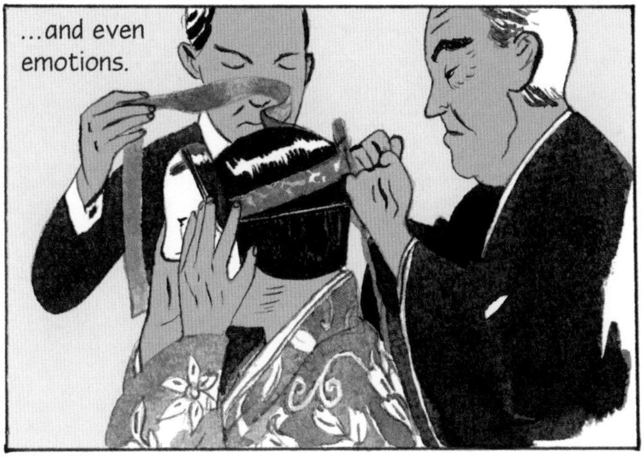
...and even
emotions.

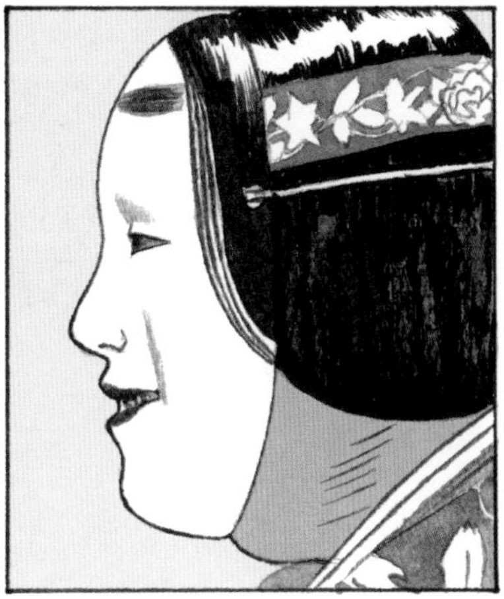

This is a transformation in a ritual sense,
to be totally possessed by the theater, or to be subject to it.

In order to express its idea of a transcendental world,
one must put one's heart and mind in total resonance
with the theatrical role.

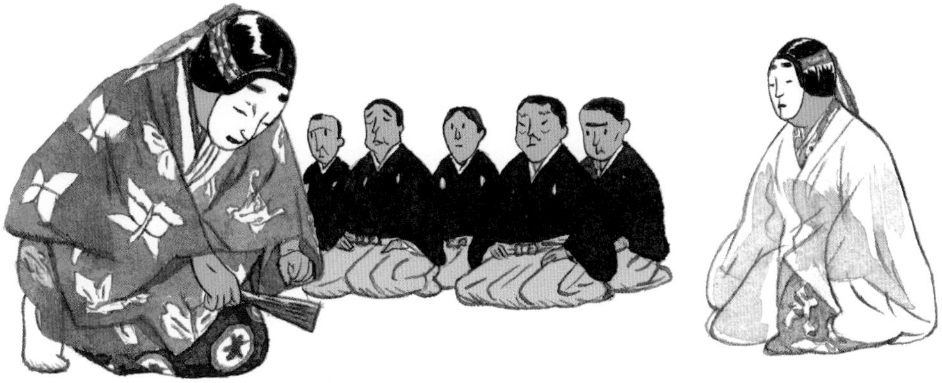

And in the process, all the natural traits are SIMPLIFIED.

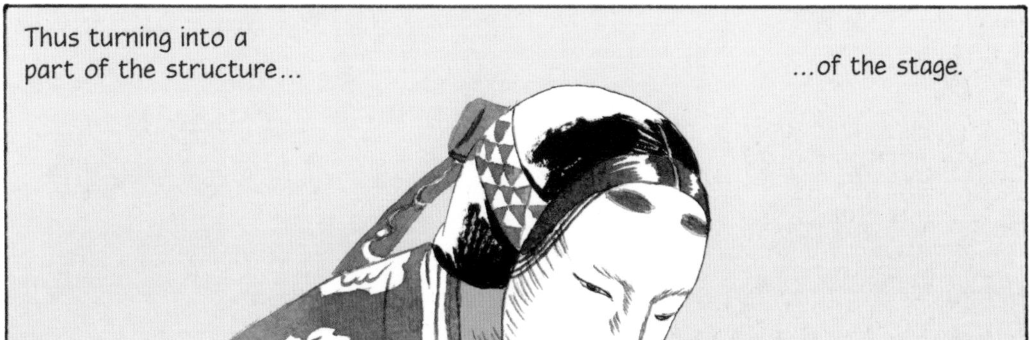
Thus turning into a
part of the structure...
...of the stage.

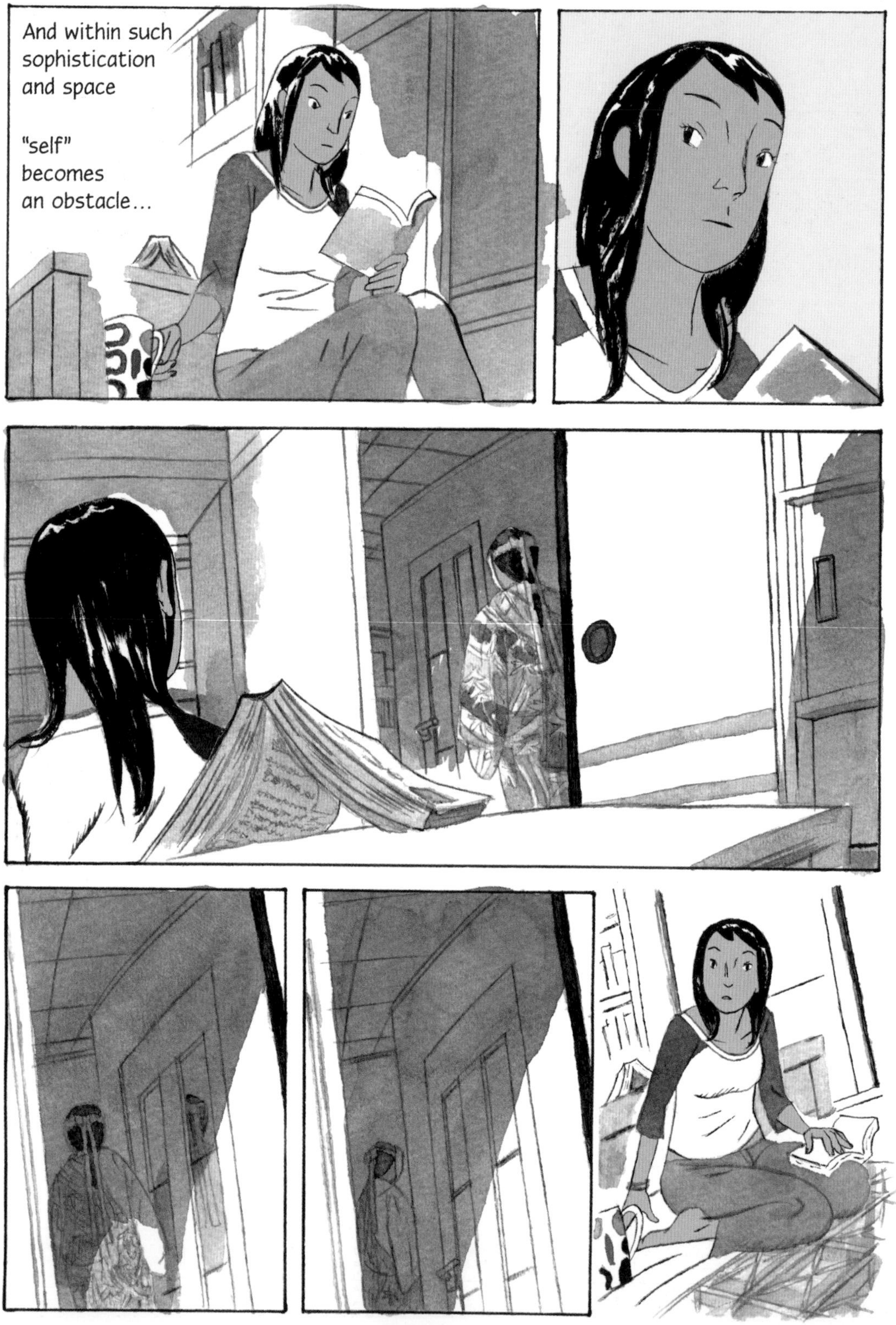
And within such sophistication and space
"self" becomes an obstacle...

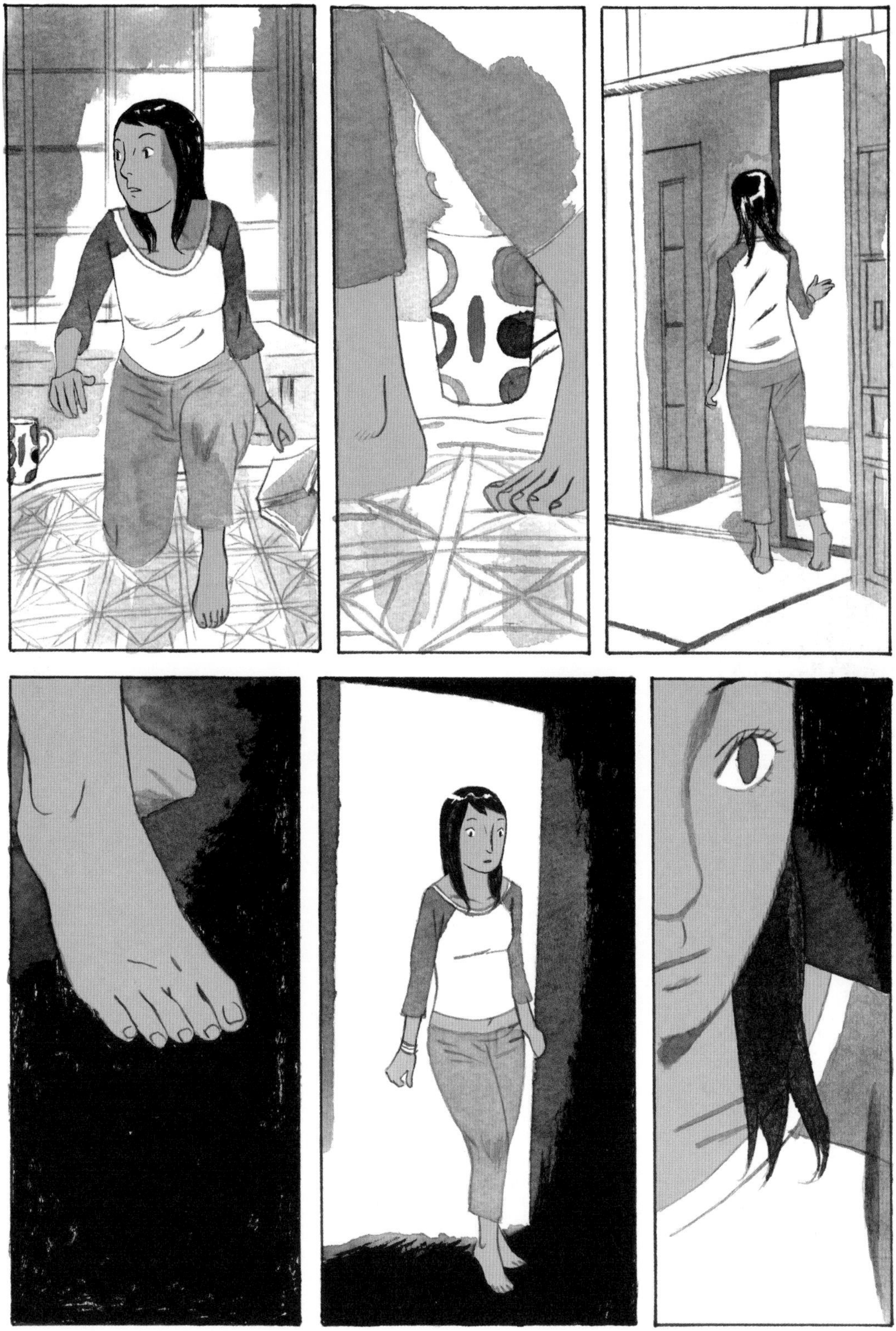

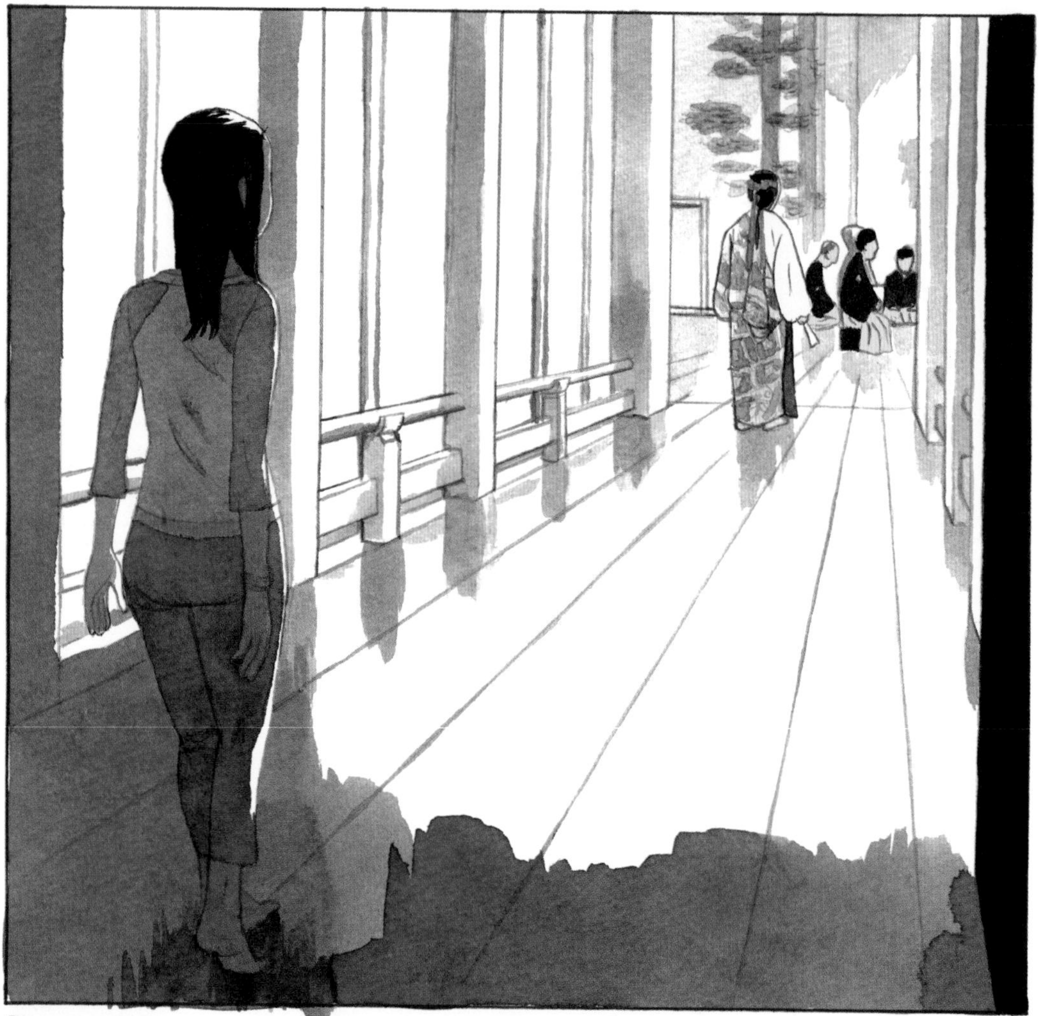

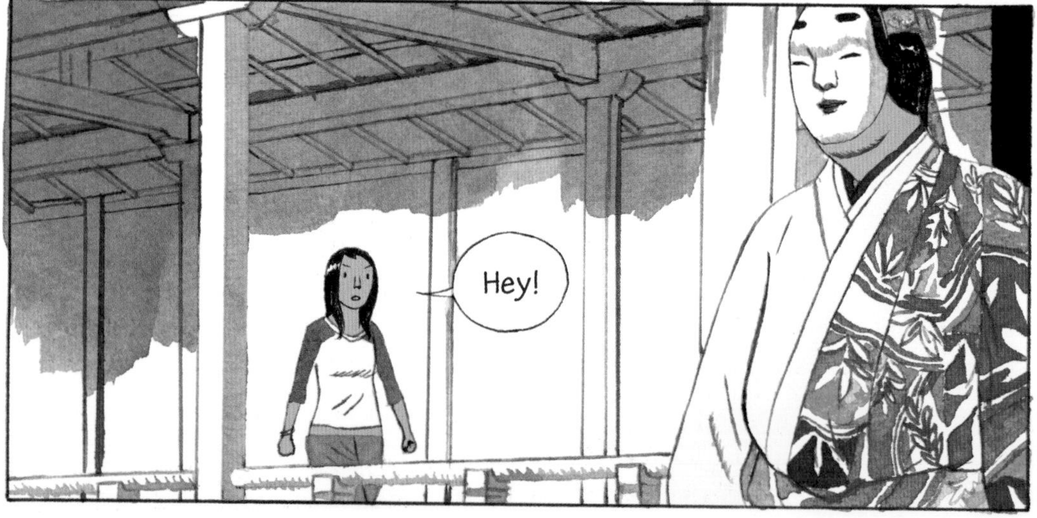
Hey!

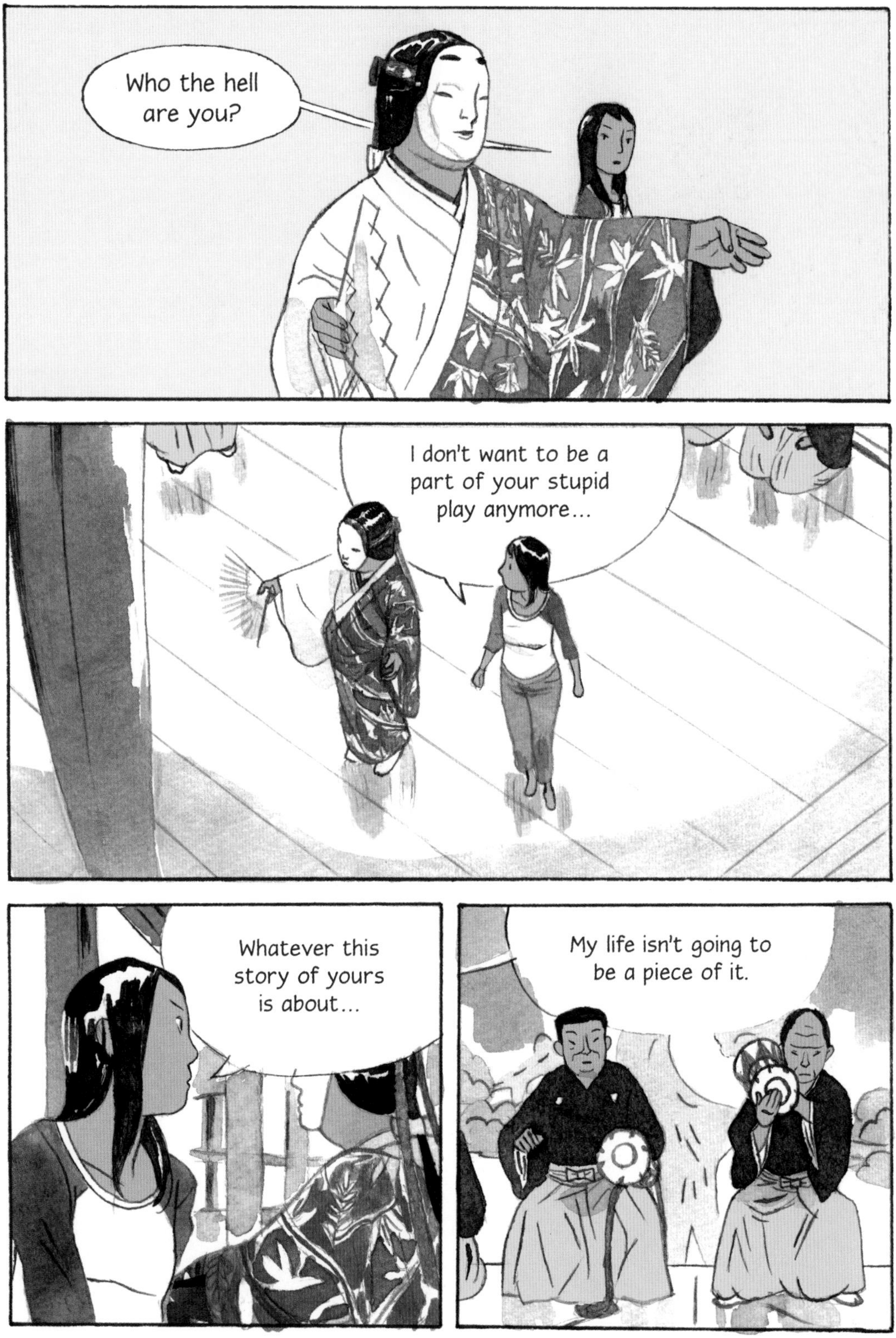
Who the hell are you?
I don't want to be a part of your stupid play anymore...
Whatever this story of yours is about...
My life isn't going to be a piece of it.

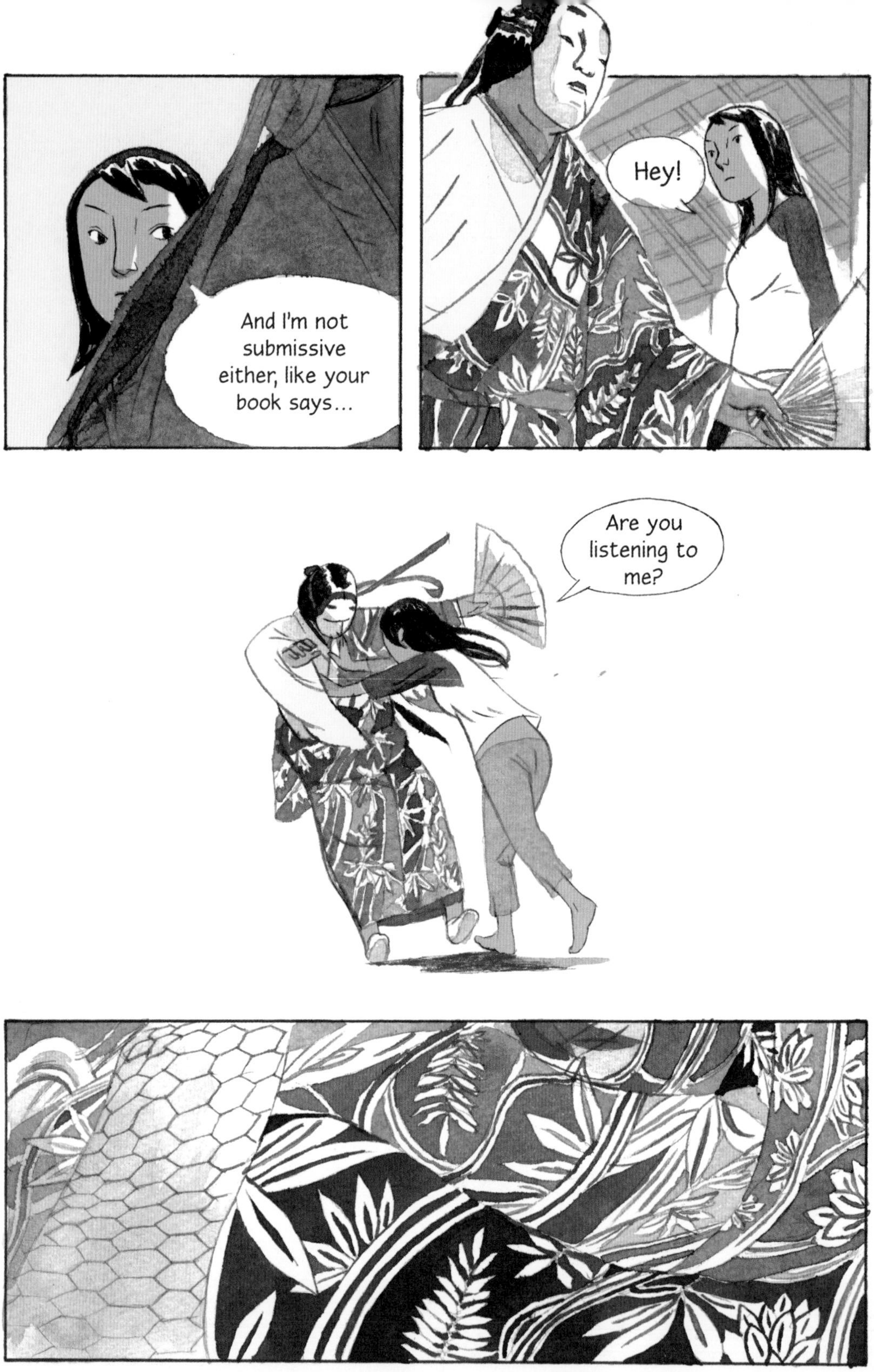

And I'm not submissive either, like your book says...
Hey!
Are you listening to me?

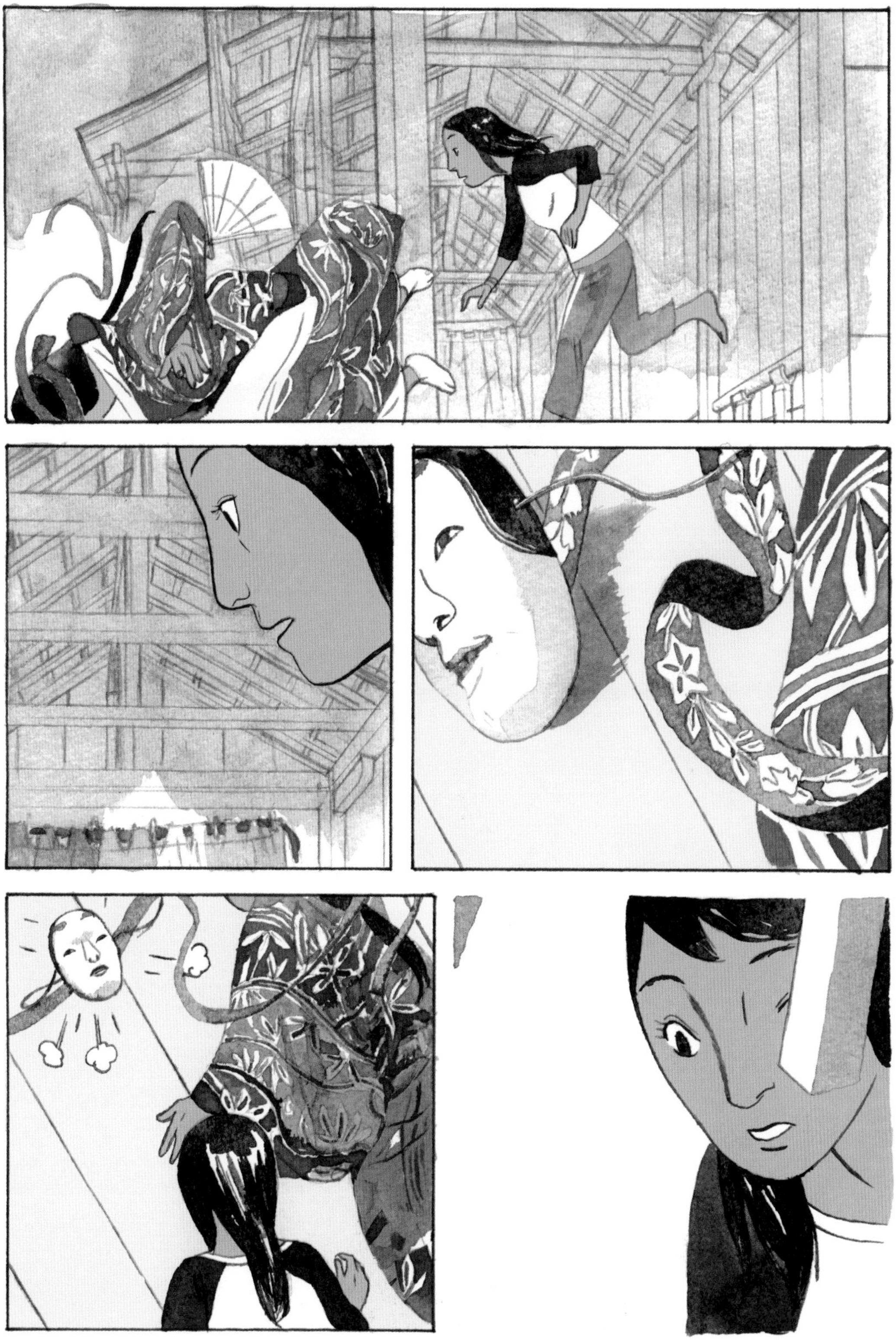

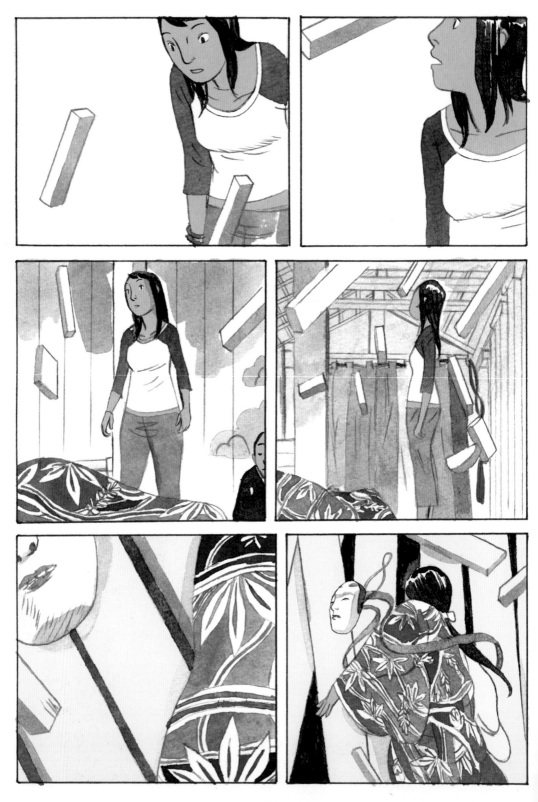

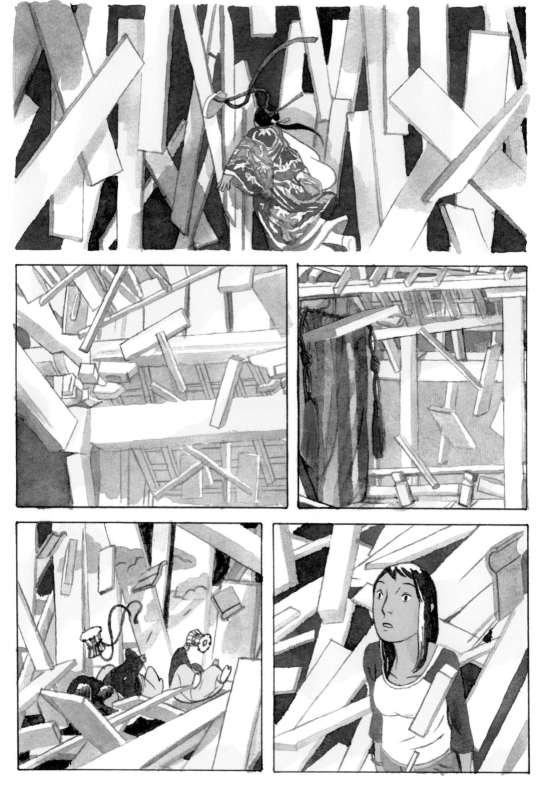

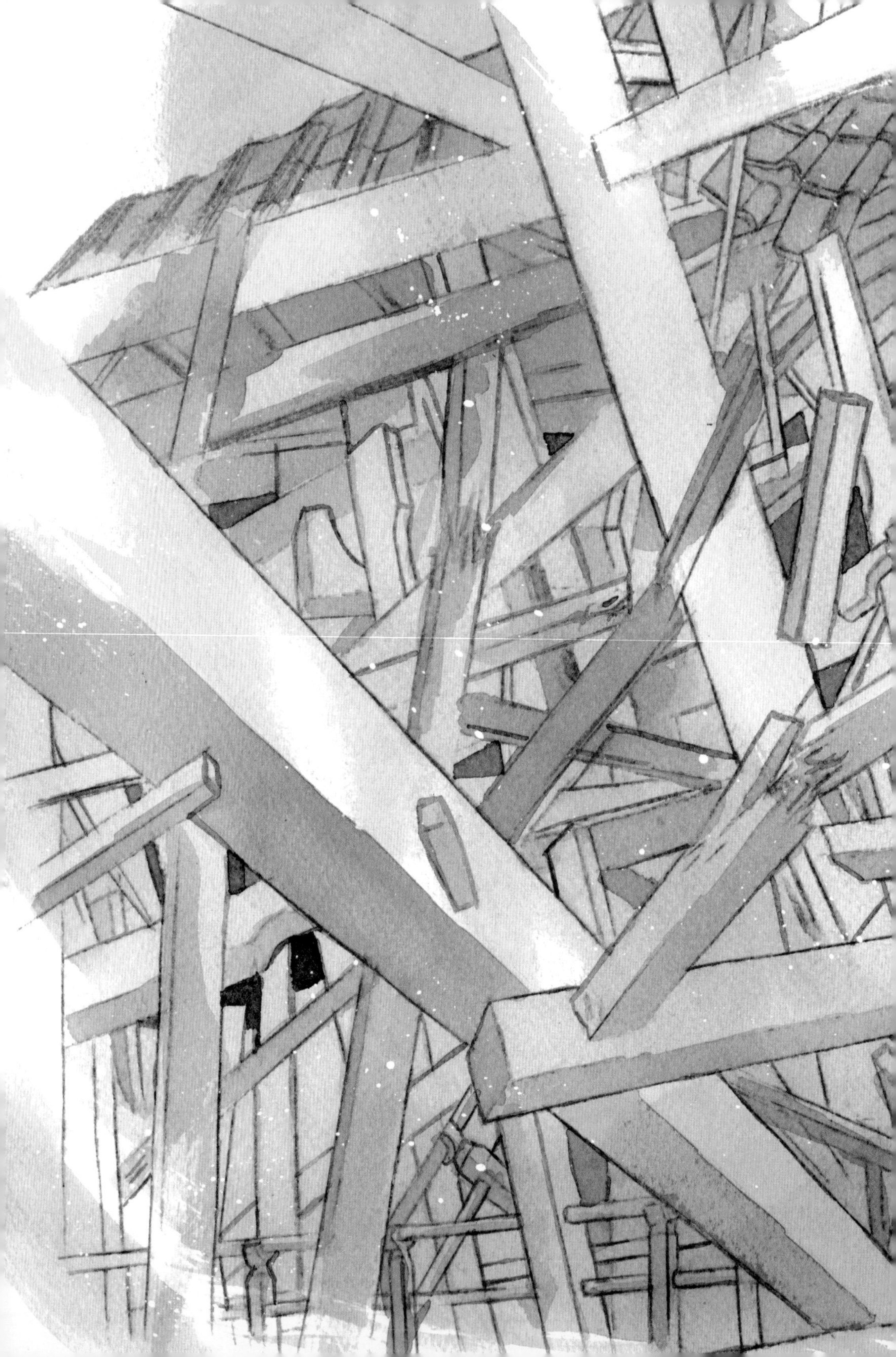

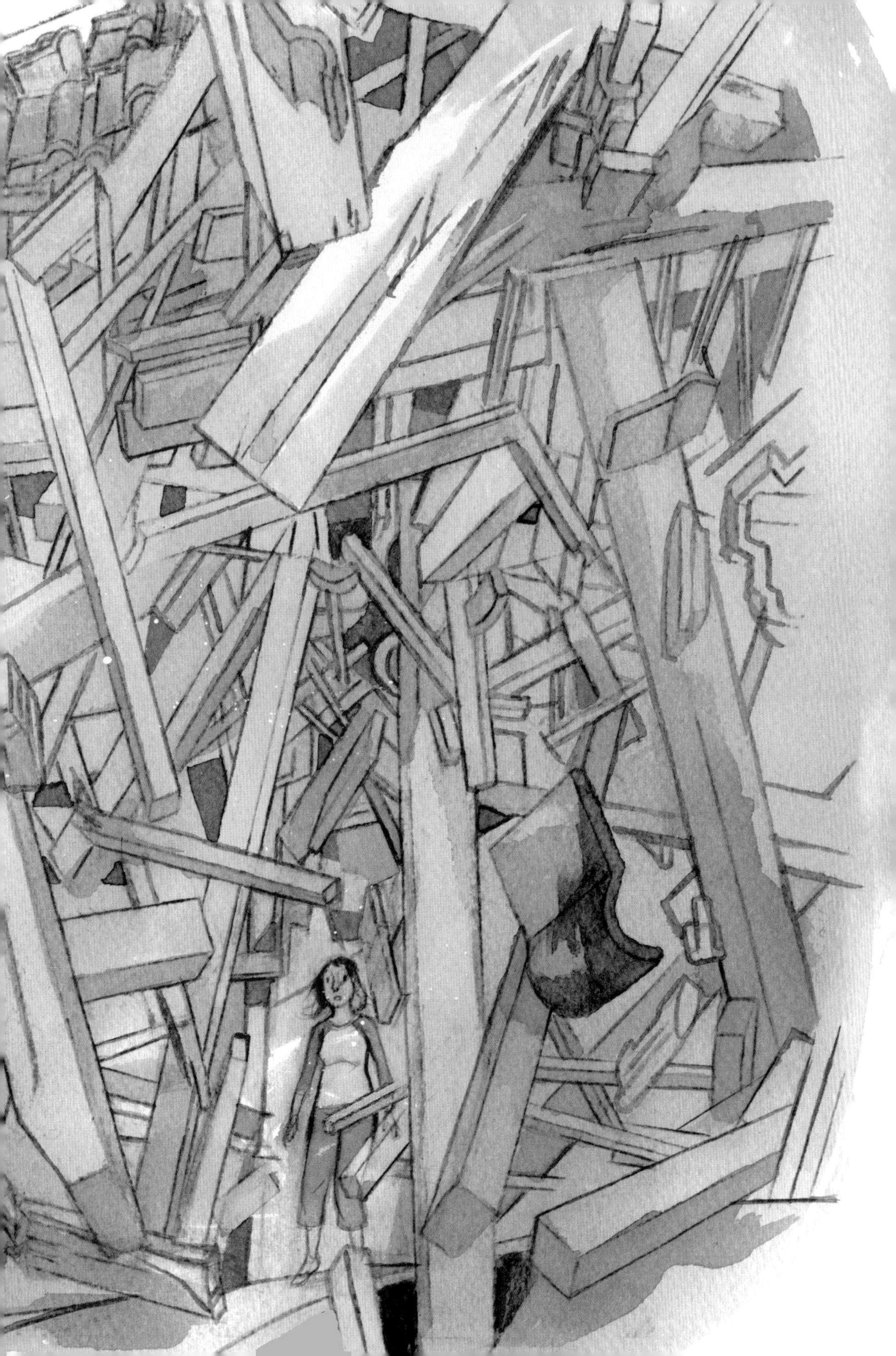

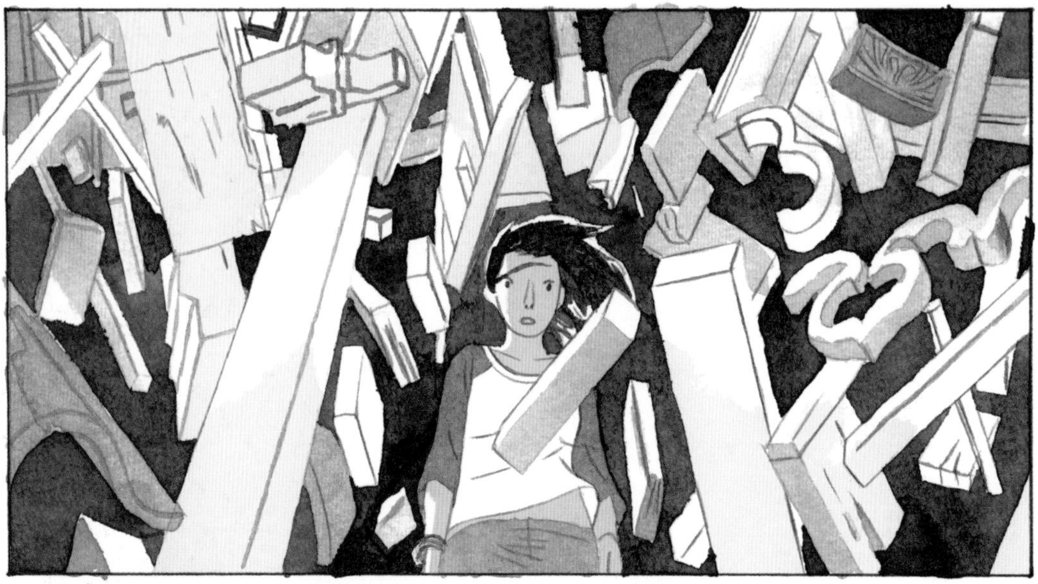

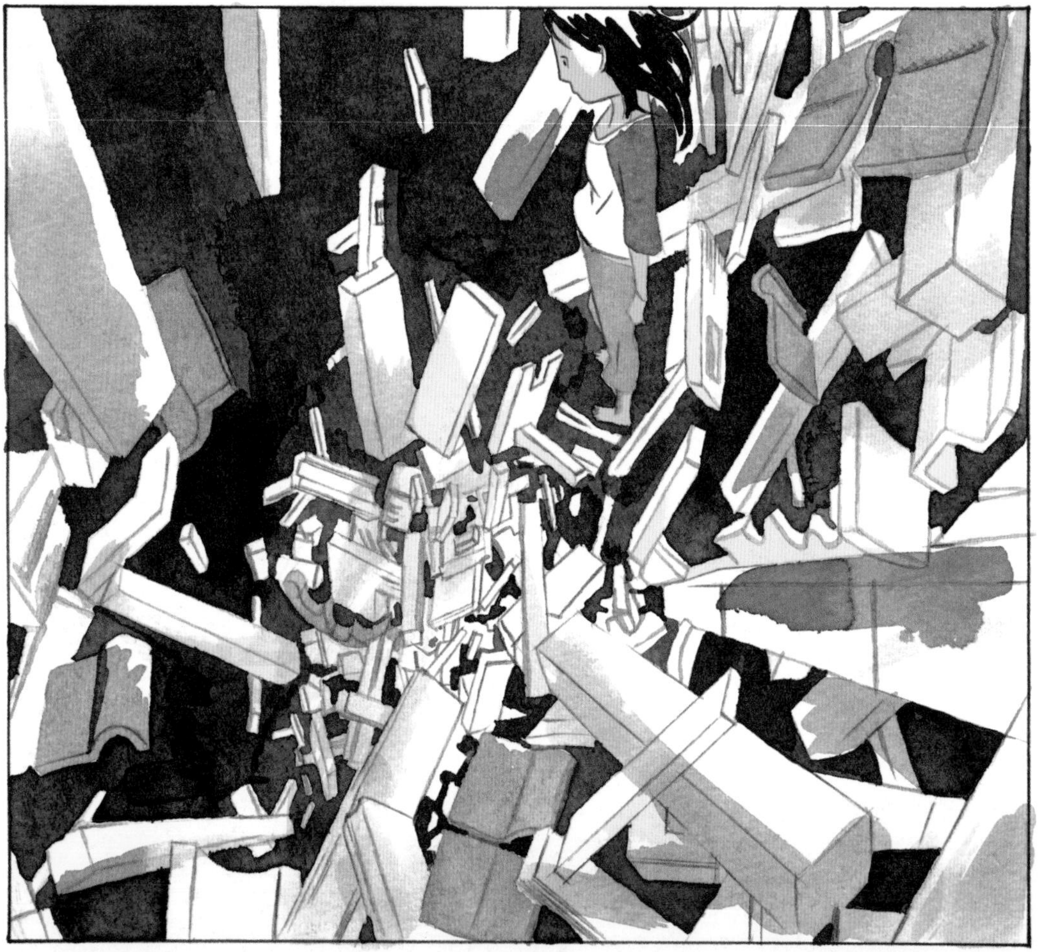

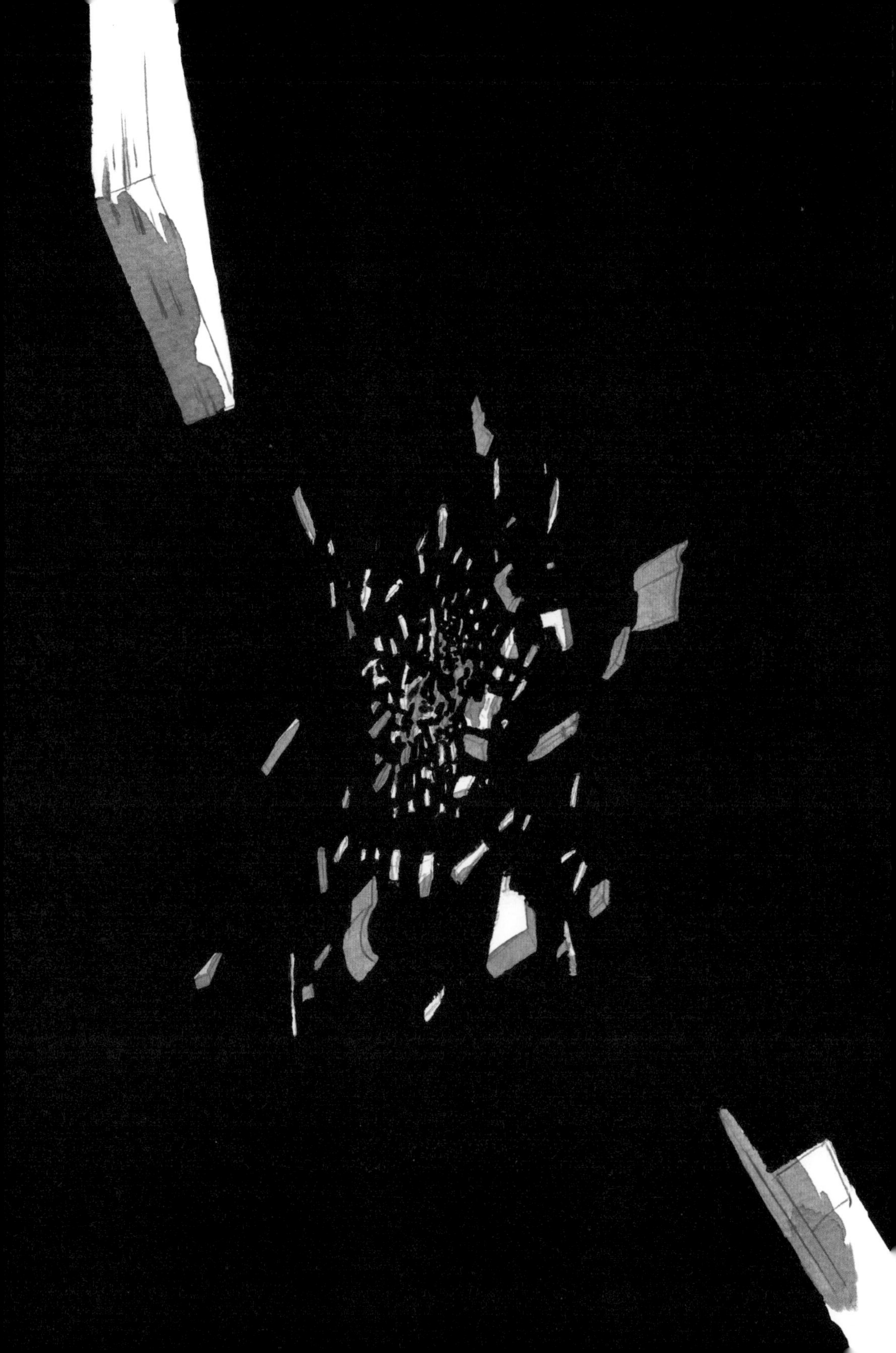

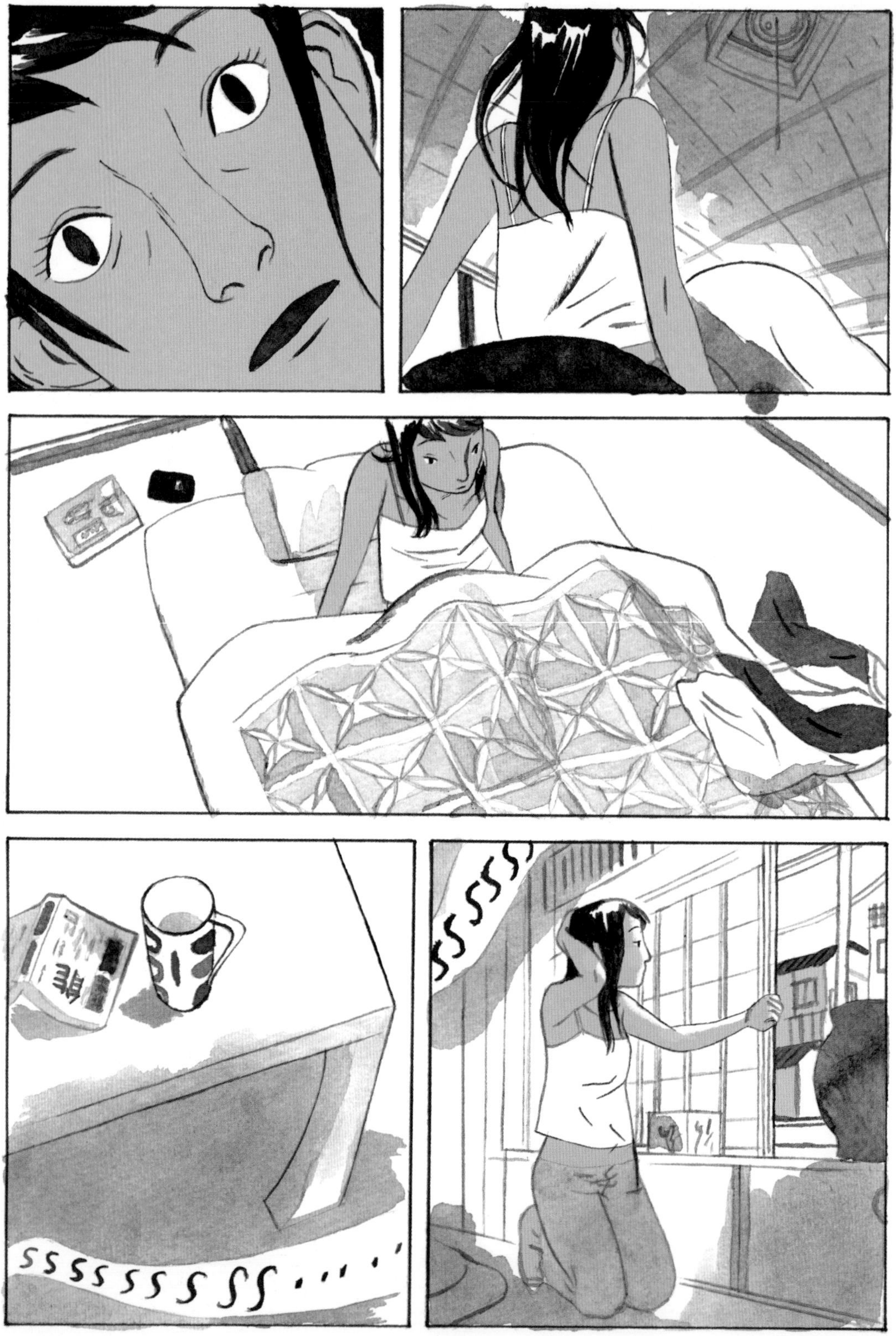
SSSSSSSSSS.....
SSSSSS

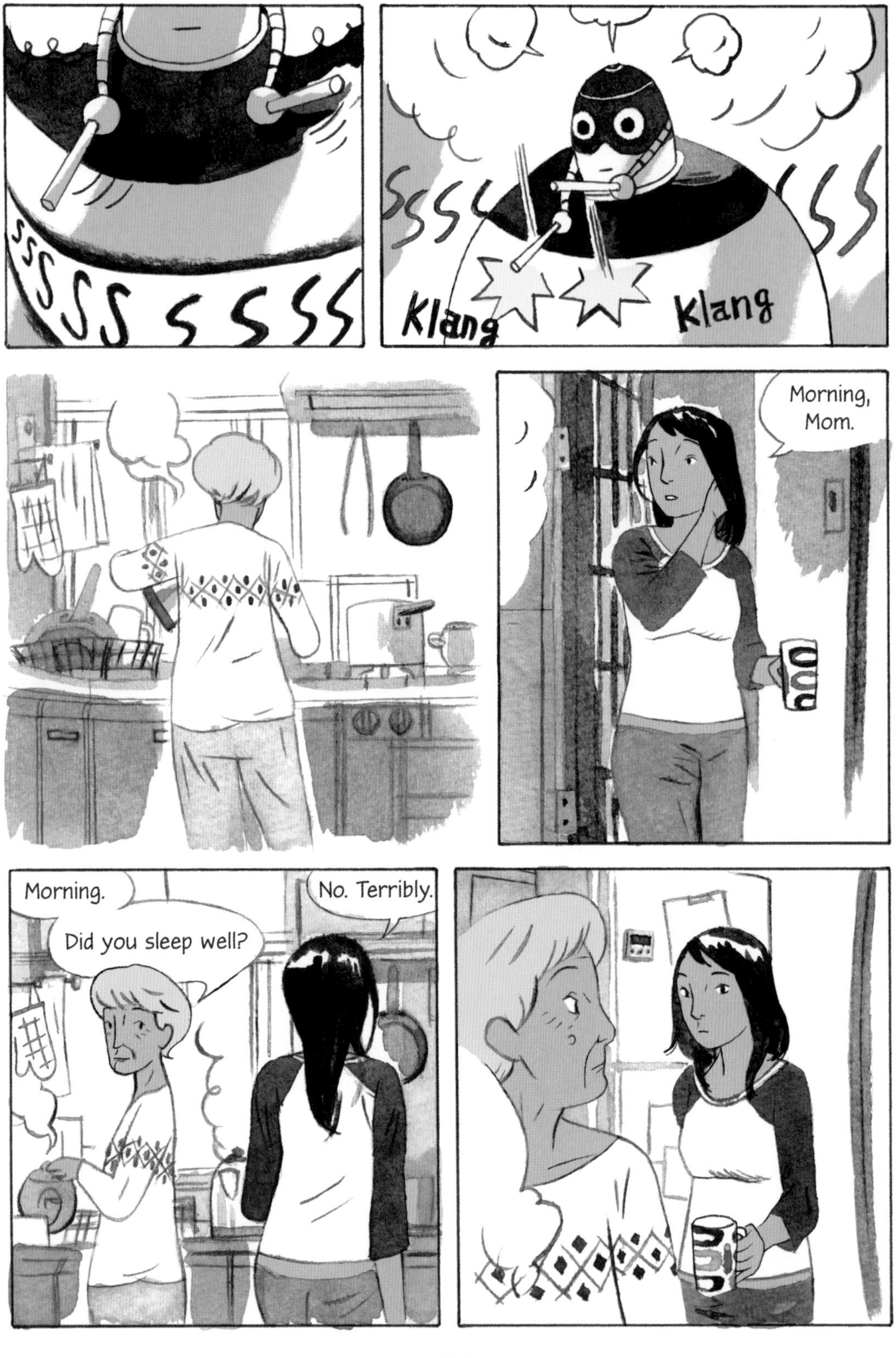
SSSSSSSS
SSSS
SSS
Klang
Klang
Morning, Mom.
Morning.
Did you sleep well?
No. Terribly.

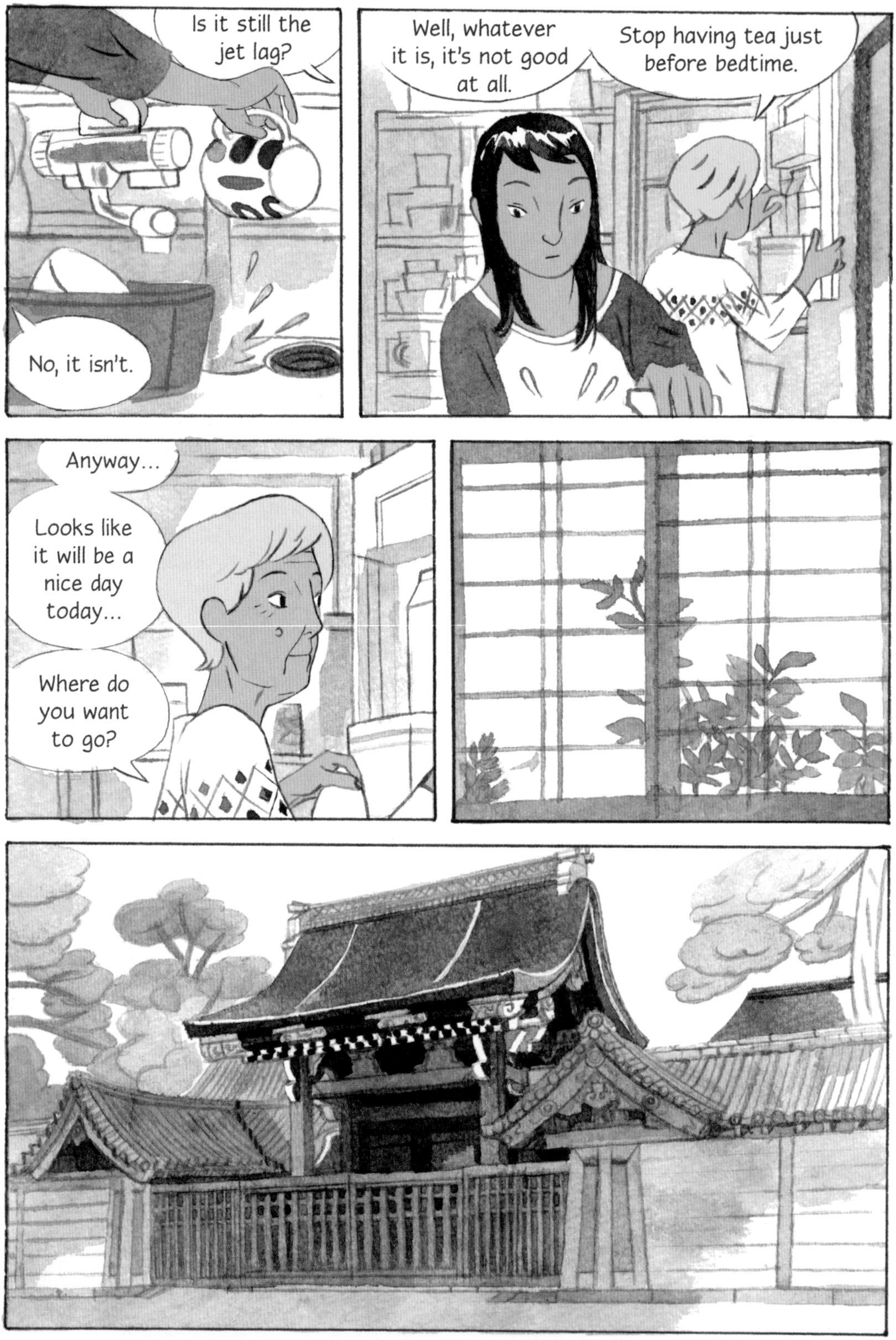
Is it still the jet lag?
No, it isn't.
Well, whatever it is, it's not good at all.
Stop having tea just before bedtime.
Anyway...
Looks like it will be a nice day today...
Where do you want to go?

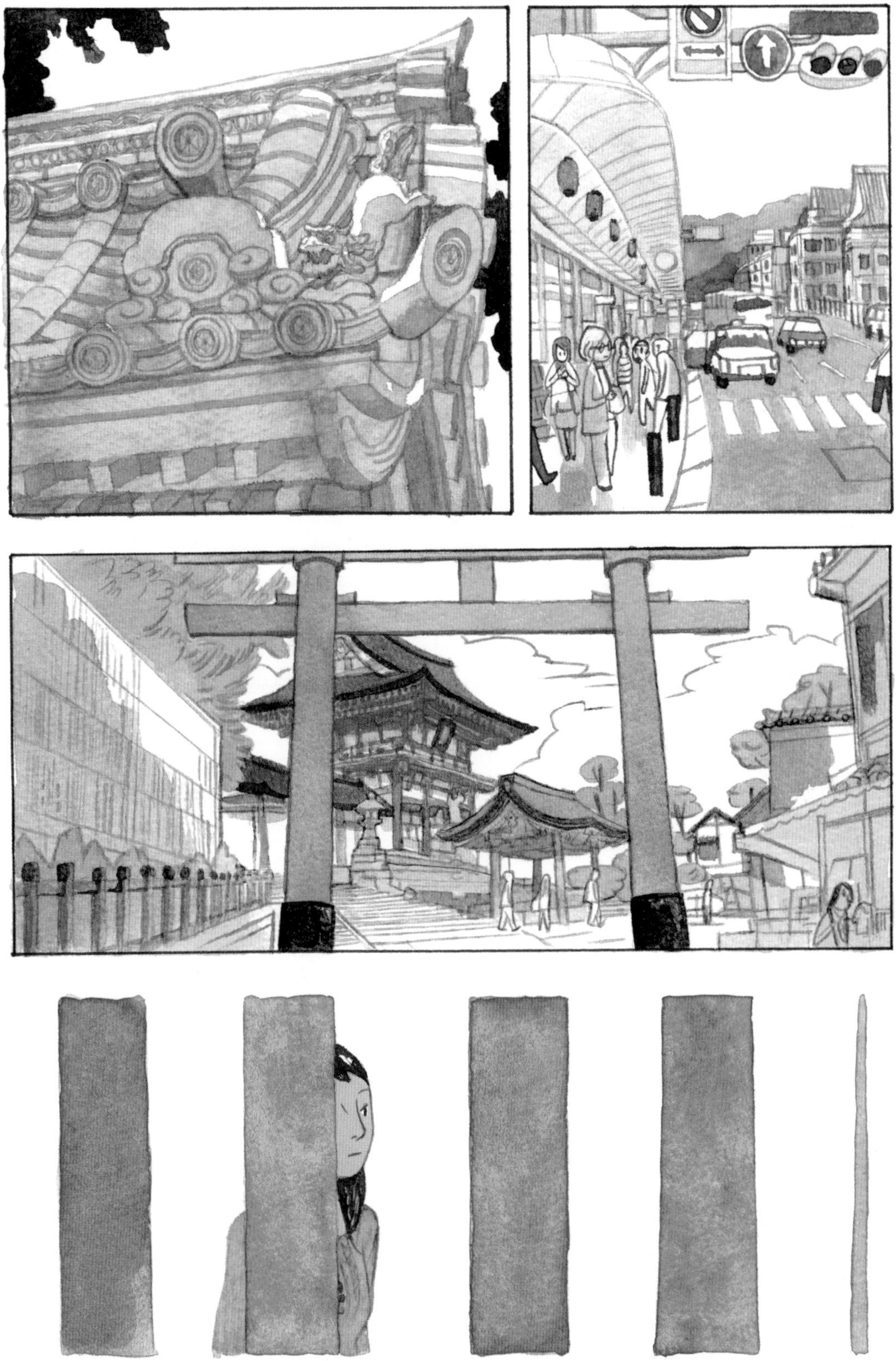

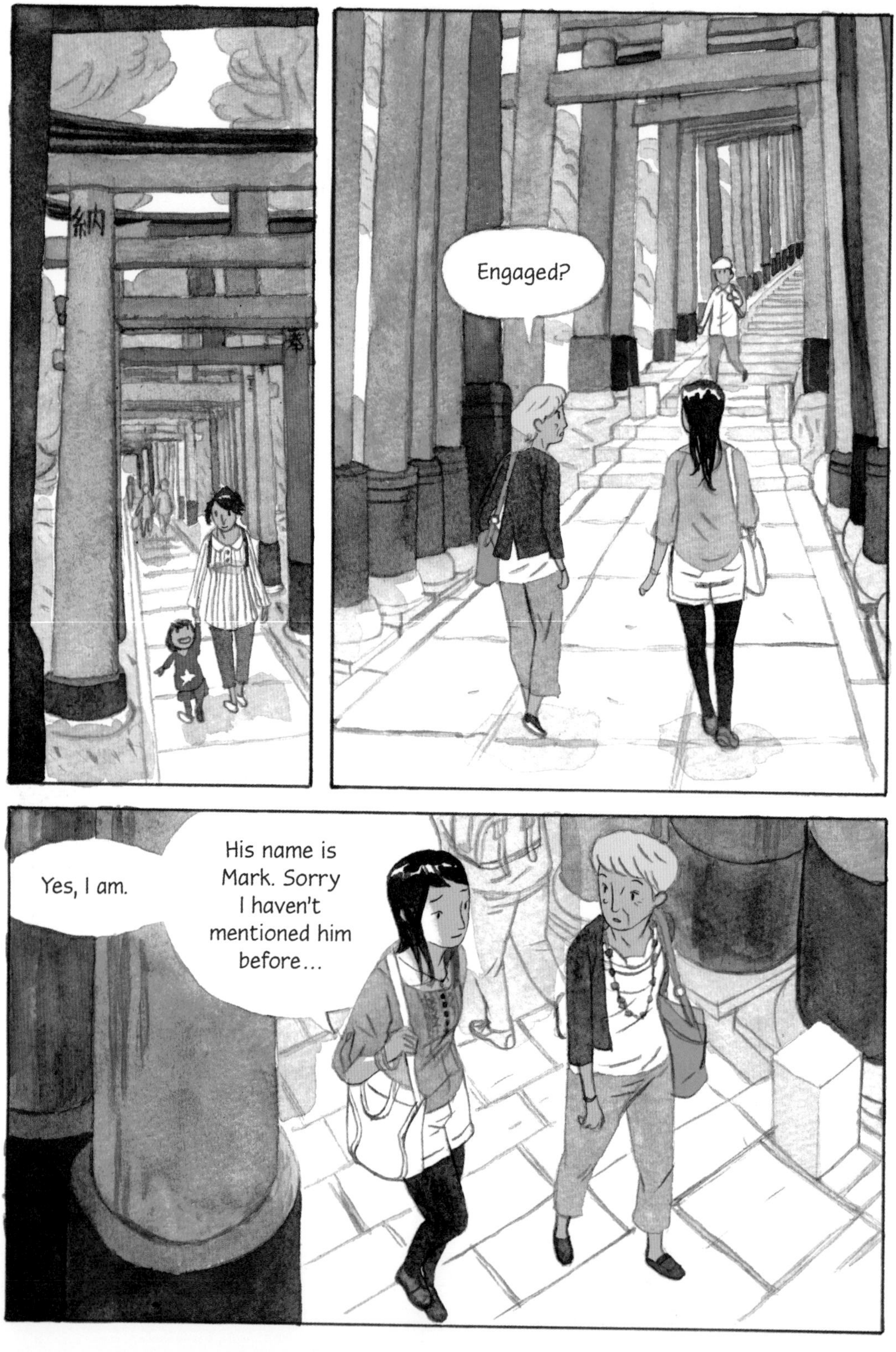
Engaged?
Yes, I am.
His name is Mark. Sorry I haven't mentioned him before…

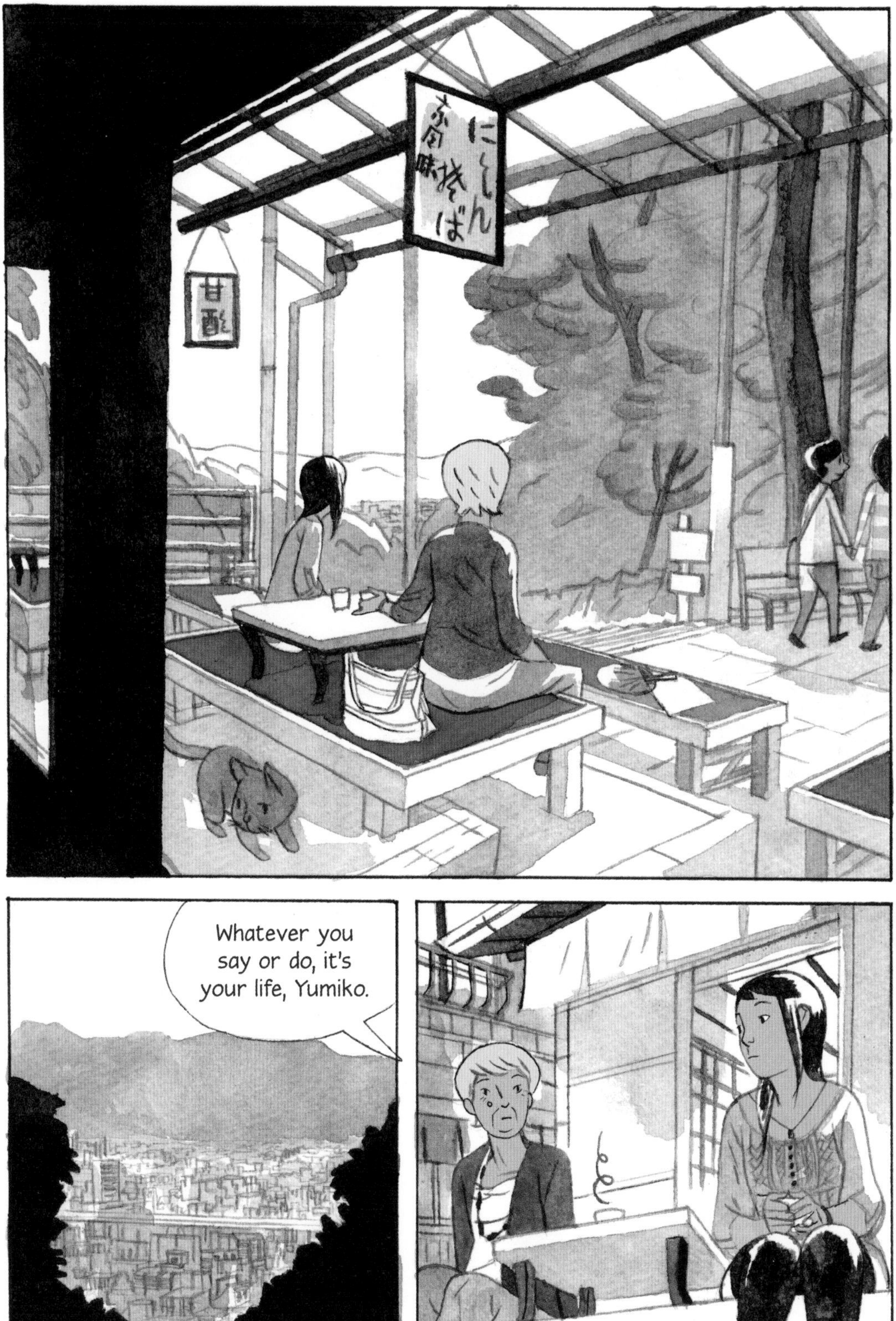
Whatever you say or do, it's your life, Yumiko.

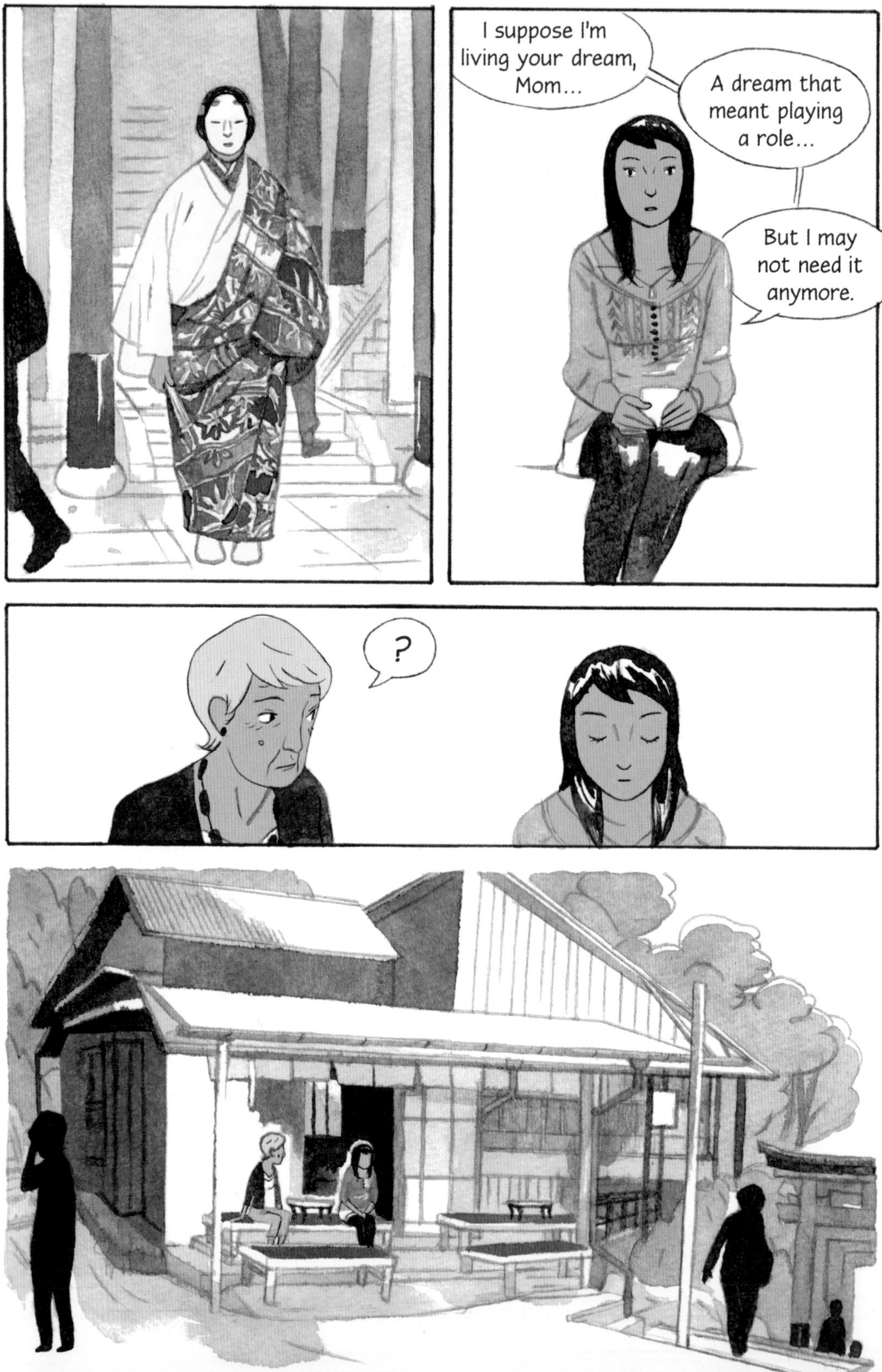
I suppose I'm living your dream, Mom...
A dream that meant playing a role...
But I may not need it anymore.
?

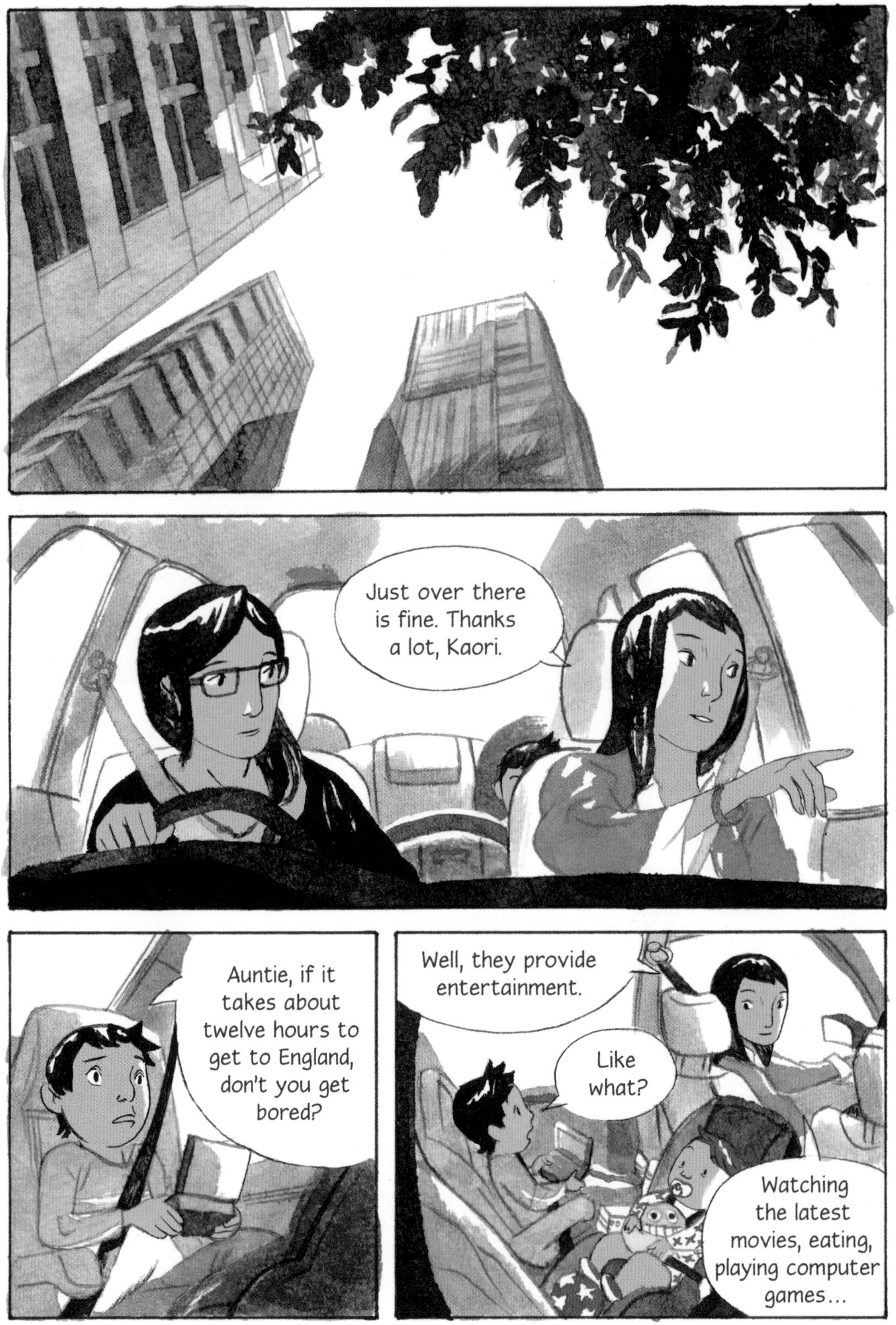

Just over there is fine. Thanks a lot, Kaori.
Auntie, if it takes about twelve hours to get to England, don't you get bored?
Well, they provide entertainment.
Like what?
Watching the latest movies, eating, playing computer games...

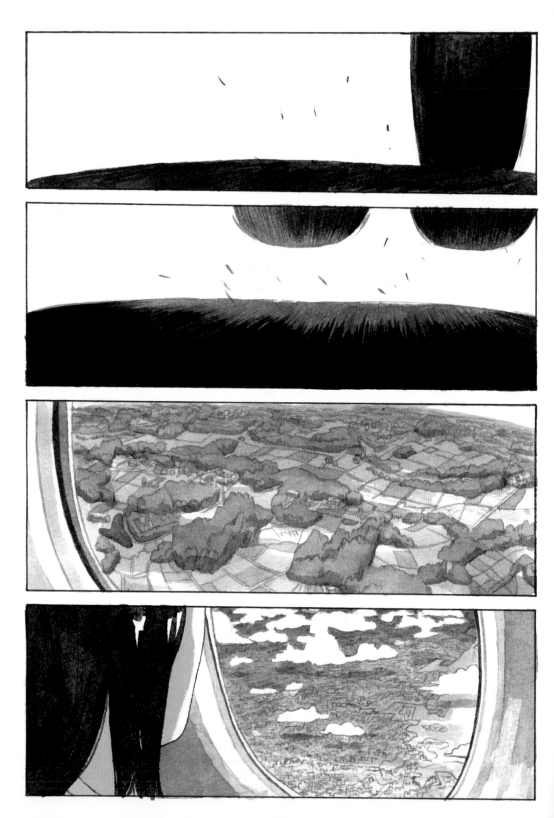

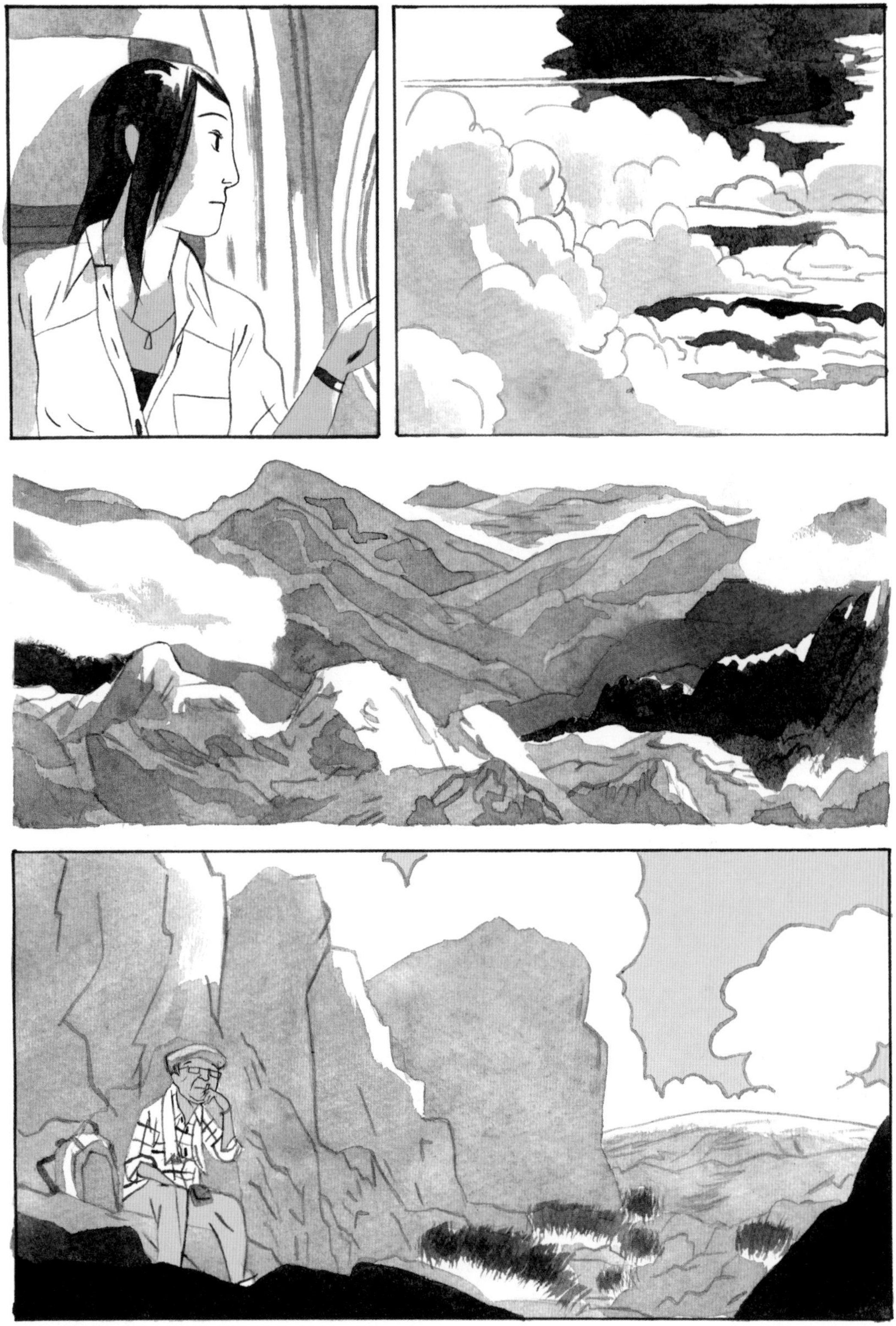

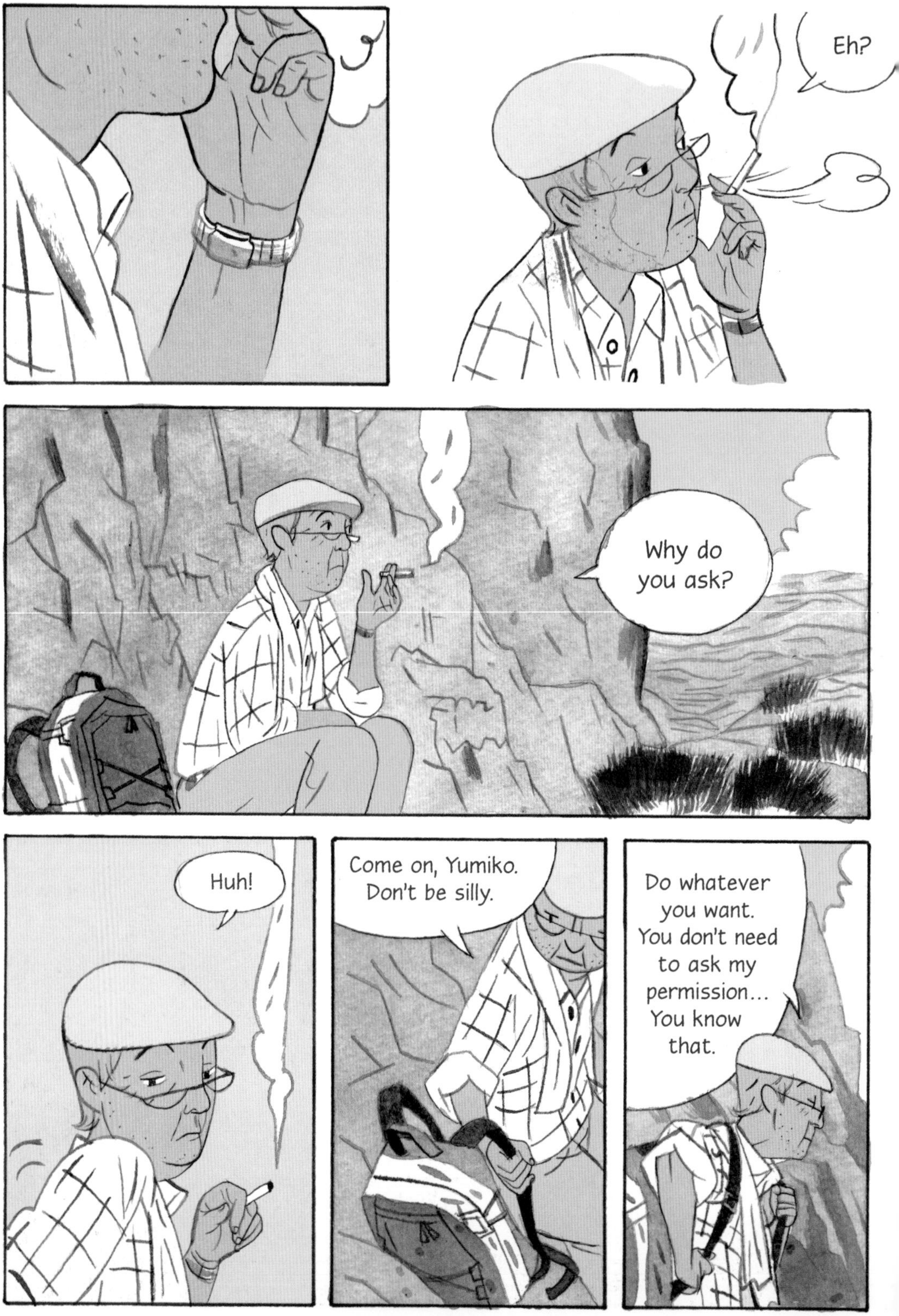
Eh?
Why do you ask?
Huh!
Come on, Yumiko. Don't be silly.
Do whatever you want. You don't need to ask my permission... You know that.

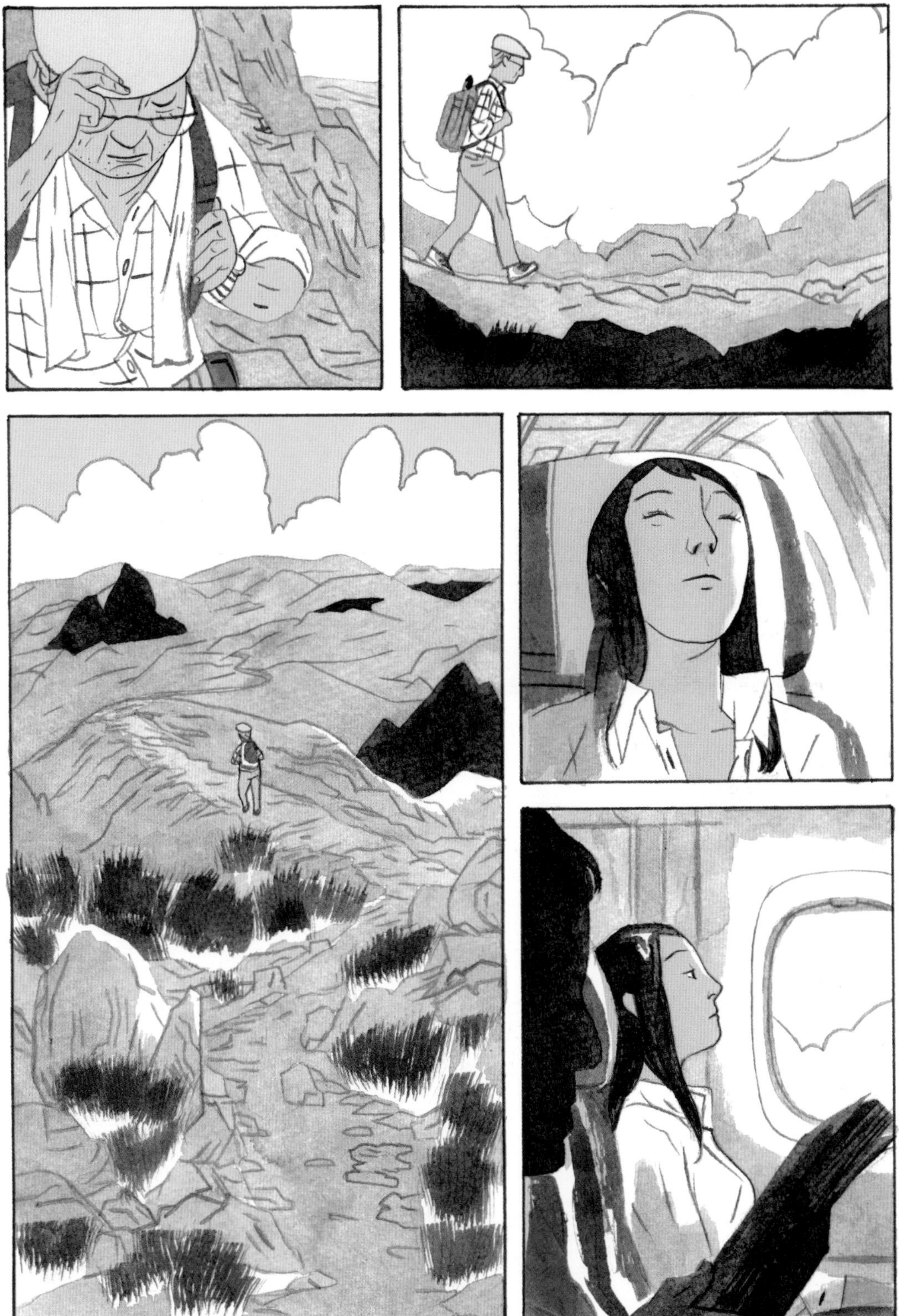

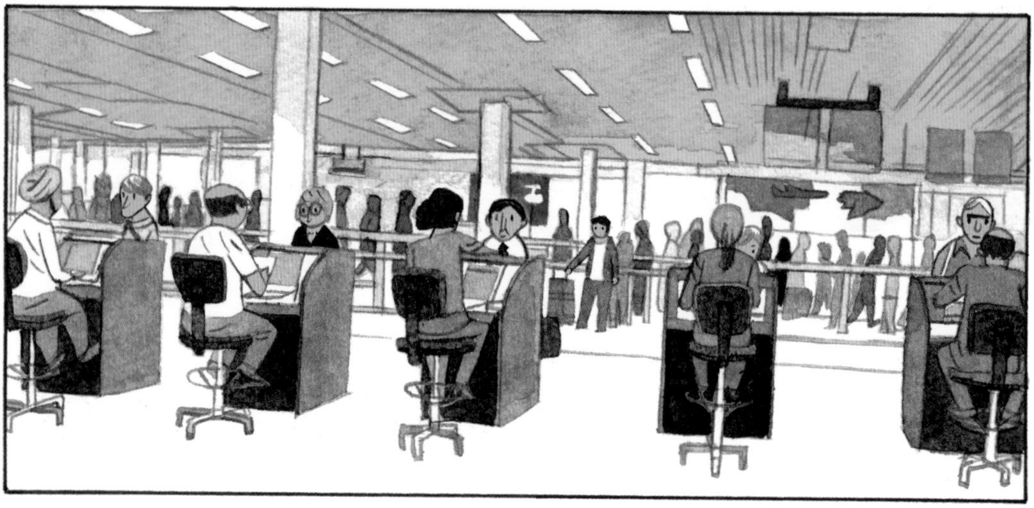

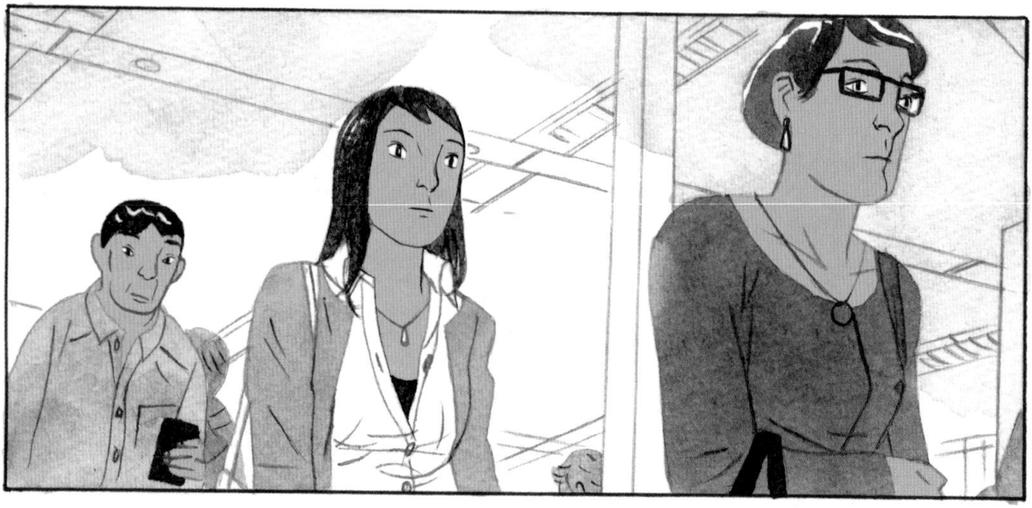

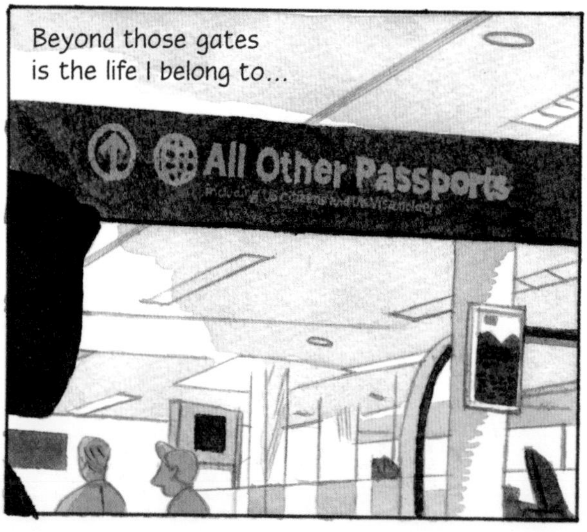
Beyond those gates
is the life I belong to...
All Other Passports

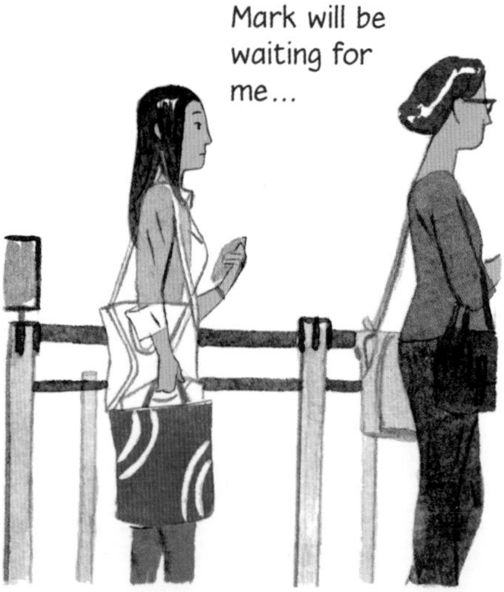
Mark will be
waiting for
me...

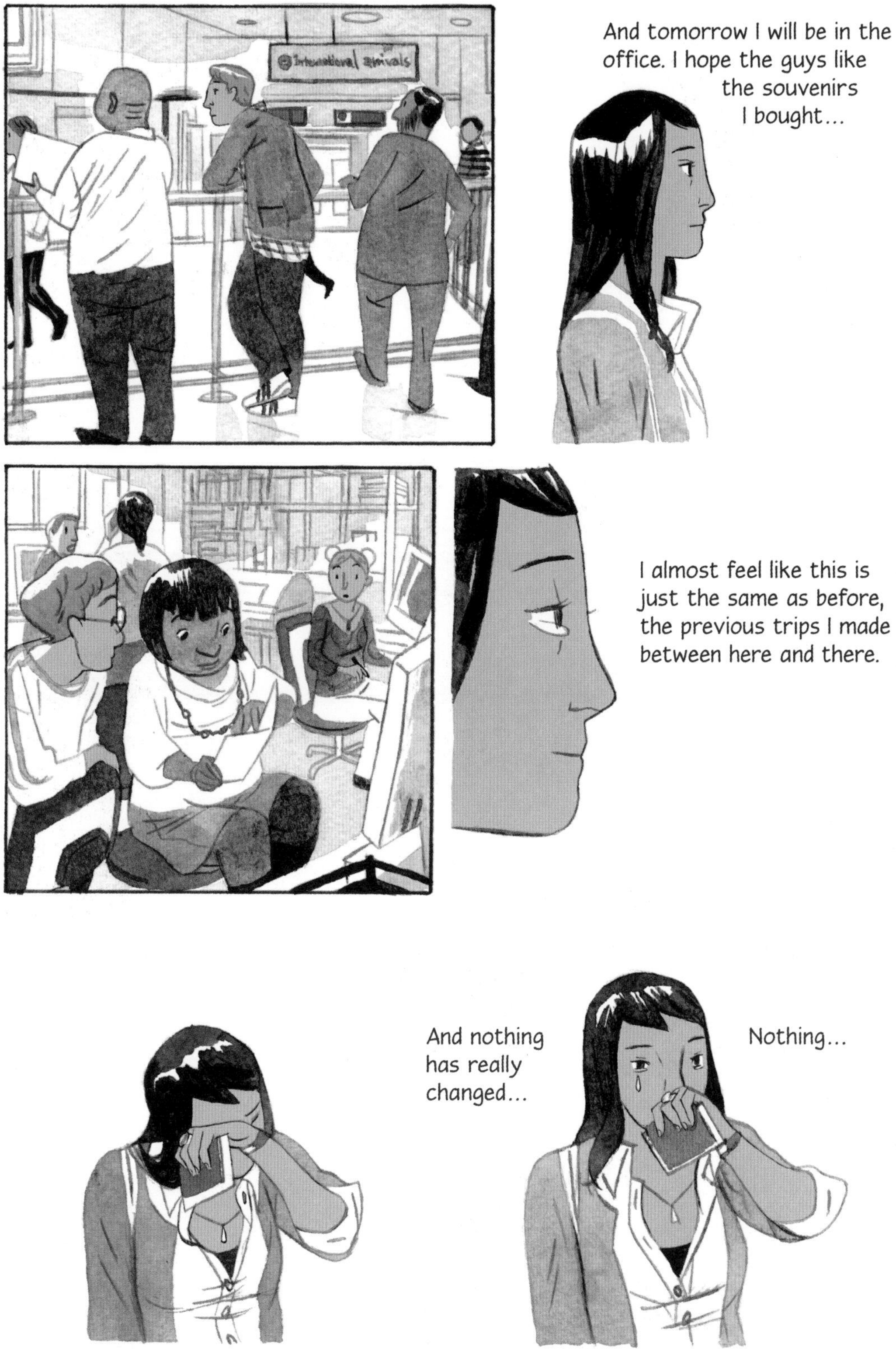

And tomorrow I will be in the office. I hope the guys like the souvenirs I bought...
I almost feel like this is just the same as before, the previous trips I made between here and there.
And nothing has really changed...
Nothing...

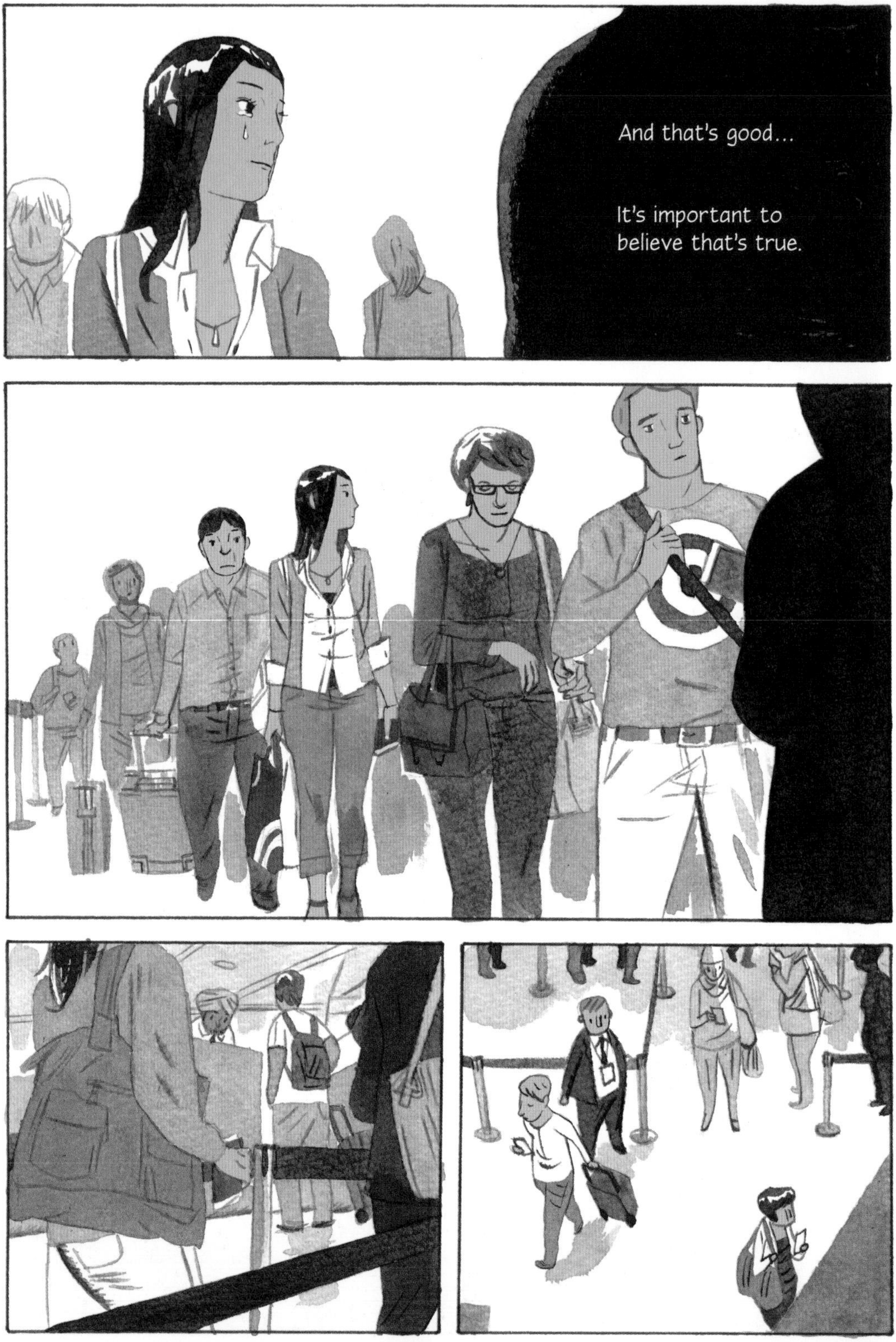
And that's good...
It's important to believe that's true.

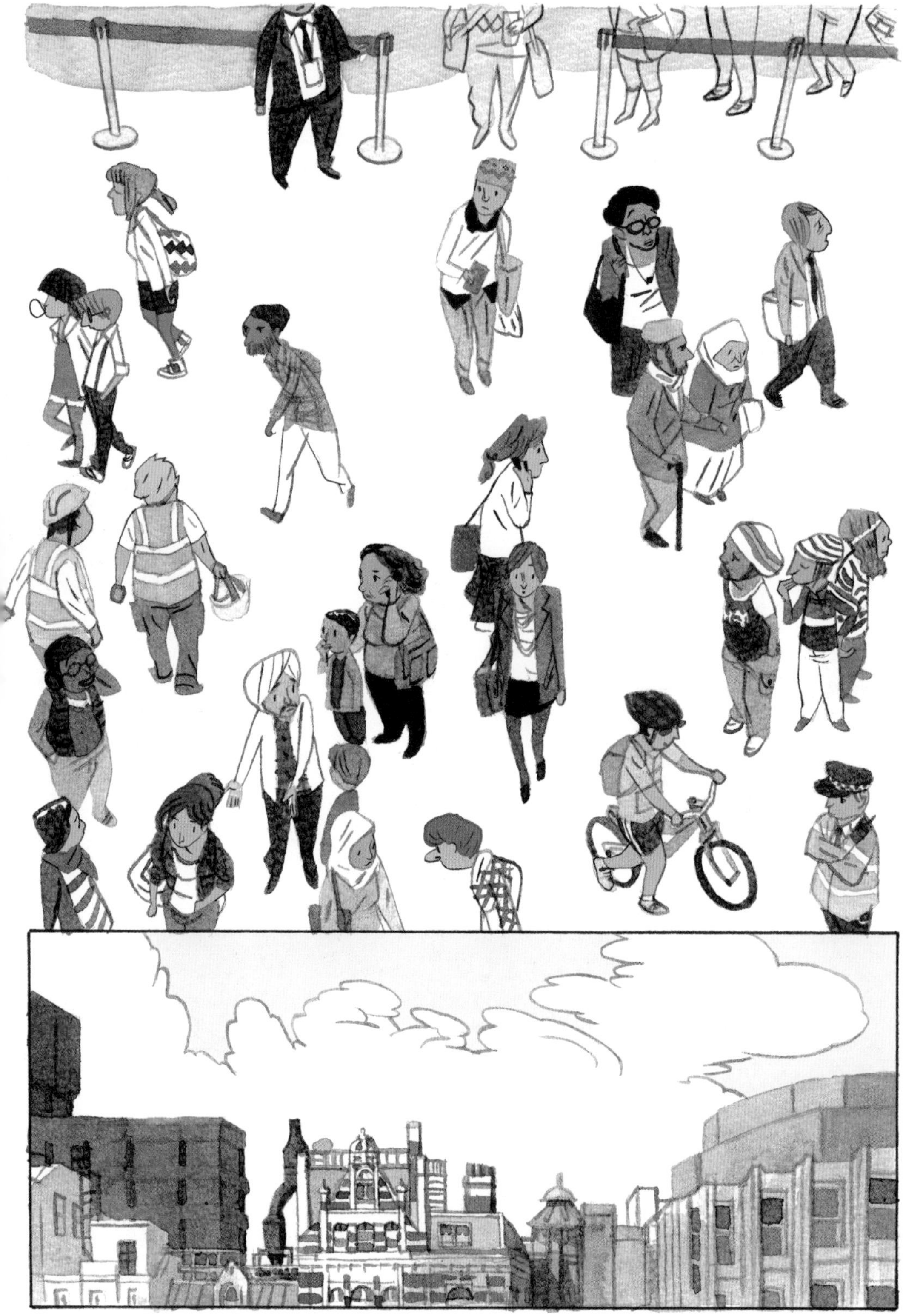

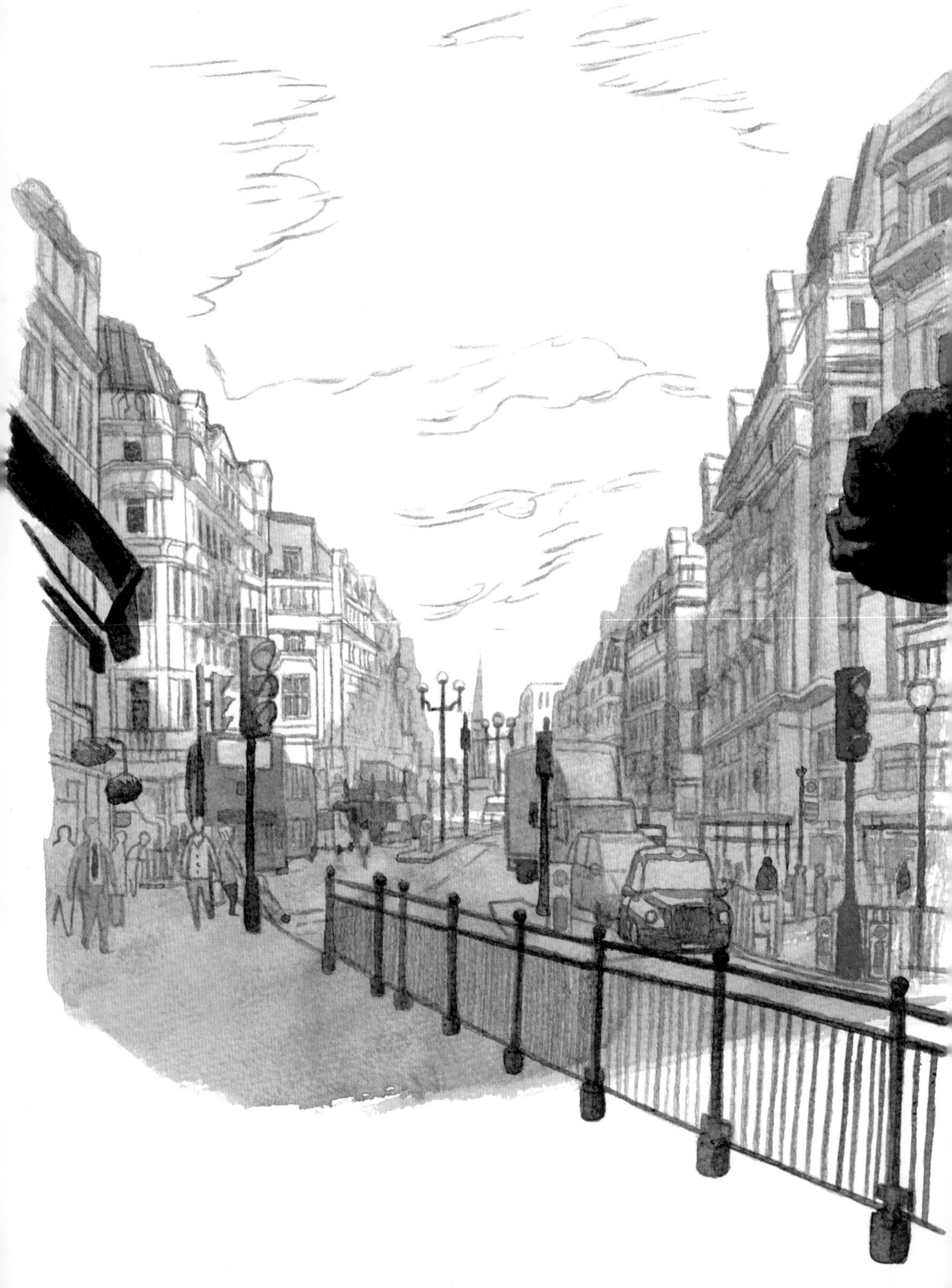